EXPLORATIONS IN WORLD ETHNOLOGY

ROBERT B. EDGERTON and L. L. LANGNESS
University of California, Los Angeles

General Editors

Blood
Is Their Argument

WARFARE AMONG THE MAE ENGA TRIBESMEN
OF THE NEW GUINEA HIGHLANDS

Mervyn Meggitt

 MAYFIELD PUBLISHING COMPANY

Manufactured in the United States of America
Mayfield Publishing Company
285 Hamilton Avenue, Palo Alto, California 94301

This book was set in Aster by Chapman's Phototypesetting
and was printed and bound by Malloy Lithographing.
Sponsoring editor was Alden C. Paine, Carole Norton
supervised editing, and Muriel Bell was manuscript
editor. Michelle Hogan supervised production, and the
text and cover were designed by Nancy Sears.

Contents

Preface

The major part of this book comprises an ethnography of the traditional military practices of the Mae, a division of the Central Enga people of the western highlands of Papua New Guinea. I describe modes of warfare undertaken by the local clans, the motives that impel them to fight, the outcomes of their confrontations, and the ways they re-establish peace. I conclude my account by tracing the consequences for Central Enga of the Australian colonial Administration, in particular its effects since the 1950's on intergroup fighting. In presenting this material both as synchronic description and in a historical framework I have two aims in mind, the one largely academic, the other, no less important in my view, rather more practical.

On the one hand, I wish to record the kinds of evidence that anthropologists can employ in constructing and testing explanations of so-called tribal warfare. In 1949 Turney-High published *Primitive War*, a valuable collation and analysis of the information then available about warfare in simpler societies, and a book whose systematic organization and sound common sense have greatly aided me in my own work. Turney-High's painstaking survey of the earlier literature led him to emphasize both the exiguity of reliable, unambiguous testimony on this subject and the prevailing lack of anthropological concern with warfare among "non-literate folk" (1949:xiii).

Since then there has been a noticeable efflorescence of anthropological interest in "primitive war." In particular, the war in Vietnam persuaded a number of anthropologists in the United States of the importance for their discipline of understanding the causes and effects of warfare in all societies, whatever their degree of political and economic complexity (see, for instance, Fried, Harris, and Murphy 1967). Although the participation of the United States in World War II had earlier directed the attention of some anthropologists to the study of war, their concern then was primarily with its occurrence between nation-states, and their explanations tended to be more psychological than anthropological.

Also in the past few years there has been a growing predisposition among anthropologists to utilize cultural-ecological and cultural-materialist approaches to the analysis of social institutions. Such functional and systems-oriented theories emphasize the salience of substantive variables and their interactions, and have led anthropologists to regard the incidence of warfare, especially in small-scale societies, as being of considerable significance. Such views have drawn the fire of opponents and skeptics, who have proposed a range of alternative hypotheses to account for "tribal" warfare and its various forms. The dust raised by this combat has tended at times to obscure the vision of adversaries and onlookers, but some idea of the issues in contention can be gained from Chagnon 1974, Fried, Harris, and Murphy 1967, Hallpike 1973, 1974, Harrison 1973, Koch 1973, 1974, Netting 1973, 1974, Rappaport 1968, 1969, and Vayda 1971, 1974. I do not intend here to review these arguments, much less to assess their individual validity; but I should state that the assumptions of cultural ecology have informed my ethnographic description.

It may, however, be remarked that the extreme diversity of the propositions referred to above (some of which are wholly antithetical) does not merely indicate a diversity of theoretical viewpoints and methodological preferences: I believe that anthropologists have asserted so many different, indeed, idiosyncratic and conflicting, hypotheses about warfare in "tribal" societies in part because the relevant data available are so scanty. Despite a few notable exceptions stemming from recently published field research in New Guinea and South America, the bulk of the evidence that polemicists have adduced is, in specificity and pertinence, hardly better than that which Turney-High criticized twenty-five years ago. We still know far too little about warfare (and that little only with respect to a handful of societies) to test effectively what purport to be general explanations of the cause, conditions, and functions of this institution. Thus I believe it important to present as complete an ethnography as I can of Central Enga warfare in order to augment the anthropologists' corpus of reliable and usable data. Moreover, as an ethnographer I am not concerned to employ this material to add to the existing tangle of theories; I leave that to my colleagues.

The other aim I have in writing this book is to meet a deep obligation to the Enga people by providing the fullest account I can of some of their institutions—especially, in this context, of the social usages connected with warfare—and of the changes that have overtaken them since the arrival of Europeans in their land. My reasons are simple. Many Enga helped me acquire this information; it is my responsibility to ensure that it is not lost to them.

Of particular relevance is the circumstance that, at the time when much of this history was unfolding, few Enga were in a position to record it for their posterity. Many of the people who participated in the events I describe are now dead, and the first-hand knowledge of those who survive is fast becoming fragmentary memories. Meanwhile, a generation of young people is growing up in a culture of literacy, and some of them now want historical testimony that they may interpret as a basis for decisions about their society's future course.

For these new scholars the written sources are essentially government files, mission archives, and anthropologists' notebooks. Obviously, all three kinds of data are in some degree biased. Administration officers, for instance, responded to events in terms of their obligation to impose peace and maintain law and order; missionaries went to the western highlands to engage in a cure of souls, which inevitably predisposed them to partial judgments about their parishioners' customary practices and values; the anthropologist, in my case a middle-class, white, Australian academic, had his own ethnic, masculine, and "liberal" assumptions, which influenced his wide-eyed naïveté. Nevertheless, I believe the anthropologist can serve a useful purpose by offering his version of what he saw and learned as a counterbalance to the assertions of government officers and missionaries. No one of us is right; but at least the Enga historians and anthropologists of the future, a future that is rapidly approaching, will have three bodies of "facts" to choose among and to test against one another, and to that extent will be better equipped to fulfill their own intentions.

The field research in Papua New Guinea on which this study is based was carried out in 1955–57, 1960, and 1961–62 with a W. M. Strong Fellowship and other monies from the University of Sydney, in 1967 with a Horace Rackham faculty research grant from the University of Michigan, and in 1970 and 1973 with grants from the Wenner-Gren Foundation for Anthropological Research. In 1973–74 I had the good fortune to be a Fellow at the Center for Advanced Study in the Behavioral Sciences at Stanford, where I organized my data and began writing this account. I thank all these institutions for their encouragement and generous financial assistance.

While working on my material I was invited to discuss it in lectures and seminars at Stanford University, the University of California at Berkeley, Duke University, the University of Maine, Harvard University, and at York and Queens Colleges of the City University of New York. The responses of faculty and students at these meetings contributed greatly to the clarification of my ideas and persuaded me that the venture was worthwhile. I thank my colleague Robert Glasse for his help in preparing the photographs for the book, and Muriel Bell for her editorial advice.

Joan Meggitt accompanied me on all but one (1960) of the sojourns in Papua New Guinea. Not only did she solve the inevitable logistical problems that arise in the field, she also undertook archival inquiries and investigations into the life of Enga women. Her work, which has been invaluable, is incorporated in my publications, and I am deeply grateful to her.

Throughout our visits to Papua New Guinea we have ever and again received extensive cooperation and practical aid from officers in many government departments, both in Port Moresby and in the district centers, from missionaries in the western highlands, from members of the University of Papua New Guinea, and from anthropologists and other workers in the field. In addition, the hospitality given us by these people and their families has been memorable. There have simply been too many occasions for me to cite the names of all our hosts, but I assure them all that we recall with pleasure their manifold courtesies.

I have saved for the last my expression of our indebtedness to the Enga themselves, especially those Mae Enga in whose neighborhood we have lived, above all the people in "our" clan, who over the years have so patiently instructed us in the matters they consider important while assisting us practically in our daily activities. I will not pretend that our relations with our extraclan neighbors were always amiable—in Enga society this is not possible. But we have learned from the Enga, friends and others, much about living, knowledge that has benefited us in non-academic ways, and we thank hem all.

We dedicate this book to a Mae Enga man who, alas, is now dead: Anggauwane of Sari, demanding mentor, generous host, and dear friend. Kaimio, we have not forgotten all you taught us.

Editors' Preface

In spite of the recent efflorescence of anthropological interest in "primitive war," there remain all too few detailed accounts of it. What is more, in those few accounts which offer some richness of detail the author's point of view too often intrudes to the point of making us suspicious of the facts. Not so in the account that follows. Mervyn Meggitt has followed the fortunes and misfortunes of the Enga for over twenty years. His account of their warfare is not only detailed but without bias insofar as that is an ethnographic possibility. Although he makes some assumptions of an ecological nature, these assumptions are stated at the outset. His materials can be analyzed by anyone, regardless of theoretical predisposition. This is ideally what an ethnographic account should be. *Blood Is Their Argument* is therefore an unusually valuable work that will be of interest to anyone concerned with the subject of warfare whether "primitive" or "civilized." Indeed, it goes a long way toward illustrating just how absurd such value-laden terms as "civilized" really are—especially when applied to such phenomena as warfare.

This book has special relevance, of course, for those who work in the Pacific region and, more specifically, in Melanesia. Professor Meggitt has done much to clarify the nature of New Guinea warfare by highlighting the difference between "great fights" and the more vicious type of warfare that also occurs. An emphasis in the past on "great fights" has led to an unfortunate neglect of this much more important problem of "real" warfare. Above all, Dr. Meggitt must be given credit for putting to rest the often stated or implied proposition that the New Guinea Highlanders somehow simply "like to fight," that they are "unafraid to die," and that warfare for them is "merely a game."

Mervyn Meggitt was educated at the University of Sydney, where he received his Ph.D. in anthropology in 1960. His extensive first fieldwork with the Walbiri Aborigines of Australia resulted in his book *Desert People: A Study of the Walbiri Aborigines of Central Australia* (1962), as well as in a monograph and a number of journal articles. His even more extensive fieldwork in New Guinea began with a fifteen-month trip during 1955–57, with shorter trips in 1960, 1962, 1967, 1970, and 1973. In addition to *Blood Is Their Argument*, he has published *The Lineage System of the Mae Enga in New Guinea* (1965), a monograph entitled *Studies in Enga History* (1974), and a large number of journal articles. All of this makes the Mae Enga probably the most extensively documented group in New Guinea to date. Since 1968 Professor Meggitt has been conducting research in the western Andalusia region of Spain.

Robert B. Edgerton
L. L. Langness

Blood Is Their Argument

Traditional Mae Enga Society

1

The ethnographic present here refers to Mae society as it was until the 1950's. Since then there has been an increase in both the magnitude and the tempo of changes stemming from interactions of the Enga with the arms of the central government and with Christian missions, from the Enga's expanding participation in a money economy through wage labor and cash cropping, and from the substantial growth of the total population.[1]

The Enga-speaking peoples of the western highlands of Papua New Guinea number well over 100,000 (now perhaps 150,000) in all and fall into several localized cultural subdivisions, which can readily be distinguished by customary differences in dialect, dress, dwellings, crops, and rituals.[2] The two largest sections (comprising more than 70,000 people) are those of the Mae (including the Yandapu) to the west and the Laiapu (including the Syaka) to the east. Together they constitute what I call Central Enga, as distinct from the surrounding Fringe Enga. Population densities among the Central Enga are high by New Guinea–Melanesian standards, being in places over 300 per square mile, as contrasted with less than twenty per square mile among some Fringe Enga. These demographic differences significantly affect the social organization and structure of the respective groups (see Meggitt 1965a).

The Enga language is clearly related to those of other peoples of the western and southern highlands. Despite the mountainous terrain, some Enga groups have long maintained intermittent trading connec-

1

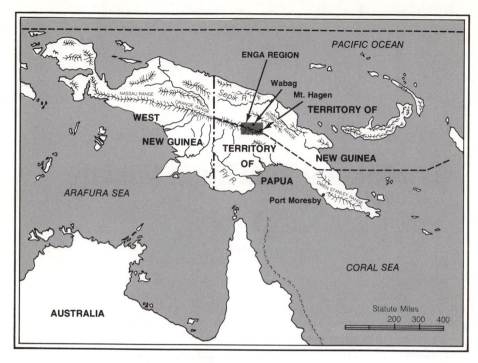

Figure 1   Map of the Enga Region

tions with such non-Enga neighbors, contacts that have not only promoted
the limited diffusion of cultural elements but have also led to occasional
intermarriage.

The Mae Enga, numbering over 30,000 people, belong, like other
Central Enga, to named and sharply localized patrilineal clans, that is,
clans whose male members are generally recruited on the basis of common descent from a male ancestor. Clan territories, whose boundaries
are known, and defended, literally to the last yard, are usually between
one and two square miles in area. They lie along the sides of valleys
from about 6,000 to over 8,000 feet above sea level, so that each clan
domain samples a variety of resources ranging from the fertile but limited river flats through poorer slopes up to wooded mountain crests. The
last are important sources of building materials and provide foraging
for pigs.

There are no villages. People live in solidly constructed houses or
homesteads dispersed through the clan territory on sites that can readily
be defended from attack. Men and women occupy separate dwellings,
partly because men have a deep-seated fear of sexual pollution (see

2

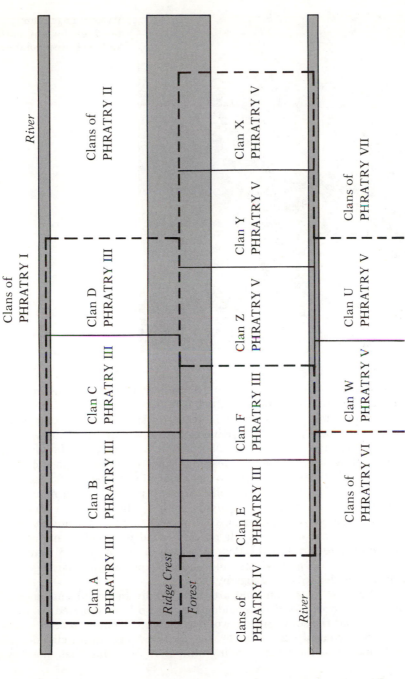

Figure 2 Territorial arrangements of Mae Enga phratries and clans

Western Enga country, too high for the cultivation of sweet potatoes

Meggitt 1957a, 1964a). Ideally, and largely in fact, patriclans are exogamous (that is, wives are recruited from outside the clan), politically autonomous, and self-sufficient in terms of subsistence. A clan parish (that is, the local group of clansmen, their wives, and their unwed children) of average size has about 350 members. Clans are subdivisions of named phratries, the largest descent group the Mae Enga recognize. There are on the average seven to eight clans in a phratry, and the range is from about four to twenty. Each clan comprises about four named subclans (the range is from two to eight), each of which includes about two named patrilineages (the range is from one to five). Within the patrilineages are both elementary families, headed by a monogamous man, and composite families, headed by a polygynist. About 25 percent of married men are polygynists, and about 92 percent of marriages conform to the ideal of clan exogamy.

Rights to patriclan land are patrilineally inherited and normally may not be transferred to outsiders. Men who have married women of the clan, and the sons of these women, may occasionally receive temporary, specified usufructuary and residential privileges in the clan domain, while incurring the corresponding obligation of aiding their hosts eco-

4

Mae Enga sweet potato gardens in various stages of growth, with pandanus nut trees in foreground

nomically and politically; but, on the average, about 85 percent of the resident males of a Mae clan parish are putative agnates, i.e., related only through the male line.

Each localized, hierarchically organized set of patrilineal descent groups making up a phratry is a segmentary lineage system, subject through time to fairly predictable processes of fission and segmentation in response to changes in group size. In this way within the clan a balance among subgroup status, functions, and size is maintained, and constant readjustments are made between group membership and land resources. Between clans of different size, however, recourse to warfare generally achieves the necessary rearrangements.

The founding ancestor for whom each phratry is named is thought to have descended from the sky people, who reside in celestial surroundings that parallel in important respects the terrestrial environment of contemporary social groups. The sky people in turn are children of the male sun and female moon, the "father and mother" of all Enga. The patrilineal genealogies of clan and phratry members provide a structural basis and rationale for complex ancestral cults, and for rituals designed to placate the malevolent ghosts of dead kin; in addition the genealogies serve

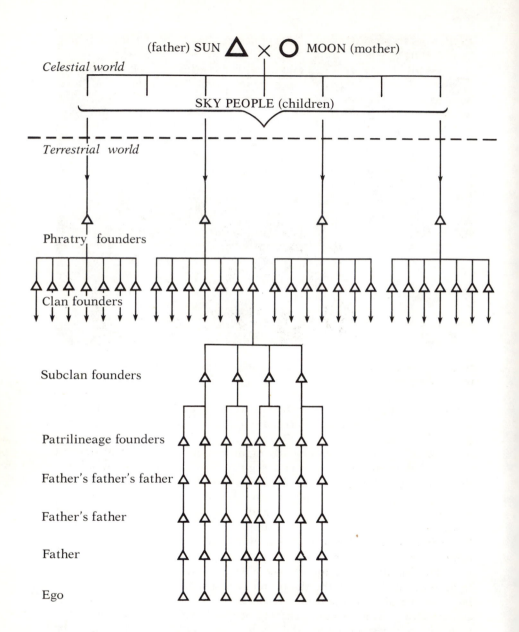

Figure 3   Ideal genealogical structure of Mae Enga descent groups

as charters that validate the rights of descent groups to patrimonial land (see Meggitt 1965b).

Despite constraints of climate, altitude, soils, and topography, the Mae are efficient gardeners who produce their staple crop, sweet potatoes, in a complex system of long fallowing. Beans, leaf vegetables, bananas, sugar cane, and pandanus nuts are important supplements; taro, which in this latitude does not thrive above about 6,000 feet, is less significant. Yams, which other Enga grow at lower altitudes, do not appear in Mae gardens. Practical forestry or silviculture is pursued, especially the establishment of casuarina plantations to provide firewood and timber for houses and fencing (see Meggitt 1958, Waddell 1972).

The Mae devote much energy and skill to pig husbandry and, by New Guinea standards, have substantial herds (on the average about five beasts per married man). Pigs, however, are raised primarily as valuables to be circulated in prestige-enhancing exchanges; they are rarely

Newly planted mounds in Mae Enga sweet potato garden, with grove of pandanus nut trees

Intensively cultivated section of Mae Enga territory, with stands of casuarina trees

killed and eaten outside ritual and ceremonial occasions. Hunting, largely an ineptly pursued pastime, contributes little to the daily diet; pork is the people's prime, albeit limited, source of animal protein.

There are no hereditary chiefs or formally elected leaders. In the main, men of influence and power resemble the Big Men commonly encountered in Melanesia. Military prowess can help a clan leader achieve and maintain his position, but more important at all times has been his role in the circulation and distribution of such valuables as pigs, pork, shells, axes, and plumes (see Meggitt, 1967, 1974).

The movement of various commodities, including those regarded as valuables, into and through Mae society is effected by trading activities and ceremonial exchanges. Trade is obviously linked to local diversity and specialization in production. Although trade does not occur on a grand scale, it is important not only in facilitating distribution throughout the Enga area of economically useful commodities (such as salt and stone axes) but also in replacing valuables (such as shells and plumes) desired primarily for prestige-building distributions.

Trade relations are contingent, finite, and private transactions between individual Mae. They lack ceremony, do not involve the extension of credit, and are not formally connected with the networks of public exchanges or prestations; they provision the latter in a relatively unsystematic way. The formal prestations, on the other hand, are elements in a system of delayed exchanges which include the notion of credit, are highly elaborated or ceremonialized, and usually occur with maximum

8

publicity between related groups of people (although non-relatives may sometimes participate). Even though in the last analysis individual Mae give or receive the valuables, the proceedings are mediated through the actions of the Big Men who represent the groups concerned.

All Mae men and groups (which are represented by their Big Men) are necessarily involved from time to time in exchanges at various levels in the hierarchy of prestations, any of which may express actual, or create potential, partnerships between particular men in the great Te exchange cycle that recurs about every four years. Not only is it to a man's advantage to participate in all distributions in the hope of extending his personal network of exchange partners; the overlapping sets of relationships thus formed also draw the various distributions together as elements in a wider system. Moreover, the aim of the Mae is constantly to exploit these situations in order to increase their holdings of, and subsequently their credits in, the more highly ranked valuables, with the further goal of maximizing their standing in the Te cycle itself. That is, the clan (and hence its members) tries to engage publicly in the greatest possible number of Te transactions in pigs with its neighbors so that in time its credits will exceed its debts.

Nevertheless, it would be a mistake to assume that success in the Te is the ultimate value in Mae culture. The Mae do not compete for prestige for its own sake. Prestige achieved through prestations helps a clan maintain its territorial boundaries by attracting military allies, as well as wives who will produce future warriors and workers. The basic preoccupation of the Mae is with the possession and defense of clan land. Participation in the Te, as in other prestations, is but a means to this end.

Mae Enga Warfare: Preliminary Considerations

2

Definitions

Throughout this account I use a straightforward definition of war as "a state or period of armed hostility existing between politically autonomous communities, which at such times regard the actions (violent or otherwise) of their members against their opponents as legitimate expressions of the sovereign policy of the community."[1] Warfare I take to be the actual military operations effected by representatives of these groups.

Among the Central Enga the social unit that commonly makes war is the patriclan—or, more accurately, the able-bodied men of a clan parish, aided from time to time by allies drawn, either individually or in groups, from currently friendly or neutral clans. On rare occasions, all the clans of a phratry combine as one loosely organized force to engage the clans of another phratry. Subclans within a large clan also fight each other for much the same reasons as do independent clans, although in doing so they contravene the generally held view that fraternal subclans should coexist peacefully and that the waging of war is an activity proper to clans.

Should this last situation be regarded not as war in any strict sense, but instead as feud, in that the contending parties, the subclans, are components of a wider polity, the clan?[2] I believe that here also we are dealing with war and not with feud. This is not simply because the reasons for these conflicts and the tactics employed in them are substantially the same as those involved in interclan fighting. In addition, such engage-

10

ments are an attempt (frequently successful) by at least one contesting group not only to secure a material advantage, but also to assert its autonomy and thus publicly to redefine its position in the lineage hierarchy. That is to say, although the groups in question are until the fighting breaks out considered both by themselves and by their congeners to be interdependent subclans of a superordinate clan, one of them in initiating warfare rejects that characterization and, in acting as a clan does, claims the political and economic status of a clan. Whether or not a subclan succeeds in this depends on such factors as the population and land resources it can command relative to those of its neighbors. Moreover, the achievement by the aggressor of clan rank in the hierarchy of descent groups could force a correlative structural elevation of the opposing subclan(s), providing the latter escaped complete defeat and eviction.

Finally, there is the question of what to call the fighting that now goes on among Mae Enga clans. Since the 1940's all Enga have come increasingly under the control of a central government—at first that of the Commonwealth of Australia, and now that of the independent nation of Papua New Guinea. For about a decade, 1950–60, the Mae generally heeded the exhortations of Administration officers to give up fighting, especially over land, and instead take their disputes to the newly established courts; but eventually it became apparent that the kind of litigation available did not resolve such problems to the people's satisfaction. In consequence, a growing number of clans have returned to traditional forms of violence, in order to secure or extend territorial boundaries. The bitter fighting that continues, despite the government's vigorous attempts to suppress it, I also regard as warfare and not as feuding. Again I do so not solely on account of the scale, duration, and intensity of the combat, but also because, by persisting in these actions, Central Enga are trying to retrieve, at least in one arena, the political autonomy of their clans. In this context of disputes over land they are in effect asserting that group violence remains a legitimate means of achieving group aims, and they are rejecting the government's claim to have jurisdiction over such matters.

Disputes: categories and frequencies

Among the Mae, disputes over substantive issues are frequent between individual clansmen and between sets of people at various levels in the local descent group hierarchy. Such a state of affairs is not surprising, given that for an unknown but obviously long time before the imposition of Australian Administration, the Mae were numerous and spatially somewhat crowded, and that they were explicitly interested in competing for relatively limited resources (be they land, pigs, or other valuables) whose possession they regarded as essential to personal, domestic, or group

11

well-being. Indeed, as analysis of actual instances indicates, whatever the ostensible or immediate reason given for a quarrel, whether between two clansmen or between two clans, many, perhaps most, of these clashes are expressions of the politics of property; that is, they concern the rights claimed by particular people to control or utilize particular commodities.

Moreover, in many of these encounters disputants quickly resort to physical violence in attempts to intimidate their opponents and secure their own ends. Nevertheless, the upshot of this ready recourse to force is not a continual Hobbesian "warre of every man against every man." Even while or after two men or groups fight over an issue, others may intervene to urge negotiation and compromise, however temporary and partial the settlement may prove to be. Whether, however, noncombatants initiate some kind of conciliation or simply stand by and watch the fighting spread, depends on a complex set of conditions whose configuration changes from one occasion to the next.[3] The range of the relevant factors, which can be structural or contingent, is considerable. They include, for instance, the importance conventionally ascribed to the object in contention (is it a pig or a sweet potato garden?), the number of antagonists, the kinship, affinal, or exchange connections among some or all of them, and between them and interested noncombatants, whether or not the contending parties are identified as representatives of specific local descent groups, the size and hierarchical status of such groups, their current political and economic relationships, and the degree of power or authority exercised by their leaders.

By and large, the only safe generalization to be made is that quarrels within the clan (and, more emphatically, within the smaller groups it comprises) are more likely to end in compromise and peaceful settlement than those between members of different clans. Even in the first category, however, strong arms usually make for strong cases.

Before examining Mae warfare in detail I shall present some figures that suggest the incidence and causes of intergroup fighting among these people in the recent past. Later I shall analyze for comparative purposes figures that relate to battles in which the Mae and other Central Enga have lately been engaged. Obviously, given the nature of the subject and the associated problems of sampling, such tabulations cannot bear too much evidential weight; but they should help orient the reader in the discussions that follow.

The first set of figures (Table 1) refers to armed conflicts that occurred between 1900 and 1950 and mainly concerned members of some 14 clans (a population of, say, 5,000) that the area in which I have worked comprises. Clearly, the sample does not include all the fighting that involved groups in that area during that time. There must have been many combats about which I was not told, just as there are some (at least 11) for whose outbreak I do not know the reasons. Thus, for the clan with which I reside I have information of varying quality about 28 interclan

12

Table 1 Intergroup warfare among Mae Enga, c.1900–1950

| | Groups involved | | | | | | | |
| | Clans of different phratries | | Clans of same phratry | | Subclans of same clan | | Total | |
Ostensible reason	N	%	N	%	N	%	N	%
Land	25	56.8	13	65.0	3	42.8	41	57.7
Theft of pigs	6	13.6	4	20.0	2	28.6	12	16.9
Avenging homicide	6	13.6	2	10.0	0	—	8	11.2
Homicide payments	3	6.8	0	—	0	—	3	4.2
Pandanus theft	3	6.8	0	—	0	—	3	4.2
Title to trees	1	2.2	0	—	0	—	1	1.4
Garden theft	0	—	0	—	1	14.3	1	1.4
Rape	0	—	0	—	1	14.3	1	1.4
Jilted suitor	0	—	1	5.0	0	—	1	1.4
Subtotal	44	100	20	100	7	100	71	100
Unknown	9		2		0		11	
Interphratry tourney	2		—		—		—	
Total	55		22		7		84	

Reasons for conflict

Groups	Land	Other property	Homicide	Sexual	Total
Of different phratries	25	10	9	0	44
Of same phratry	16	7	2	2	27
Total	41	17	11	2	71
Percentage	57.7	23.9	15.5	2.8	100

Note: This table includes figures reported in Meggitt 1965a, Table 91. Group affiliations refer to those of the primary contestants whose disagreement is the "root" of the conflict, the "owners of the quarrel." In most cases each side is supported by individual allies, a number of whom may be relatives from other phratries; sometimes whole clans offer their aid. Nevertheless, even if the fighting spreads, the primary contestants continue to be identified as such and must afterward pay compensation for the deaths of enemies and allies.

wars in which it participated in that period of forty–fifty years, whereas I have only scanty evidence about the engagements of other clans, especially some that have been long-term enemies of my clan.[4] If all the clans in this sample fought, both among themselves and with other neighbors, as often as the group I know best (and there is every reason to believe they did), then the total number of intergroup wars in which they were concerned during the period approximated 200.

However that may be, the 84 known eruptions of fighting among these 14 clans alone in that time confirm the Mae view of themselves as fairly violent people, people for whom "blood is their argument." Moreover, for the 73 confrontations for which reasons were given me, the significance of disputes over land, as well as other property issues, is patent. It is true that provocations such as rape, homicide, and the refusal to pay compensation for homicide, in addition to the stealing of pigs or pandanus nuts, can be an immediate stimulus to warfare as well as being "acts of war" in themselves—that is, incidents in an ongoing sequence of overt and covert hostilities between opposed groups.[5] Nevertheless, the information I have about past or recent conflicts indicates that in many cases the ostensible motives for the launching of combat merely rationalize a more basic concern to seize or defend a descent group's patrimonial estates. Thus, when the Mae say that they commonly fight over land, they not only mean it, they are also correct.

Further analysis of the 41 instances in which occupation of land is given as the immediate reason for war reveals several features of considerable importance in understanding the Mae's readiness (and that of other Central Enga) to take up arms over this issue (see Table 2). For 34 of these conflicts I have reasonable knowledge of the outcome. In only nine cases (26.5 percent) was the result a standoff in which the aggressors achieved none of their aims. In 19 (55.9 percent) of these wars the invaders managed to secure at least a portion of their opponents' territory, with the area thus acquired ranging from a few acres of arable land to a quarter of the losers' domain. The remaining six (17.6 percent) collisions led to the complete eviction of the losers and the seizure of their entire territory.

In short, Mae groups that feel themselves to be in need of more land to maintain their members have good reason to believe that violence is a fairly effective means of acquiring territory. Given that the initiation of warfare generally in this sense pays off for the aggressors, it is not sur-

Table 2 Outcome of warfare over land among Mae Enga

Combatants	Losers wholly evicted	Victors secure some land	Standoff	Outcome unknown	Total
Subclans of same clan	1	3	1	—	5
Clans of same phratry	3[a]	3	2	5	13
Clans of different phratries	2[b]	13	6	2	23
Total	6	19	9	7	41
Percentage	14.6	46.3	21.9	17.1	100
Known outcomes	6	19	9	—	34
Percentage	17.6	55.9	26.5		100

[a]In at least one case, the victorious clan enlisted a clan of another phratry to attack the losers simultaneously.

[b]In both cases, the victorious clan enlisted a clan of a third phratry to attack the losers simultaneously.

14

prising that by and large the Mae count warfare as well worth the cost in human casualties.

Finally, these figures have obvious significance for any examination of highlands warfare as a mechanism for redistributing populations within a determinate region. The six total defeats and evictions dispersed 1,500 or more people to live with relatives in clans elsewhere with land to spare for their support.[6]

Kinds of Fighting among the Mae
3

The Mae recognize four main contexts within which numbers of men join battle, and these they define largely in terms of the combatants' descent-group affiliations: (a) fighting within the clan; (b) fighting between clans of one phratry; (c) fighting between clans of different phratries; and (d) fighting between phratries as such. They tend ideally to associate a particular mode of fighting with each situation. As we shall see, however, these normative correlations do not always hold good in practice. Because warfare between phratries has certain formal and substantive characteristics that set it apart from the other modes of combat, I describe it first.

Warfare between phratries

I remarked earlier that the Enga comprise a number of cultural divisions differentiated by variations in dialect, dress, house forms, and the like. These segments are relatively sharply localized. Thus, the Laiapu Enga reside along the middle and lower reaches of the Lai River, the Mae in the upper Lai and the Ambumu valleys, the Yandapu around the headwaters of the Lagaipu River.

In some cases, for instance, those of the Maramuni and the Waka Enga, the populations are separated from other Enga by such natural boundaries as an uninhabited, forested mountain range—a condition

16

that does not, however, prevent sporadic interaction for trade and marriage (see Meggitt 1958). In other cases, for example, that of the Taro and the Yandapu, the Yandapu and the Mae, and the Mae and the Laiapu, the populations are contiguous, and adjoining clans of the different divisions are in frequent contact. Here, the common border may be a zone a mile or two deep, occupied by clans whose members share cultural characteristics of both segments. An outsider may be hard put to categorize these groups, although they themselves when asked have no difficulty in nominating their "true" identities as Mae, Laiapu, etc., because normally phratry membership does not cross cultural boundaries.[1] The Enga clearly recognize these local cultural divisions, which in any case are named, and membership in them is accompanied by, indeed provokes, mild ethnocentrism. Nevertheless, the segments are in no way political entities; clans of one never all combine as a unit to contend with the clans of another. Although individual clans or even a whole phratry of one division may go to war with neighboring groups of another, and though the combatants may refer in their gibes to the cultural differences between them, this warfare is not to be distinguished in motive or intensity from warfare within a cultural division.

In short, the largest military assemblage known to the Enga is that in which all the clans of one phratry combine to fight all the clans of another. Such "great fights" appear to have taken place only among the more densely settled Central (Mae and Laiapu) Enga, and those rarely. Moreover, these contests are very much in the nature of tourneys, bounded by conventions that minimize casualty rates in relation to the large numbers of warriors involved.[2]

In the neighborhood of Mae clans with which I am most concerned, men aged 60 years or more in the mid-1950's said that only about four such great fights had occurred in their lifetimes, and that their fathers had told them of another four or five that had happened in earlier times. In most of them only two phratries participated, meaning that the average size of each force was on the order of 500 men; but around 1930 two phratries related as "brothers" combined to oppose a coalition of two unrelated neighboring phratries. If on this occasion all the clans concerned were mobilized (and they probably were), there must have been some 2,000 men in the field.[3]

Great fights are deliberately planned affairs (I use the present tense for convenience, although none has taken place in my area since the 1940's), whose main purpose or function appears to be display. That is, they are designed to serve as tests of strength and as opportunities for individual warriors and groups to enhance their prestige. The initial stimulus to mount a great fight varies. Sometimes the men of a clan are angered by continued thefts of their pigs, or are affronted because another clan has ignored them when disbursing valuables at weddings, funerary distributions, or during the Te cycle; there are in Mae social life many situations that touchy egos can interpret as intended insults. The offended men react by calling a meeting of their clansmen, at which the usual refrain is: "Who do these people think they are? It is time someone humbled them!" Sometimes no explicit provocation is needed. Times have been good, and the men of the clan are simply spoiling for a fight. Then almost any clan in another phratry nearby is an appropriate target. During the clan's discussions the recognized fight leaders in particular push for a confrontation, whereas those Big Men who are not also fight leaders may seek to temper enthusiasm with a realistic appraisal of the odds. However, if everyone is obviously eager to fight and the clan has no other current military or ceremonial commitments, the Big Men accede to the fight leaders on this issue.

The would-be aggressors quickly send word of their intentions to the men of their fraternal clans, who in turn indicate whether or not they are interested in participating in a great fight. If the response is positive, the men of the first clan gather on a convenient hillside, where they chant boastful and insulting songs and call out challenges to their opponents. The message, wrapped in a wealth of metaphor and allusion, is generally: "We have beaten you before and we can do so again! Are you willing to try conclusions with us?" Their opponents reply in kind, and a suitable day and place are agreed on for the meeting.

Early on the appointed day, decorated and armed warriors from both phratries assemble at the lists. The site is a gently sloping, grassy down that lies on the phratries' common border (not necessarily in the domain of the challengers) and offers plenty of room for maneuvering. Directed by their fight leaders, the forces form extended lines along opposite sides of the arena, arranged more or less by clans. The two clans that initiated the confrontation, naturally enough, stand opposed, while the others single out as opponents groups with whom they have bones to pick. However, individual men may change their place if they find themselves facing close relatives in the other force. There is no restriction barring friends or kinsmen in other phratries from taking part, and a number, especially younger bachelors, do join in, either to help their relatives, to gain combat experience, or just for the hell of it. Sometimes, because of different kin connections, volunteers from one clan may fight on opposite sides; naturally they take care not to harm each other. Women, children, and the elderly belonging to each phratry may observe the fight from a safe distance (out of bowshot); they are not expected to participate, for instance by retrieving spent arrows, and they should be immune from attack.

Proceedings open with a period of massed chanting, the shouting of insults, and stylized displays of aggression (brandishing of weapons, feints, and the like). Then fight leaders of each side challenge men of comparable reputation from the other to duels. Each pair may begin by

18

firing arrows and then, using shields and spears, fight at close quarters in the middle of the field. These encounters are rarely fatal, partly because the antagonists are evenly matched, partly because they are more concerned to wound than to kill.[4] The duel ends when one man is wounded or weapons have been expended. The champions congratulate each other, embrace, and exchange decorations, which may include plumes, shells, and the lethal stone axes that they carry but should not use in such contests; they then rejoin their own forces.

During these balletic episodes the remaining warriors are simply interested and knowledgeable spectators who shout advice and encouragement. On no account should they fire on an enemy duelist. If a man were to do so, angry Big Men or fight leaders of his own group might well attack him, for his action, especially if he killed the opposing champion, could easily convert the tourney into serious warfare. Furthermore, in the subsequent fighting the dead man's clansmen would single out the offender for special attention, from which his own clansmen might not protect him. The enemy, moreover, would not be content merely with shooting him with arrows but would try to cut him down and hack open his chest, planting there, as a mark of obloquy, a pandanus or casuarina seedling.

Once the dueling is over, the two lines open fire with their bows, and rapid movement up and down the field ensues as men shoot, dodge, advance, and fall back. Despite this mobility, each side tries to preserve its extended skirmishing line, and each clan group attempts to maintain its position *vis-à-vis* its opponent. The aim of each force is to turn a flank of the other and so expose the crowded enemy to a heavy, death-dealing crossfire. Because both forces have the same goal but neither is supposed to move off the field into the trees and gardens or among the houses to achieve it, there generally results a prolonged stalemate. At times, however, men are so carried away that they leave the arena and try to steal around the enemy's line and take him in the rear, hoping thus to disorganize one wing and enable their own line to execute a rapid turning movement. This is a risky operation, for the watching noncombatants may cry out warnings to the intended victims, who can readily cut off the outnumbered intruders. Moreover, because infiltration is considered outside the rules, the enemy may indicate their disapproval of unsporting behavior by killing the intruders and mutilating their corpses, decorating them with seedlings and leaving them there for onlookers to carry home. Again, such an outcome may so anger the clansmen of the deceased that the fighting gets out of hand.

During the skirmishing, which goes on at a great pace, tired men withdraw from time to time to catch their breath and replenish their arrows; in doing so they form a changing reserve force that the fight leaders or Big Men can use to strengthen weak points in the front line. Big Men who are not fight leaders generally stay in the rear throughout. The

19

fight leaders alternate between observing and advising from behind and rushing into the fray to rally faltering groups. Ideally, when in action fight leaders should fire at their counterparts, and ordinary warriors should not strive to injure them. But sometimes "rubbish men," those of little worth or merit, in the hope of magnifying their own names take advantage of the confusion to dog and shoot an opposing fight leader or Big Man. If such men succeed in killing an opposition leader, his clansmen make every effort to slay and mutilate them.

For the rest, hand-to-hand combat is largely avoided, and most casualties result from arrows fired at a distance. When a man falls, the enemy should not prevent his clansmen or allies from dragging the corpse from the field, although they may seize the opportunity to shoot anyone who leaves himself open in the process. Wounded men move or are carried to the rear, where the less seriously injured have arrows removed before returning to the front. A man wounded in the limbs two or three times may keep on fighting.[5]

Skirmishing in this set-piece fashion continues throughout the day. Given the numbers involved and the style of battle, it is unusual (I know of no instances) for one side to suffer such disproportionate losses that it unilaterally breaks off the engagement and withdraws. Should the weather hold, the fighting goes on until dusk, but usually it is halted by the late afternoon rain. In either case, men fear that in the poor light not only will their shooting be less accurate and thereby endanger opponents, i.e., relatives, they do not wish to harm, but also the latter will be less able to see and dodge the arrows. Moreover, the downpours are miserably cold and uncomfortable, and they do great damage to highly prized plumes. Accordingly, when the fight leaders and Big Men judge that it is time to draw stumps, they counsel their forces to fall back in an orderly manner into their own territory, if necessary thumping the heads of young enthusiasts who wish to prolong the contest. If weather permits, some of the fight leaders may formally close the proceedings by engaging in duels.

Once the action is broken off, the Big Men of each force make speeches touching on the day's events and their outcome (a drawn match) and listing the dead.[6] In these orations, aimed at their opponents as well as their own followers, they also set the scene for future exchanges of valuables between the two sides. Then everyone hurries home, satisfied that he has vindicated his honor and upheld the clan's prestige. My informants did not dwell on the feelings of those who lose close kinsmen in the fighting.

Subsequently, it becomes the task of the Big Men (and not of the men who are merely fight leaders) to organize promptly the large-scale meetings at which the contestants (especially the clans whose challenges led to the great fight) exchange pork in considerable quantities to mark the re-establishment of peace between them. These assemblies also serve as the occasion for allocating responsibility for the deaths that occurred in the encounter and settling claims for homicide compensation.

20

In theory, the two clans that initiated the great fight, being the "owners of the quarrel," cannot expect compensation for their warriors' deaths, no matter who killed them. Moreover, each of these two clans must pay compensation for all the men lost by its fraternal clans. Whether such a clan is also obliged to compensate for the deaths of uninvited, non-fraternal allies is doubtful; on balance it appears that if such payments are made, they are voluntary, and depend on the importance of existing ties between the groups concerned.

However that may be, even if some fraternal clans waive their claims to compensation (which is unlikely), and even if some opponents are willing to compensate an initiating clan for some of its dead, the latter often stands to pay dearly for provoking the great fight. Not only does it suffer losses of men that are in no way compensated, it also incurs a heavy load of pig debts that will take a long time to discharge—circumstances that may well discourage that clan, for a while at least, from undertaking further military or other homicidal ventures. An awareness of such consequences is probably one reason why great fights occur so rarely.

Great fights between phratries contrast strikingly with the vicious warfare over land that takes place between clans, especially between clans of different phratries. Whereas the latter is an expression of Realpolitik in which almost any action is acceptable if it will effectively dispossess the enemy, the great fight is more a social event in which the participants are bound by generally recognized constraints. I have already indicated some of these—the rules that noncombatants are safe from attack, that equals should engage each other, that fighting should be confined to a delimited area. In addition, warriors should not burn down houses or damage gardens and valuable trees near the battlefield. Finally, and this is perhaps the most striking aspect of a great fight, even if one of the contending forces is so badly mauled that it must withdraw, the victors may profit only in terms of glory and the knowledge that they have weakened potential enemies. They have no right to turn the retreat into a rout and to invade and occupy the losers' territory. And indeed I have not heard of this happening.[7]

A Mae great fight thus in many ways conforms to the participants' recollections of it—good sport pleasantly spiced with danger, a day of splendid fun for all, during which men (especially the young) can demonstrate their skill and win their spurs as warriors. All this is true enough but we, in the comfort of our armchairs, should not forget that men die in great fights, painfully.[8]

Intraclan fighting

The Mae, like a number of New Guinea highlands societies, distinguish between fighting within the major autonomous local unit, in this case

21

the patriclan, and fighting in which whole clans engage. Because the former concerns men who, as co-resident agnates, are close "brothers," it should not, say the Mae, result in serious bloodshed and certainly should not cause deaths.[9] Accordingly, clansmen should not carry obviously lethal weapons (spears, bows, or axes) into such domestic affrays but instead simply use whatever objects are at hand. Because these are frequently fenceposts and gardening poles, a great deal of blood is in fact spilled in intraclan brawls, and I know of several men who subsequently died after the blows inflicted on these occasions.

Their deaths are regarded as homicides, and the killer and his descent group (that is, his lineage or subclan) must pay appropriate compensation in pigs to the corresponding agnatic group of the victim, much as would be required following an interclan killing. However, whereas the receipt of compensation for an interclan homicide still leaves the victim's clansmen free to attack the killer's clan at will, the payment of such compensation within a clan is thought to close the matter, and indeed it often does. Other members of the clan, particularly the Big Men, can bring strong moral and economic pressure to bear on the deceased's agnates not to retaliate, arguing that taking the lives of more "brothers" would weaken the clan and make it vulnerable to its external enemies.

So long as the contestants avoid using "lethal" weapons and do not burn each other's houses, the Mae do not consider fighting within the clan to be true warfare, even when it draws in whole lineages or subclans and results in deaths. Apparently for them also warfare is an activity in which politically autonomous groups—that is, clans—engage. When the men of a local group fight among themselves within the conventions of "non-military" brawling, they are publicly indicating that they recognize their common clan membership, which they gloss as "brotherhood," and the restraints this places on their actions. This in turn invites other people (generally clansmen) to intervene to compose the quarrel.

Nevertheless, despite this generally held view that warfare should only be directed across clan borders, it occasionally happens that subclans (never, apparently, the component lineages) of one clan make war on each other. To judge from the seven intraclan wars of which I have knowledge, the circumstances in which they occur are fairly predictable. In all cases the clan concerned is larger than average (that is, having more than 350–400 members), and its component subclans are markedly unequal in membership, so that at least one of the subclans is increasingly short of arable land while smaller subclans have enough or more than enough. Whereas normally the landholdings of subclans are more or less interspersed throughout the clan territory, in large or rapidly growing clans the domains of each subclan tend to form a unitary, clearly demarcated block. The men of land-hungry subclans encroach on the fallow areas of smaller subclans. The members of these in turn become more vigilant in marking and overseeing their boundaries, and disputes over the occupation of gardens and the trespassing of pigs multiply. Even though the clan appears to act as one in its dealings with outsiders, the growing incidence of domestic dissension erodes its internal solidarity. The ideal of clan brotherhood carries less weight in the settlement of quarrels, and men begin to behave toward members of fraternal subclans as they would toward outsiders.

Such tensions may persist for some years without coming to a head, especially if the clansmen perceive serious threats to their borders from other clans. Indeed, the clan may suffer in such interclan warfare enough casualties or evictions of families to relieve, at least temporarily, the population pressures at home; and this diminution, together with the need for clansmen to cooperate in providing the pigs required for consequent funerary distributions and homicide compensations, may lead to a decrease in internal disputes. Moreover, the substantial transfer of pigs out of the clan's territory may in itself lessen the demand for land.

If, however, there are no such countervalent forces to reduce or at least to confine the pressures leading to frequent quarrels within a large clan, then inevitably the day comes when what begins as a brawl rapidly increases in scale and ferocity until all the clansmen are drawn in on one or the other side and reasonable compromise is precluded. Commonly, such escalation occurs when exasperated men of one subclan have committed a serious offense against the men of another, for instance, stealing and eating a pig,[10] blatantly occupying and tilling some of their fallow, or, more rarely, raping one of their wives—actions which on occasion may quite properly be directed at enemy clans but which are deplored among clansmen.[11]

Thus, when such hostilities do erupt at home, they indicate the emergence of apparently irreconcilable differences between subgroups of the clan and a rejection of the right, and obligation, of the remaining clansmen to mediate the dispute in the name of common fraternal interests. At this point the onlookers have little choice but to take sides as well. Battle lines form on a subclan basis, and the combatants employ military weapons and tactics. The two groups are at war. Individual allies may come from neighboring friendly clans to help particular relatives or exchange partners for longer or shorter periods; and open skirmishing, raiding, and counter-raiding may go on intermittently for weeks, until either one group routs the other and evicts it from the clan territory or a stalemate is reached and both sides call a truce in the face of mounting and roughly equal numbers of deaths.

Casualties in such intraclan warfare can be surprisingly high.[12] Thus, the number of deaths recalled as occurring in seven intraclan conflicts ranges from one to 16, with the total 29. Even so, men believe the antagonists should feel constrained to keep the fighting from developing into the kind of all-out warfare that can occur between enemy clans. One should give one's own clansmen at least a sporting chance to survive arrow or spear wounds. It is bad form, for instance, to use axes to cut down or dismember disabled opponents. Mutilation of a wounded enemy is the ultimate expression of contempt for the victim's group.[13]

Similarly, decent men should not in these conflicts try to kill the wives and children of the "brothers" who oppose them; in particular, they should not set fire to women's houses in order to incinerate the occupants, as may be attempted in interclan warfare. Moreover, the burning of men's houses and the destruction of the gardens, trees, or pigs of one's clansmen are better avoided or kept to a "reasonable" minimum. Nevertheless, when the fighting is protracted and the contestants see several of their close agnates wounded or killed, they cannot easily restrain themselves. They do considerable damage to their opponents' property, and from time to time, to everyone's discomfort, a woman or child is killed.

An outbreak of warfare within the clan distresses men in related clans, especially those in the same phratry, and indeed offends their sense of propriety. Even as some of these men fight as allies in the intraclan engagements, they urge their hosts to refrain from shedding their "brothers'" blood and to contain the violence before their clan is irrevocably split or so diminished that even the victors will be vulnerable to enemy clans. Self-interest as well as morality inform this plea, because the weakening of one clan in a phratry prejudices the fortunes of its fraternal clans, which can no longer depend on it for effective aid in wars with enemy clans or in public distributions of wealth. If, for whatever reasons, the contending subclans agree to stop fighting, the men (particularly the Big Men) of fraternal clans actively join with the uncommitted men of that clan in pushing for, and contributing to, early interim exchanges of homicide compensations in pork between the two sides in the hope that these prestations will sustain the temporary truce until formal and final compensation in pigs lays the foundations for a more lasting peace within the clan.

Obviously, if the casualties or evictions of men and pigs have been high, this may alleviate for a time the underlying pressures on horticultural resources, which in turn may lead to a lower incidence of disputes over rights to garden land, even though bitterness over deaths may well persist. Thus domestic peace may be achieved, but clearly its duration is in part a function of the recovery rates of the local human and porcine populations. When they increase, the same troubles will probably recur.

On the other hand, if from the start of the conflict the opposed subclans are significantly imbalanced in size (if one force, for instance, is twice the size of the other), then the odds favor a speedy defeat of the weaker side and its ejection before enough allies can enter the combat to equalize the number of men fighting. Should such a rout occur, the

24

vanquished take refuge with friendly, related clans.[14] Given the distribution and density of the Mae population, the local topography, and the altitudinal limits on the cultivation of sweet potatoes, there is effectively no virgin or unclaimed land within the Mae domain on which a dispossessed group can settle and survive. Unless the victims migrate across the mountains into the sparsely inhabited valleys occupied by Fringe Enga (as Mae with appropriate connections have done in the past), they have no choice but to turn to neighboring Mae groups.

Because the Mae are not required to marry outside their own phratry, and because people tend to marry most often into adjacent clans, the fugitives' fraternal clans are likely to contain men who are simultaneously their agnates and their affines or maternal kin. It is to these that the losers should, and generally do, apply for succor. Related men in nearby clans are under a strong and explicitly stated obligation to provide their "brothers" with shelter and access to gardens for an indefinite period. Naturally enough, the emigrants prefer to move as a subclan group, or at least as lineages, in the belief that remaining together will improve their chances of regaining their land. Whether they can do so or not depends largely on the distribution of their affines and cognates among their fraternal clans and on the amounts of land their hosts have available for longterm usufructuary grants. It happens, therefore, that a dispossessed subclan must disperse, its component families taking up small parcels of land wherever they can.

If, as a result of war or sickness, a host clan is declining in population, its Big Men may well encourage newcomers to settle in order to enhance the clan's military and economic strength; to this end the clan may be generous in its concessions of usufruct. In most clans, however, the hosts are likely to consider their land resources barely adequate for their own needs, so that they are sparing in their generosity and wish to see the immigrants go home without undue delay. Accordingly, the Big Men of these clans take the lead in interceding with the victors, pressing for peace and the return of at least some land to the losers. At the same time they also urge the latter to arrange for homicide compensation to the winners as quickly as possible, not merely the interim payments of pork but also the full payments of pigs, to which they themselves may contribute handsomely. The losers also petition relatives and exchange partners in other clans for substantial donations of pigs and pork, all of which (including those of their hosts) they must eventually repay either through participation in the Te exchange cycle or by contributions to their creditors' marriage and funerary prestations. Even though the refugees may have lost many pigs in the rout, they are likely to have others in the care of relatives elsewhere. In addition, they still have pigs, pork, and other valuables owed them from prewar transactions with men of other clans. Their task is to manipulate these credits advantageously to build up resources

25

for the impending payments of compensation.

The aim of the dispossessed is to offer their opponents larger amounts of homicide compensation than the latter would ordinarily expect, in the hope that this gesture, together with a statement of their willingness to wait for or even to forgo compensation for their own dead, will generate among enough of the victors a sympathetic attitude to their recovering their patrimonial gardens. The losers must rely more heavily on the efficacy of such material inducements than on the moral disapproval their fraternal clans direct at the victors for having so seriously injured their "brothers."

Although an outsider might well regard the offer of extra homicide compensation to the victors as disguised ransom for the land in question, the Mae men with whom I discussed the matter did not phrase it this way. In their view, despite the conflict and subsequent eviction, the antagonists are still clansmen and "brothers." Communication between them should continue; the losers have the right to press for a hearing and the victors have an obligation to listen. Here the Mae differ from the Laiapu Enga to the east, who recognize the possibility of the losers in a war making payments (explicitly distinguished from homicide compensation) to recover occupied territory, although in fact this does not happen often (I know of only one instance). Moreover, some Laiapu men have told me that on occasion the victors in an intraclan or intraphratry fight who seize the land of their "brothers" and refuse to vacate it may during the exchange of homicide payments voluntarily make an additional gift of valuables to the losers to compensate them in part for their loss. Acceptance of the gift in some degree validates the usurpers' title to the property. I have never heard of such an arrangement among the Mae.

Whether or not the men of the victorious Mae subclan accept the offer of compensation and accede to the losers' request for reinstatement is largely up to them. The ousted clansmen have no obvious way of forcing their hand. Given the initial imbalance in numbers that led to the conflict, the refugees, even if settled elsewhere as a group, have no hope of mounting a successful counterattack alone; and their fraternal clans will not go to war on their behalf because, as they say, to do so would simply cause the deaths of more "brothers." Later, perhaps, an adjacent fraternal clan, forced by an increase in population to extend its borders, may occupy some of the weakened clan's territory—but it would do so for its own advantage and not to restore the refugees to their homeland.

In view of the situation that originally impelled the victors to dispossess their "brothers," they are not likely at once to ask all the latter to return; in the four instances of such evictions with which I am familiar, the pattern has been for the victors to refuse to enter into any public negotiations for some years. Then from time to time individual men within the group who find they have acquired more than enough land for their own families quietly invite particular families among the refugees to come home. They meet the objections of clansmen by arguing each case on its merits, pointing to the closeness of agnatic ties, to the existence of former exchange connections and friendships, to payments of homicide compensation, to the availability of land, to the need for a strong fighting force to defend it—and usually the Big Men support them. Nevertheless, the outcome of intraclan warfare leading to eviction of the losers is typically that only some of the dispossessed ever return home and that they recover only part of their land. The remaining refugees stay with their hosts, into whose clans they, or rather their descendants, are eventually absorbed.

During the period 1955–1962, a time of relative peace for the Mae (and other Central) Enga, Administration officers made considerable demands on them to provide unpaid labor to build and maintain roads, rest houses, and aid posts, as well as to furnish (for payment) materials for new houses at Wabag, the subdistrict administrative center. The officially appointed representatives of the clans, the *luluais* (many of whom were also Big Men), had to ensure that the able-bodied adults of their clans devoted half a day a week to these tasks, a charge whose implementation often tested the luluais' powers of command and persuasion. One consequence of this requirement was that some luluais argued strongly with their followers that clansmen who, because of former quarrels and evictions, were living elsewhere should be invited with offers of garden land to return and so augment the clan's labor force. Their followers, who would have had to donate most of the necessary land, did not always welcome such suggestions, and as far as I can tell few expatriates received invitations at that time. In the later 1960's, however, as the incidence of interclan warfare increased, the same clansmen agreed to cede unused land in order to bring back men who could bolster the fighting force needed to defend clan territory.

To summarize thus far: although in Mae opinion clansmen are "brothers" who should live together amicably and present a united front to the outside world, quarrels within the clan, especially over property, are common, and they often lead to bloodshed and occasionally to killing. Nevertheless, in most cases the Big Men of the clan can achieve rough, if not necessarily just, compromises; they urge the contestants to exchange valuables, and peace is regained. But from time to time, largely because of intensifying population pressures on domestic resources, the antagonists reject all attempts at mediation, and what starts as conventionally acceptable brawling expands into warfare between armed groups, with numerous casualties ensuing. Sometimes the losses themselves help resolve the dispute by restoring a material balance between the contending groups, and an uncertain peace follows the payment of compensation. At other times the opposing sides are so ill-matched that one routs the

27

other and seizes the land of the losers, some of whom never regain their patrimony. In all these armed encounters within the clan, however, the combatants operate under self-imposed constraints that effectively prevent the fighting from developing into the kind of thoroughly destructive total warfare that, the Mae believe, should be directed only at external enemies, men who are not "brothers."

Fighting between clans of one phratry

It is with intraphratry dissension that a considerable discrepancy emerges between Mae norm and Mae practice, a conflict between the moral obligations explicitly attached to "brotherhood" on the one hand, and the self-interest of individual descent groups suffering critical shortages of material resources on the other.

The spatial contiguity of fraternal clans is a significant variable. A Mae phratry of average size comprises seven or eight clans (about 2,500 people), usually occupying a continuous line of demarcated territories along one side of a river valley. Larger phratries, which can include up to twenty clans and about 5,500 people, may, however, hold land on both banks of a major river or on both slopes of a mountain range. The important point is that, of the four or five clans with which a particular clan shares common borders, at least two are likely to be of its own phratry.

The founders of the clans of a phratry are thought to have been brothers, sons of the founder of the phratry, and all their descendants in the male line (who form the most extensive set of agnates that a man recognizes) are also "brothers." Moreover, because the phratry is not, either ideally or in fact, an exogamous group and because marriages tend to be made close to home, in many cases distant agnates are simultaneously close cognates or affines. Recurrent and intricate exchange relationships should be, and are, maintained with such people, and visits back and forth are fairly frequent. In addition, men of fraternal clans are entitled to participate in the other clans' rituals in which clan ancestors are propitiated, and their bachelors may join in the others' purificatory seclusion and rituals.

In short, fraternal clans, even though they are regarded as largely autonomous politically and self-sufficient in subsistence terms, should deal with one another in amity, freely offering support when needed in warfare and in public distributions of wealth. Obviously, in view of this conventional definition of their mutual obligations, they should as far as possible avoid coming into conflict.

Nevertheless, fraternal clans do fight—and relatively often. Table 1 (p. 13 above) indicates that, of the 84 instances of intergroup warfare I have recorded for the period c.1900 to 1950, 22 (26 percent) involve clans of the same phratry (setting aside the seven that are within clans). The

28

reasons for this substantial divergence from the ideal of an enduring fraternal comity are not difficult to perceive. Of the twenty intraphratry clashes for which the reasons are known, 19 arose out of disputes over property, and 13 of these overtly concerned land. The fact that the contending clans are usually also neighbors illuminates the figures. Shared boundaries inevitably make for frequent collisions.

The Mae themselves are naturally aware of this state of affairs, and they characterize it in much the same terms I do. Indeed, men analyze the unfortunate reality of conflicts within the phratry rather as they do that of violence within the clan. "Brothers" should not quarrel, they say, but of course there will always be reasons why they do. When they quarrel, noncombatants or people related to both sides should try to persuade them into compromises that will quickly restore order. Mutual payments or exchanges of valuables between the opponents provide the best way to achieve a truce and at the same time to ratify the ensuing peace. However, because fraternal clans are in effect autonomous and jealous of their independence, it is not easy for conciliation to be effective across their borders, that is, for the members of one group to accept wholeheartedly resolutions proposed by Big Men of the other, even when the Big Men of both press for an accord. And if the leaders of the two clans disagree and strongly support the claims of their own clansmen, there is little hope of a bloodless settlement.

It is accepted, therefore, that, however regrettable this may be, quarrels between men of fraternal clans very often lead to fighting, fighting that rapidly escalates to out-and-out warfare between the clans. But once again it is explicitly assumed that "brothers" should set limits to the kind of fighting in which they engage, albeit limits somewhat wider than those thought to constrain intraclan warfare.

Thus, if the men of an aggrieved clan attack an offending fraternal clan in force, they should do so by day after giving the latter fair warning.[15] This they do by shouting insults and chanting boastful songs as they move toward the common border. Their opponents reply in kind, and the continuation of this hostile interchange gives them time to arm and assemble.[16] In addition, the general noise and confusion serve to alert neighboring clans (including those of other "brothers") to the impending battle, so that men who wish to do so have an opportunity to enlist as allies with either group. All allies from one clan do not necessarily fight together as a unit; rather, each visitor chooses the side that, for whatever reason, he wants to help on that occasion—perhaps because it includes his mother's near kinsmen or a valued exchange partner, perhaps because he has personal enemies in the other force. As a result, actual brothers may find themselves in opposing camps, in which case they take care not to fire at each other or, for that matter, at any close friends or relatives.[17]

In this way the number of men fighting on each side may be more or less equalized, which means that the war, at least in its initial stages, may well degenerate into a costly stalemate, and those who began it become more ready to negotiate a truce. However, with Mae clans ranging in size from under 200 to well over 1,000 members (or from under sixty to over 300 warriors), there are obviously occasions on which the disparity between two contending groups is too great to be offset by the support of extraclan friends, if only because a very large clan generally has more potential allies than a small one has.

Whereas a clan whose fighting men are grossly outnumbered by their opponents is likely to accept any allies who offer their services, another clan not at such a disadvantage may not welcome them. In part this is because, given Enga techniques of military command, it is not easy for the host group to control the actions of its allies, who may push the fight against its "brothers" more vigorously or less selectively than the host wishes. For instance, an enraged ally, pursuing a personal grievance and not being bound by the underlying obligations of fraternity, may kill a man that his hosts would have been pleased to spare. Indeed, Mae leaders recognize that the men most ready to join in other peoples' wars are just the young hotheads who will disregard the orders of their seniors.

Moreover, according to the rules allocating responsibility for homicides, the two groups that initiate the fighting "own the quarrel." Each group must later pay substantial compensation, not only for opponents killed in the fighting but also for any of its own allies who die in combat. Hence a clan that is not wholly enthusiastic about warring with its "brothers," even in self-defense, may be loath to see the conflict expand with the consequent likelihood that, win or lose, it will afterward bear a crippling burden of pig debts. Such a clan may therefore discourage large numbers of allies from joining it.

Other constraints should also operate in warfare between fraternal clans. Thus, the requirement that these groups attack each other only by day and after giving due warning is sharply contrasted with the notion that it is proper to take other clans by surprise (by mounting nocturnal raids or, better, a dawn invasion) in order to achieve a maximum of death and destruction, especially by burning houses in the hope of incinerating their human and porcine occupants. This is intended to demoralize the enemy forces, making it difficult for them to regroup and so facilitating their complete rout.

A daylight engagement, on the other hand, almost inevitably leads to a war of hectic skirmishing by mobile battle lines, during which women, children, and pigs can evacuate the area being fought over and take refuge with friendly clans nearby. Indeed, the warriors should not seek out noncombatants as targets; and, although they shoot to kill their opponents, they should not try to cut down the wounded or to mutilate the dead. Nevertheless, even within such limits, the casualty rates in warfare between clans of the same phratry are by no means negligible; in nine cases of intraphratry fighting the numbers of deaths recalled range from one to nine, with a total (I think an underestimate) of 27.

Whereas men in these "fraternal" conflicts may well tear up and trample opponents' gardens in their path, break fences, wound stray pigs, or even put to the torch houses they pass, this is not their primary aim, and in any case the mobility of the fighting reduces the amount of damage they can do and still fight effectively. In particular, it is wrong for an attacking force to destroy the cult-house of their "brothers" or to ring-bark the great old trees that shade their ceremonial grounds, for these are the appurtenances of ancestors who also figure in the agnatic genealogies of the invaders.

Finally, there is the general expectation that warfare between fraternal clans should be limited in time, that even within a day's fighting the victors, by invading their opponents' domain, destroying some of their property, and killing or wounding some of their men, can make their point sufficiently clear. Having done so, they should withdraw into their own territory and, while the losers return to repair the damage they have suffered, enter into negotiations over compensation for such deaths as have occurred. These dealings should in turn enable both sides to reach compromise solutions to the initial grievances and thus lead to the re-establishing of ostensibly friendly relations between them.

Ideally, then, the Mae view warfare within the phratry in much the same way as they do warfare within the clan, that is, as an activity that should be amenable to certain constraints that reflect, however dimly, men's moral obligations to their agnatic "brothers." Nevertheless, they also recognize that every clan is concerned as far as possible to maintain its autonomy and to pursue its own ends, so that serious disputes between fraternal clans are even more likely than intraclan disputes to defy conciliation. This is particularly so when land is at issue. Then the pattern of events closely parallels the one I have already sketched for the development of hostilities between subclans.

My observations suggest that when the population density of a growing clan much exceeds about 250 persons per square mile, the members of that group become increasingly land-hungry. The rise in the incidence of internal disputes over garden boundaries and over the incursions of pigs helps alert them to their predicament. Given the explicit expectation that men should not blatantly encroach on the holdings of clansmen, those who feel impelled to extend their estates should do so at the expense of other, adjacent clans. However, some of these neighbors are fraternal clans and, in the light of this wider, albeit more tenuous bond, one should not overtly infringe on their territories either. Rather, the men should probe the borders their clan shares with non-fraternal clans.

By and large, the men attempt to do this. By covertly shifting their boundary markers a few yards each time they bring a new garden into cultivation, they continually gnaw away at the fallow of the weakest agnatically unrelated clan that adjoins their own. Because they are likely to have singled out for this treatment a clan considerably smaller than their own, there is a good chance that the victims will hesitate to push the matter to the point of violence for fear of provoking a full-scale invasion. Such a state of affairs can persist for years, until either the victims can no longer tolerate the losses and are forced to fight, or the usurpers, believing the odds to favor them heavily, seize on any incident as a *casus belli* and attack in strength.

The need (or at least the desire) of an expanding clan for more land may be increasing at a rate that cannot effectively be met by gradual encroachment upon the territory of one or more of the adjacent non-fraternal clans. Or these clans may themselves be growing and of such obvious strength that to incite a confrontation with them would be suicidal. With clans ranging in size from under 200 to over 1,000 members, men must weigh their chances with care before deciding to embark on a collision course with a neighboring group.

So the clansmen may have little choice but to turn their attentions to one or another of their fraternal neighbors. One device, commonly used, is for land-hungry men to use distributions of valuables as opportunities to treat with generous consideration affines, cognates, or exchange partners among more distant agnates, especially those belonging to a smaller and weaker contiguous clan in the phratry. The last, being in a vulnerable position vis-à-vis other, potentially hostile groups, welcome this support, as well as offers of fraternal aid in military defense; and sometimes they are willing to repay the helpers by allowing them usufructuary, agistment, and even residential privileges in their domain. Normally, landholders should carefully qualify the terms of such concessions, granting them only for a season at a time and reserving the right to dismiss the visitors at will. Occasionally, however, a host who has ample land to spare, or whose greed for present gains blinds him to future dangers, may foolishly let his guests cultivate year after year on fallow land that adjoins the outsiders' clan holdings—land the outsiders have shrewdly selected for its location. Eventually, when the host finds he needs the land and requests the occupants to vacate it, they (or their sons) vigorously assert that it has always been theirs, that it is part of their clan patrimony for which they are prepared to fight. Their own clansmen are, of course, usually only too willing to confirm these claims, which, if successful, will relieve some of the pressures on their estates. The men of the host's clan then have to decide whether or not recovery of the area involved is worth the risk, indeed the likelihood, of a military defeat that could lead to a more extensive invasion of their clan territory.

Even as a weak clan faces this devious kind of usurpation by men of expanding fraternal clans, it may simultaneously be suffering a straightforward erosion of its boundaries (as described above) at the hands of other "brothers" whose numbers are outrunning their resources. Border disputes multiply, brawls increase in frequency and intensity, and compromise becomes impossible as the antagonists reject the appeals of others to observe the obligations of agnatic brotherhood. The feelings of enmity solidify as men on both sides, irrespective of the merits of their cases, take every opportunity to steal each other's pigs and pandanus nuts—offenses of such seriousness that the consequent confrontation between victims and culprits inevitably explodes out of the common melée into bitter interclan fighting.

At this point, reasonably enough, each group is persuaded that its very survival as an autonomous entity is at stake. All-out warfare involving pitched battles, raids, ambushes, and arson continues, sometimes for weeks, as each side strives to demoralize and eventually to rout the other in such disorder that the losers can never regroup and regain their territory. Should one group achieve so decisive a victory, the members of the other disperse and take refuge wherever they can among friendly, related clans. The victors occupy the vacated territory and henceforth count it an integral part of their clan patrimony.

Unlike some other highlands groups, Mae clans do not perform rituals that serve to legitimize in their own or other peoples' eyes their occupation of territories taken by force. They simply rely on their uninterrupted use of the land over time to effect a kind of social amnesia through which de facto possession is converted into de jure title. Naturally enough, the rapidity with which others recognize their newly extended domain varies according to their relations with the usurpers and the losers. If victors and vanquished are members of the same phratry, men of other fraternal clans, as well as those of friendly or neutral clans nearby, may be slow to forget the facts of the matter, which they may use to score points in public oratory at interclan gatherings. (When the antagonists are of different phratries, by contrast, the "brothers" of the victorious clan, who were probably also active allies in the combat, readily and happily accept the situation.) The dispossessed families of the beaten clan, of course, long remember their humiliation (or at least their version of it), as do men of other clans of their phratry. Indeed, for a generation or so afterward, the latter may invoke the usurpation as justification for their own military attacks on the victors, even though such warfare arises out of current disputes over other land or pig thefts.

Only a few wars I know of between clans of the same phratry have ended in such clear-cut, final defeats. There are at least two reasons for this, both touched on earlier. First, when interclan fighting grows out of a brawl or small-scale engagement between lesser groups, as is likely to occur where fraternal clans are concerned, the pattern of events usually gives the weaker side time in which to arm and to assemble in sufficient numbers to blunt the initial drive of the stronger force. In the skirmishing and raiding that follow, the former can then mount a defense strong enough to inflict casualties on the attackers and to achieve a stalemate, albeit one that may cost them some land. Second, and connected with this, the capacity of the weaker force to sustain a holding action for some hours enables allies to stream in (remember that distances between Mae clans are short), so that the numbers on the two sides become more equal and the probability of a standoff increases.

Obviously, then, a clan that is determined to dispossess a fraternal clan of its land is most likely to succeed if it takes the latter by surprise— that is, if it adopts a measure explicitly condemned for warfare within the phratry. On occasion the desire of a growing clan for more land becomes so strong and its relations with a neighboring fraternal clan deteriorate so sadly that its members in council unanimously decide to invade the other group's territory without warning, and they make covert preparations for the action. Indeed, the aggressors may go further and seek as an ally in the venture another expanding clan that adjoins and is currently at odds with the intended victims. For obvious reasons they prefer to approach a clan of another phratry, whose men will be more ready to participate in such unbrotherly treachery and less likely to warn the prey.

The Big Men and the fight leaders of both clans meet in secret in a men's house of the allies' clan to thrash out the details of a bargain whereby, in return for launching a simultaneous attack on the enemy's flank or rear, the allied group is also invited to exploit the victory. The instigators do not, however, undertake to make any payment in the event the overall strategy to disperse the opponents fails other than to promise that, win or lose, they will compensate the allies for their dead.[18]

Because both parties to the agreement are motivated by a shortage of domestic resources, the initiators of the plan are careful to specify the spoils and the terms on which the allies are to share them. Depending on the relative needs of the two clans and on the pertinacity with which the allies haggle, the latter's proposed share may range from the right to seize any pigs they encounter, through the right to fell valuable timber trees or to harvest for a given period the pandanus nuts on a demarcated area of the victims' territory adjoining their border or to cultivate there for one or more years, up to an outright cession of that locality to the allies.

Once the bargain is struck, the instigators unobtrusively return home and inform their clansmen. At this meeting, which is convened quietly in order not to alert neighboring groups and which is attended by all males in their late teens or older, they plan a predawn attack in strength for the next day and ensure that everyone clearly understands the strategy and tactics to be employed. The leaders choose the early morning for two important reasons. Not only is this the time at which they expect the enemy to be least prepared and hence most vulnerable, but also an engagement initiated then can be pressed to the utmost throughout the daylight hours. Although Mae warriors will on occasion undertake stealthy raids or set ambushes by night, they dislike having to fight pitched battles in darkness among trees and over the difficult mountain terrain.

Toward evening the men check their weapons and prepare food to serve as combat rations. They move their women, children, pigs, and valuables from houses near the border to safer positions inside the clan domain and appoint the old men and the boys to protect them from sudden forays. Then the men take up their concealed posts for the night, in readiness for the signal to rush the enemy houses. Their allies, meanwhile, do likewise, and they watch at their border for the flames that will herald the start of the fighting and bring them into action.

The men of a clan assailed without warning on two fronts are likely at the outset to suffer severe casualties and to be badly shaken, so that the aggressors stand a fair chance of routing them and occupying their territory before the end of the first day. This, of course, is the attackers' aim—to force a decision before darkness brings the attack to a halt and gives the victims time to regroup and to call in allies. The defenders, on the other hand, fight desperately and try to hold out so that their families can escape to neighboring clans, and enough allies, either as individuals or as groups, can join them to sustain hostilities until dusk.

However, even if the defense survives the first onslaught and the action continues intermittently for days or weeks, the defenders usually remain at such a disadvantage that the inevitable is merely postponed. Eventually they break and scatter to friendly clans, losing much or all of their land as a result. Their best hope of avoiding this fate is that a fraternal clan, angered by the treachery, will in turn take one of the attacking groups in the rear and force these men to withdraw to protect their own estates. Should this occur, both the original and the subsidiary conflict may then develop into a stalemate of the kind and with the consequences I have described earlier.

If, as seems commonly to be the case when two clans combine to invade the territory of a third, the aggressors achieve their ends, the consequences of their victory are also predictable. Having dispersed the group that formerly separated them, the clans now share a common border; despite the careful allocation beforehand of the newly acquired resources, quarrels soon arise over the interpretation and implementation of the claims made by men of each group. Add to these the domestic pressures that the groups are likely to be experiencing and it is not surprising that before long the erstwhile allies are themselves at war.

Disputes between clans within a phratry, like those between sub-clans within a clan, can on occasion escalate into the kind of unrestrained warfare that so frequently occurs between non-fraternal clans; and the circumstances leading to this are generally the same, namely that the members of one of the contending groups believe that they absolutely must have more land to support their growing human and porcine populations.

I do not wish, however, to suggest by this statement that whenever Mae experience a shortage (actual or fancied) of land, they at once go to war. They may at first resort to other expedients in the hope of meeting their needs, such as asking for usufructuary privileges from relatives or friends in other, better situated clans; they may cut into their forest reserves or drain swampy localities to extend their arable land; they may increase the number of pigs they have on agistment elsewhere or mount pig distributions to reduce the size of their herds. Nevertheless, such peaceful devices seem at best to provide temporary solutions, and sooner or later a growing clan has little choice but to encroach on the holdings of its weakest neighbors, an action that inevitably leads to violence that in turn develops into internecine war. And often enough the targets of this aggression are phratry brothers.

Warfare between clans of different phratries

The internal logic governing the course of intergroup hostilities within clans and within phratries has forced me to touch on the kind of strenuous warfare the Mae believe appropriate between non-fraternal clans. Without anticipating here the detailed account of the mechanics of Mae warfare that is to follow, I shall at this point simply summarize the significant features of this mode of conflict.

The attributes that seem to me (and to the Mae) most obviously to mark off non-fraternal wars from those between "brothers" are: (a) the execution of surprise attacks or invasions with the aim of achieving a total rout that opens the enemy's territory to occupation; (b) the deliberate maximizing of property destruction (cult structures, houses, ceremonial grounds, trees, crops, and pigs), in the hope of demoralizing the enemy; (c) the readiness to ignore the restraints of kinship or affinity, both as they moderate the intensity of violence and as they encourage acceptance of mediation or conciliation; (d) the occasional refusal to recognize non-combatant status; (e) the mutilation of fallen enemies; (f) and, perhaps, the longer duration of these confrontations.

In 18 cases of warfare between clans of different phratries, the number of deaths for which I have information (again obviously partial) ranges from one to 24, with a total of 69.[19]

Other data relevant to non-fraternal warfare may also be adduced here. Table 1 (p. 13 above) indicates that, of the 84 instances of inter-group fighting that involved any of the 14 Mae clans in my neighborhood before about 1950, 55 (65 percent) concern opponents of different phratries. However, given that on the average only about one-third of the clans directly adjoining a Mae clan are likely to be of its own phratry, the 65 percent figure is not remarkable. That is to say, despite the stated ideals of the Mae to the contrary, the members of these clans do not appear in that period to have attacked non-fraternal neighbors significantly more often than they did their "brothers," which suggests yet another triumph of Realpolitik over social morality.

Two of the conflicts in this sample are "great fights" or interphratry tourneys, a category already described. Of the remaining 44 for whose occurrence I know the ostensible reasons, 25 (57 percent) arose directly out of disputes over land, 13 (29 percent) concerned other kinds of possessions, and six (14 percent) the avenging of homicides. These figures, like those for intraphratry and intraclan warfare, underline the Mae's preoccupation with material property and the lengths to which they will go to secure or defend it.

The data also point to the significance of propinquity in determining who goes to war. Repeatedly we find that the groups which first attack each other, the "owners of the quarrel," are actual neighbors. Given that quarrels over land are the prime cause of intergroup warfare, this makes sense. The techniques used to infiltrate or to seize coveted territory, together with the difficulty if not the impossibility of a clan's controlling terrain separated from its home base by other potentially hostile groups, obviously militate against frequent warfare between clans that are not contiguous. Moreover, in situations where land is not at issue—for instance, when one clan simply plans a destructive hit-and-run attack on another, if the intended target is not a neighbor the aggressors require at least the tacit permission of intervening groups to move in force through their domains. Unless such clans are friendly phratry "brothers" or are themselves at odds with the intended victims, they are unlikely to welcome the passage of a large company of armed men across their land. Even if they agree to this, the chances are that the attackers will have lost the important element of surprise by the time they reach the enemy's border.

This is not to say that members of non-contiguous clans, especially those of different phratries, do not come into conflict. They do so frequently, and at times bloodshed ensues. Most commonly such disputes concern the claims of specific men or groups to receive valuables in public prestations connected with marriages, deaths, or the Te exchange; and they can lead to killings whose avenging demands further bloodshed. These retaliatory homicides, however, are usually not effected during organized warfare but rather are isolated murders committed by disgruntled individuals or small raiding parties.

These attempts at self-help normally receive the approbation of the perpetrators' clansmen, either before or after the fact, despite the possibility they raise of a further round of murderous reprisals; such is the importance that Mae ascribe to asserting clan solidarity and sovereignty in the face of external injury or insult. For this reason I am reluctant to label these modes of redress among the Mae as instances of feud, even though they may appear to resemble, in scale at any rate, situations loosely characterized as feud in the African ethnographic literature. Moreover, these kinds of actions can have wider political and military consequences in that, by motivating clansmen of victims to join as allies one or the other side in other interclan battles, the outcome of those engagements may be significantly affected. Accordingly, they warrant a brief description at this point.

A typical situation is that which follows when a man (of clan X) is killed while fighting as an ally of his relatives or exchange partners in another clan (Y) that is at war with a third group (clan Z). The host clan Y as one of the "owners" of the original quarrel is by custom responsible for the death and should pay a substantial homicide compensation to the victim's agnates (clan X). Generally the host clan does so, and there the matter rests. But if for any reason, whether a lack of pigs or a fresh dispute with the clan of the dead ally, the host clan refuses compensation or unduly postpones the payment, the deceased's clansmen are likely to respond with violence. In this they are significantly motivated not only by their desire for the pigs due them and by their need to uphold conspicuously the prestige of their own group, but also by their fear that both the ghost of the dead man and the ancestral ghosts of the clan as a whole might retaliate if they failed to act.[20]

If the two clans X and Y are contiguous, the complainants may launch an attack on the defaulters, with or without warning depending on such considerations as the tenor of previous dealings and the kin or other connections between them. Should the groups be some distance apart so that continuous, organized warfare is not feasible, the deceased's agnates of X, especially his lineage "brothers," may tacitly reserve the right to avenge his loss by bringing about the death of a member of the defaulting clan Y when a suitable opportunity arises.

Because the original victim from X was merely an ally of one of the owners of the dispute (Y), clan Z, whose warriors in fact killed him, is not bound to pay compensation to his agnates in X (although if Z is the other owner of the dispute, it should of course compensate for any fatalities among its own allies and within the opposed owner, clan Y. Should the clans of the killers (Z) and the deceased ally (X) have few or no kin or exchange ties, the men of the latter generally, albeit grudgingly, concede the propriety of clan Z's not making them a homicide payment. In effect they charge their brother's death to the fortunes of war; he knew the risk he was taking when he went off to fight (see Figure 4).

But should the two clans X and Z, although spatially separated, be joined by blood or marriage (which is commonly the case), the men who are actually so related are impelled to argue for the payment of homicide compensation to preserve or extend the exchange connections between the two groups. If enough of the killers' clansmen in Z, especially the Big Men, support the proposal, that clan will offer compensation, and by accepting it the clan of the deceased publicly declares the matter to be closed. On the other hand, the refusal of the killers' clan Z to act in such circumstances is an overt denigration of existing connections. This affronts the victim's clansmen in X, some of whom may then be disposed to avenge his death and thus assuage their own feelings.

There are several ways in which the aggrieved men can take revenge on a distant group. One response, relatively rare, is to direct at some or all of the offenders putatively lethal sorcery of a kind specially imported from other regions that are noted for these products. But, as Mae pragmatists have often told me, the effect of sorcery is uncertain, and in any

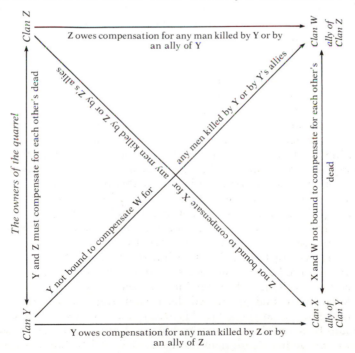

Figure 4   Responsibility for the compensation of deaths in Mae interclan warfare

case its use does not offer the satisfaction that comes from actually cutting down an enemy with an axe. If the identity of the killer is known, it is better for some of the dead man's close agnates to pay a stealthy nocturnal visit to the culprit's territory in the hope of catching him unawares. Such retaliation utilizes the basic techniques of raiding, which I shall describe more fully in the chapter on the mechanics of warfare. However, I should note here that if the preferred target, the actual killer, proves to be too wary (for instance, he may sensibly have decided to pay a prolonged visit to a friendly clan until passions cool), one of his clansmen, or one of their women, can serve in his stead—a substitution that in many cases paves the way for further bloodshed.

Such small-scale incursions into distant enemy territory obviously expose the raiders to the risk of interception by superior numbers when making their escape, and such enterprises therefore are not lightly undertaken. An alternative approach is for the victim's clansmen to conceal their anger and do nothing for weeks or months, until the killer optimistically persuades himself that the matter has blown over and he resumes his daily round of activities. As soon as he incautiously travels near the deceased's clan territory and is seen by a man, woman, or child there, a quiet signal initiates a rapid but effective ambush.[21] Custom demands that afterward the assailants announce their success with yodeling calls and invite the members of a friendly intervening clan to retrieve the corpse and take it to its home place for mourning and burial.

Sometimes the original killer, with what must be regarded as incredible foolhardiness, is so concerned to implement some profitable exchange transaction with a partner or relative in the dead man's clan that he visits this friend, trusting in the latter's hospitality and protection. Should the close agnates of his original victim learn of his presence (and usually they do so), the obligations of fraternal solidarity demand that they act, either by luring the host away with a message, for instance, that pigs are destroying his garden, and killing the visitor in his absence, or, if the stratagem fails, by overpowering the host and shooting down the outsider as he flees. The host, on the other hand, is bound by personal considerations of kinship, hospitality, and no doubt self-interest to try to prevent the death of his guest, even to the extent of fighting with his "brothers."

In one such case the host returned from a false errand to find the body of his visitor lying riddled with arrows outside his house yard. Incensed, he turned on the murderers, men of a parallel subclan, and killed one with his axe. Other clansmen intervened to stop the fight from spreading. As a heated and protracted discussion over compensation ensued, the clan of the victim, which in this instance lay nearby, attacked in force. It should be noted that in situations of guest murder, a man's attempt to save or avenge his visitor does not necessarily shield him from reprisals mounted by the latter's clan, nor does it excuse him from contributing to any homicide compensation paid by his clan to his guest's. As a member of the offending clan he must share the responsibility for its actions.

Finally, exacting revenge by inciting an agent to homicide is a recognized device. Thus, men of clan A may have been unsuccessful in avenging a "brother" who was killed by a member of clan C. With the approval of his clansmen of A, particularly of the Big Men, the father or brother of the deceased secretly approaches a relative, often a maternal kinsman of the victim, who belongs to a clan B that is a neighbor of clan C. The visitor explains that he and his clansmen have not been able to surprise the wanted man, and he entreats his relative to arrange an ambush on their behalf because (he hopes) the killer does not fear danger from that quarter. To strengthen his case the petitioner invokes the ties of blood, friendship, and exchange dealings that the dead man had had with his relative, and he plays on any injuries that the killer's group, clan C, has done to the chosen agent's group, clan B. The petitioner guarantees the support of his own clan A in any conflict that follows, and he may also promise the covert transfer of a pig or two as an individual payment for the service. If, as can happen, clans A and B are also members of the one phratry and clan C is not, the petitioner is of course in an even better position to enlist the desired aid by appealing to fraternal solidarity. If the relative agrees to entertain the request, the visitor gives him a suitably bespelled bow or spear to use.

Whether or not the relative undertakes the task depends largely on the political relations currently obtaining between his and the killer's clans. If, as the petitioner often knows to be the case, the two have been seriously at odds over land or pig thefts, men of clan B may welcome an opportunity to weaken their opponents and, even at the risk of provoking war, may urge their "brother" to act. Once the murder is accomplished, the original clan A may announce its part in the affair and offer homicide compensation directly to the victim's agnates, or the relative's clan B may pay on the understanding that clan A will quickly reimburse them.

Naturally enough, the clansmen of the new victim may take reprisals against the agent's clan B either by mounting a concerted attack or by raiding. If warfare ensues, the original clan A is morally bound to support clan B in strength. In either case, clan A is regarded as the owner of the quarrel and should compensate *both* the other groups for any deaths. However, in light of the situation that stimulated this chain of events, the "owners," although willing to compensate clan B, may well delay or refuse payment to clan C, arguing that the two groups are now even. Whether clan C accepts this unilateral rejection of responsibility is in turn contingent on factors such as the number of casualties it has suffered, the importance of its former exchange and other connections with clan A, and its current relations with clan B. The latter, B, may decide that its own interests are better served by compensating for those men of clan

C whom its members have killed; and it may suit clan C to accept the offer and temporarily relinquish its claims on clan A in order to secure a breathing space in which to acquire more economic and political allies.

The Mae distinction, ideally at least, of warfare between fraternal clans from that between clans of different phratries raises the question whether they, like some other highlands people, recognize a category of permanent or traditional enemies for a particular clan or clans and whether these are simply to be equated with non-fraternal clans. The answer is by no means simple, for several interacting factors must be taken into account.

First, given that Mae clans are locally bounded, named, and populous entities that persist identifiably through time (in many cases for at least a century), Mae social structure is fully compatible with relationships of long-term enmity between specific groups. In addition, the overt folk distinction between fraternal and non-fraternal clans and the assertion that "brothers" should remain on friendly terms could well point to the groups toward which enduring hostility is appropriate.

On the other hand, as my figures indicate and as the Mae themselves realize, warfare tends to erupt most frequently between neighbors, and it very often involves fraternal clans. There are, as we have seen, good ecological reasons for this. Topography, types and distribution of resources, population pressures, and the like make it inevitable that contiguous clans, whatever their agnatic links, constantly come into conflict. The Mae frequently say "we marry the people we fight," and this popular stereotype is supported by the evidence. Analysis of a sample of 311 marriages made by members of three clans in my neighborhood reveals that over half of them took spouses from adjacent clans (see Table 3), that is, from the groups with which they are most likely to be at war. In roughly the same period one clan for which I have more detailed information made at least 182 marriages with 41 other clans, and was involved in disputes with them that resulted in at least 36 homicides. With respect to the variable of intervening distance the correlation ($rho_{m,k}$) between the rates of intermarriage and killing is $+.65$. Moreover, 61 percent (111) of these marriages and 69 percent (25) of the killings concerned immediate neighbors, both fraternal and non-fraternal.

Table 3 Propinquity and marriage among the Mae Enga

Number of marriages	Distance of spouse's clan from reference clan			
	Contiguous	Next but one	More remote	Total
Intraphratry	72	12	17	101
Extraphratry	92	59	59	210
Total	164	71	76	311
Percentage	52.7	22.9	24.4	100

42

Nevertheless, although these figures confirm the view that for a Mae clan all neighboring clans (and especially those directly adjacent) are always potential and often active opponents, Mae men themselves declare that at a given time they regard only some of the non-fraternal nearby clans as "real" enemies, with whom they feel impelled to fight bitterly and often, and that these patterns of enmity shift over the years. From what I have been able to learn about the "histories" and reported attitudes of several clans during the past fifty or so years, I am persuaded that something of the kind is so. Even as a clan engages for various reasons in intermittent hostilities with numerous other clans, there is generally one, perhaps two, of its non-fraternal neighbors with whom for a period of five or ten years it contends strenuously for land. Then as circumstances change, either suddenly or gradually, each of the clans directs its aggression or defense toward another clan.

Population differences are obviously a significant factor here. Thus, the two groups may be so evenly matched that recurrent warfare simply ends in a stalemate, or one may be just strong enough to occupy a small part but no more of the enemy's territory.[22] Each clan is likely then to reduce its commitment in that direction and begin testing the borders of other contiguous non-fraternal clans. In the process it generates with one of them a corresponding relationship of long-term, intense enmity. Moreover, while the first two groups have been locked in continuing contention, it often happens that a previously neutral neighbor of one of them has become, in a relatively short time, effectively larger and more powerful than the latter as a result of differential rates of marriage, fertility, and mortality from warfare and illness. The encroachments of this clan now begin to threaten seriously the security of its neighbor, which has little choice but to damp down hostilities with its habitual enemy in order to meet the new danger. Mae men have frequently told me how greatly they fear having to fight on two fronts simultaneously; they know that this means almost certain defeat on a grand scale.

In short, not even among non-fraternal Mae clans do we encounter fixed relationships of enmity. The focal point for the military activity of any Mae clan continually shifts through time. That is to say, within the broader context of expectations that all other clans, be they fraternal or not, are potential opponents, the Mae recognize that for any given period only one or two of these groups (most often nonfraternal neighbors) are one's "real" enemies, with whom constant combat is the proper mode of behavior. Furthermore, percipient Mae men are aware that the identity of one's current enemies and allies is largely dependent on the interaction of two kinds of variables: namely, (1) the moral constraints ascribed to the norms of kinship and of exchange, which themselves are interpreted variably in the light of pragmatic considerations, and (2) the material stimuli of population pressures and land resources, which of course are never wholly stable.[23]

Hostility and mobility

The ever-present threat of violence abroad has had serious consequences for personal mobility. In this respect it is necessary to consider three fairly clearly defined periods: that up till about 1950, when the Australian administration imposed general peace on the Central Enga; the decade from about 1950 to about 1960, in which most of the people turned to the official courts to settle their disputes; and the next ten or twelve years, which have seen a noticeable resurgence of intergroup warfare, mainly over land, and a great deal of individual turbulence sparked by alcohol. I shall deal with the last two periods in their appropriate historical contexts in later chapters.

In the past all movement outside one's own clan territory was hazardous, and in general men made such excursions only in armed groups and for compelling reasons, in particular to attend distributions of wealth, to negotiate exchange transactions, to trade, and to assist friends and relatives in battle. Casual social visiting by lone men was not common, not only because it exposed the wayfarer to the dangers of ambush and murder en route, but also because it violated Mae notions of personal privacy and group security. A man who unexpectedly appeared at the house of even a close kinsman in another clan was viewed with some suspicion by the latter's clansmen as a potential spy, who might carry home information—about that clan's defenses (palisades, ditches, secret escape passages, and the like) or about the disposition of its pigs—that could be used in planning a night raid or theft. Accordingly, it was the duty of his host to keep the guest from loitering about the host's territory during his stay and to escort him directly to the clan border on his departure.

Nevertheless, on occasion one or two men might, at the explicit invitation of a maternal kinsman or a wife's agnate, have to go to a relative's house—for instance, to discuss arrangements for a death compensation or to receive a preliminary gift for the Te distribution. If their destination lay at some distance, the travelers had to choose carefully a route, however roundabout, that took them along the public tracks of currently friendly or neutral clans. Even if they avoided their enemies on the way, they could still encounter unforeseen trouble on their arrival. I know of several instances when a visitor walking with his host was killed in a surprise raid or ambush aimed at the latter by a neighboring clan. That this man was a stranger to the attackers was irrelevant; they would not chance letting the host escape in order to spare the visitor. In such circumstances the host's clan should later offer homicide compensation to the visitor's agnates.

Naturally enough, women did not travel abroad unless they were in the company of armed men from their fathers' or their husbands' clans, an elementary precaution that effectively limited their contacts with extraclan relatives. In general women, whether married or single, visited

44

other clans only on relatively formal occasions, as when members of their clans of residence were required to participate at weddings, the making of compensations, the distribution of Te valuables, and the celebration of fraternal clans' rituals.

Given the network of cognatic, affinal, and exchange relationships in which the clans of a Mae neighborhood are embedded, together with the shifting patterns of interclan hostilities discussed earlier, it follows that often a clan which is mounting a distribution of wealth (for instance, a death compensation to matrilateral kinsmen) has simultaneous binding social obligations toward two clans that are currently "real" enemies. Thus, one might include agnates of the deceased's mother, the other the mother's sister's husband's agnates; both have the right to attend the meeting and to receive valuables. Conventional propriety demands that, out of deference to their hosts, the opposed groups should keep apart during the ceremonies and then depart separately and peacefully. But obviously, if the groups have recently been skirmishing and in particular if one has a death to avenge, the encounter is fraught with possibilities of violence.[24]

Much depends on the strength of the host group. If it is relatively numerous and there are enough other uncommitted guests present, all these men combine to keep order as the donors hurry through the prestations, although even this haste can elicit vigorous responses from men ready to take affront. No matter how numerous or persuasive the keepers, they cannot hope to induce the visitors to give up their arms on arrival; even to suggest this could provoke a riot.

Clansmen going to another clan's distribution almost always know beforehand whether their enemies will also be there. Not only are they acquainted with the kinship and other connections of the people concerned, they can also hear the singing and yodeling by which invitations are transmitted from ridge to ridge, and they make their plans accordingly. Whoever the other visitors are to be, each group will include women (and even children) as a sign to its hosts of ostensibly peaceful intentions. Indeed, should a visiting party comprise only armed men, the hosts, assembled in force, would turn them back at the border and postpone the distribution. Therefore, when a clan knows that its current enemies are also to be present, it musters a considerable number of fighting men but only a few women for the excursion.

Before they set off, the Big Men and military experts carefully brief the travelers, warning them to keep close together during the ceremonies and to watch their opponents constantly. If the enemy contingent greatly outnumbers them, it might well seize on an altercation as an excuse to attack, so that the women have to be ready to flee while their men make a fighting retreat. On the other hand, during the visit their own leaders may judge that a clear advantage lies with them, and one covertly alerts the party by, for example, shifting his decorated head-scratcher from one side of his wig to the other. At this signal the noncombatants prepare to decamp, while the men quietly loosen their weapons and await the command to fall on the enemy. In these melées the aggressors cannot expect to kill or disable many of their opponents before the hosts and other guests come to the aid of the latter. Consequently, their aim is to cut down one or two of the most important men in the enemy party and then to run in a group for the border, turning now and again to fire a volley of arrows to deter their pursuers.

Even if both parties, or at least their leaders, have decided to keep the peace at the assembly, it is always possible that a member of one group will recognize in the other the actual slayer of a son or brother and will feel compelled to take vengeance there and then—for instance, by stalking and killing the offender when he withdraws to relieve himself. In the uproar that follows discovery of the corpse, the homicide's agnates are bound to support him, thus immediately converting the issue into inter-clan combat.

However it comes about, if enemies fight and kill at such a gathering, the ensuing complications are considerable. The two contending groups are in a real sense the "owners of the quarrel" and are therefore liable to pay compensation for each other's dead, as well as for anybody else who is killed during the fray. Nevertheless, the agnates of slain neutral bystanders are likely to demand compensation from the hosts on the grounds that they are responsible for the safety of their guests. The situation is obviously one in which the seeds of future disputes are sown, disputes serious enough to lead to warfare between hitherto friendly or neutral clans.

The Mechanics
of Mae Warfare
4

Here I am mainly concerned with the practical aspects of serious warfare among the Mae, matters to which I gave only passing attention in earlier chapters.

Material considerations

I begin with a brief account of the material equipment the Mae employ in military offense and defense, for technological considerations obviously both constrain and motivate their choices of strategy and tactics.

Pattern of residence

Residential arrangements clearly have a bearing here. It will be recalled that the Mae do not live in compact villages that can be walled about and hence readily defended by relatively large groups of inhabitants. Instead, their houses, separately occupied by men and by women, are dispersed in homesteads throughout the clan domain. The dwellings are not, however, randomly distributed. Social and topographical factors determine their locations.

47

A Mae clan territory typically comprises a polygonal block of dissected land, extending more or less at right angles from a major river up to the crest of the containing ridge; in some cases it continues over the ridge and down to the river in the adjoining valley. The lateral borders of the territory are generally tributary creeks, and the upper boundary runs through a zone of fairly dense forest crowning or abutting the ridge. This forest not only provides timber and other commodities for the clan, it also impedes and noisily signals the movements of those who would pass through it in force and without warning. For this reason the clansmen maintain there only one or two narrow, tortuous tracks, which must be traversed slowly in single file and which can easily be guarded at their proximate entrances in troubled times.

If the clan can spare the land, along the banks of the lateral boundary streams the men foster belts of trees or dense stands of cane grass. It is almost impossible to move quietly through the cane grass, which is also an effective barrier to snipers' arrows and at the same time furnishes necessary materials for the manufacture of arrow shafts.

Should the main river at the lower border separate the clan from a currently friendly clan, especially a fraternal group, men from both may combine, if there are no reasonably safe fording places, to construct a suspension or an arched bridge to facilitate visiting. Although the boulder-strewn rivers are not very wide or deep, they can rise quickly and run fast following heavy rain. Because few Enga know how to swim, crossing swollen rivers presents a real hazard and drownings are common.

In general, however, people are reluctant to build bridges, for fear that they encourage trespass, theft, and sudden attack. Indeed, the first move of a clan mounting a surprise invasion of a neighbor's territory is to seize any bridge between them and to place pickets there to secure a line of retreat. The defenders in turn try to force the bridge and cut it. Accordingly, if relations become strained between two groups connected by a bridge, usually one will dismantle the structure, both as a precautionary measure and as a gesture symbolic of social distance. The almost inevitable dispute that follows over the ownership of the salvaged timber fans an already smoldering fire.

Within the defensive perimeter of the clan territory, men place their own and their wives' houses with several considerations (positive and negative) in mind.[1] These include (not in order of importance) ready access to springs of drinking water, the avoidance of damp ground, current locations of family gardens and food trees and their stages of maturity, the desire for domestic privacy (especially for the women's houses, in which the family pigs shelter), the distribution of existing men's houses of the lineage and subclan, suitability for the establishment or extension of a ceremonial ground, distance from the clan's cult house, and security.

The outcome of such calculations is that men generally erect their

48

Mae Enga homestead complex of men's house and associated women's houses

own houses a hundred yards or more below the edge of the upper forest, scattered across terraces or spurs that stand high above the river. The military virtues of such a position are manifold. The houses are at a fairly safe distance from the borders across which attacks may be expected; and they command good views of neighboring territories, as well as of the lower slopes and alluvial flats where most of the clan's gardens are established and where the women spend much of their time. With the men's houses thus overlooking some two-thirds of the clan domain, not only can their occupants guard the women working below, but also, if an enemy group launches a raid, the odds are the defenders will have the recognized advantage of counterattacking downhill. Men also construct on suitable knolls or spurs small, unwalled shelters, where in times of tension they gather to plan raids or counter-raids. From these they can survey the territory of their enemies and detect their movements. In particular, they can espy the incautious traveler who is a likely target for a quick ambush.

The house of a woman, especially of one who is her husband's only wife, tends to be within call of the men's house in which her husband habitually resides, although, to ensure privacy, it is usually separated by a narrow and uninviting track from the main path that links that men's house with others. A man with several wives is likely to have widely separated garden plots, in which case one or more of the women may live some distance from the men's house. If, however, there is any danger of an incursion in that quarter, the woman removes to the comparative safety of her co-wife's house near the men's residence.

By and large men build their own and their wives' houses on land belonging to their own patrilineage or at least to their own subclan, although occasionally, given the location of his gardens, a man may find it convenient to ask a man of a parallel subclan for permission to place

Mae Enga woman's house and sweet potato gardens

his wife's house on fallow land belonging to the latter. Commonly, most of the men of a patrilineage (that is, close agnates "who share one blood") are distributed among two or three houses, although some may for longer or shorter periods reside with friends in other men's houses of the clan. In a sample of 57 Mae men's houses belonging to three clans censused in 1956, the total number of occupants was 256 men and 53 boys; the mean number of occupants per house was 5.4 (including 4.5 men), and the range was from two to 16. Ideally, and usually in fact, each married woman in the clan parish has her own house, which she shares with her children and the pigs. In the three clans mentioned above therewere in 1956 155 women's houses, whose occupants comprised 235 women, 266 children, and nine elderly men. The mean number of occupants per house was 3.3 and the range from one to eight.

The Mae do not rely solely on the undoubted sturdiness of their double-walled houses to protect them. For one thing, the thick grass thatch on the low roof invites the torch of the raider who can get close to it. Consequently, outer lines of defense are essential. The bananas, pandanus, casuarinas, and other trees that generally surround each house help, but more effective is the fence of stout palings and growing cordyline and saccharum that encloses the house site. Sometimes stakes are set at an angle along the fence so that their pointed ends project outward to impale or at least impede nocturnal assailants. This fence may also be supplemented by dense screens of cane grass and by ditches two or three feet deep (in which grow taro and the reed elaeocharis), crossed by logs that are removed at night.[2]

As a further precaution the ground outside the external fences may be sown with needle-pointed bamboo slivers, which penetrate the toughest feet and cripple the unwary. Once lodged in the flesh the bamboo breaks off and disintegrates into fibers, whose presence stimulates singularly painful and lingering infections. The householders, of course, take good care to avoid these traps; but often their children stumble on them and incur injuries that plague them the rest of their lives.

The front porch of a woman's house opens into a series of two or three fenced courtyards, the entrance to each of which is through a low and narrow gateway. The main approach to the courtyard of the men's house is through a small doorway set in a heavy timber palisade some six or seven feet high. Sometimes, with the addition of walls and a roof of living cane grass, this doorway serves as a gatehouse, from which the archers' fire can sweep the path leading to it.

Occasionally a men's house and four or five ancillary women's houses are clustered to form a complex encircled by a continuous and substantial fence, inside which the component houses are connected by lanes dug three or four feet below ground level and lined with cordylines and palings that extend well above head height. Similarly sunken and sheltered lanes may lead to gardens nearby and separate the holdings of individual families. These serve several functions: they enable people to move unobserved to their gardens, keep wandering pigs away from the crops, and act as drainage ditches.

The Mae have a lively fear of being incinerated in their houses—and with good reason. Not only are accidental blazes common, taking a number of lives over the years, but arson is a recognized military tactic. Accordingly, in addition to the small front doorway (about thirty inches square), the typical woman's house has a narrow weakened section in the rear wall of her sleeping quarters. In the event of fire the occupants, including the pigs, are supposed to break through this panel to safety; but often the combination of tough cane-grass insulation in the panel, smoke, and panic delays them long enough to cause asphyxiation. Moreover, because such exits are standard, raiders may simply wait beside them to cut down the fugitives as they scramble awkwardly through them.

Men's houses do not always have these rear safety hatches, partly because their presence is expected, partly because a clever enemy may enter through them. Some do have special exits, however, which take either of two forms. If the house is close to a declivity, a tunnel just wide enough for a man is made from inside the house to emerge in the bank.[3] Otherwise a ditch, later roofed with timber and soil, is dug from the house to a clump of trees nearby. The householders prepare the tunnel secretly at night, taking care to hide all debris and to camouflage their handiwork with grass and shrubs. Stout wooden trapdoors conceal both ends of the passage, the outer one, if this is feasible, also being covered with earth and plants. The tunnel's whereabouts is kept from the wives and children, as well as from outsiders, lest they inadvertently betray it. Nevertheless, visitors to men's houses of other clans are always on the alert for evidence of these devices, and they store away the information for future use.

Such a tunnel is not meant merely to be a means of escape from a burning men's house. Theoretically it also enables besieged occupants to take their attackers from behind while the latter are dazzled by and silhouetted against the flames. My general impression is that, given the confusion men experience on waking to find their house ablaze and the enemy on their doorstep, they rarely succeed in thus turning the tables on the raiders.

The dispersed residential pattern of the Mae affects the style and effectiveness of their warfare. It poses no serious communication problem with respect to calling together the men of a clan for an attack on a neighboring group. Clan territories are not so extensive that warriors cannot be readily convened at a particular place and time for briefing and dispatch.

But once an assault is under way, the distribution of the enemy's houses obviously does affect the outcome of the venture. It is by no means easy for the leaders of an invading force, even one of considerable size, to deploy component units so they can simultaneously strike most or all of the dwellings. Inevitably, the besieging or burning of the first few houses warns the occupants of those in other parts of the territory, who then have some time in which to act (whether they choose to flee or to fight). On the other hand, the invaders can concentrate their efforts to ensure that those first victims at least will not escape, that their houses will be well ablaze before other clansmen can come to their aid.

Thus, although on balance it may seem that the advantage must generally lie with the attacking forces, this is true only if they are prepared to seek limited gains. If they spend too long in dealing with the first houses and then move on to the rest in the hope of inflicting total defeat on their opponents, the latter may well be ready to meet them in some strength or to outflank them and cut off their retreat. Then it can become difficult for the scattered invaders to regroup and fight their way home. Moreover, the surrounding zones of forest and cane grass now become dangerous obstacles for men trying to escape from hostile territory, slowing their movement so that their pursuers can fire at them.

All the foregoing suggests that in general the placement of Mae dwellings reduces the likelihood of heavy casualties among the intended victims and gives them some chance to equalize the circumstances. This in turn increases the probability of a military standoff, in which, although both sides suffer some losses, the attackers fail in their full intention and have to withdraw. Certainly, what I have learned of Mae warfare points to a significant frequency of inconclusive engagements.

Weapons and personal accoutrements

Mae warriors going into battle do not affect a uniform in any Western sense. Nevertheless, their style of dress on these occasions is indeed relatively uniform. Men turn out in what is essentially their everyday costume, namely, a cincture or belt, with two or more heavy aprons of netted string hanging from it in the front, and with long cordyline leaves tucked into the back as a rump cover. The leaves are arranged to pull free easily if seized, and the belt itself may be fastened with light string so that it comes away when sharply tugged. Although men dislike revealing their genitals in public, they say that in combat it is better to suffer momentary shame than to be held and cut down. Those who are old enough to be warriors may make and wear for daily adornment narrow but heavy armlets and wristlets of plaited rattan. These do not, however, function as archers' wristguards.

Men ordinarily wear their hair compacted to form a dense mushroom-shaped cap which, when it becomes unbearably lousy, is cut off in one piece, cleaned, and converted into a wig. In either mode the pad of hair provides useful protection against glancing blows from axes or arrows. It is usually topped with a sheath of dirty brown bark-cloth tapa that effectively camouflages the owner when he is lurking in the cane grass. Sometimes a small headdress of brown or black cassowary plumes also surmounts the hair.

The only other item regularly worn during fighting is a small net bag attached to the belt or slung over the shoulder, which contains battle rations and perhaps a bamboo knife and some arrow points.

Warriors blacken their faces with a thick layer of soot or powdered charcoal, explicitly to conceal their individual identities from their enemies. In addition they may smear their torsos with soot or with dark earth or clay. Some men also paint their noses red, to enhance the ferocity of their appearance.[4]

This generally utilitarian costume is adequate for most military occasions. For the infrequent event of a "great fight," warriors, especially the fight leaders, get themselves up more lavishly, adding plumes, shells, and other ornaments to their basic attire of wig, apron, and rump leaves. Those entitled to do so also sport the knotted strings that serve as "coup counters," each knot recalling an outstanding achievement in battle. The string may be attached to the butt of the spear or hang from the back of the headdress. In effect, the men dress as they would to attend a public ceremony such as a pig distribution or a clan ritual.

In the past the Mae, like other Enga, used no body armor of any kind apart from shields. Nowadays, however, although most men still prefer to fight wearing traditional costume, some younger warriors don European clothing, namely, two or three shirts and a couple of pairs of short trousers, as protection not only against cold and rain but also against

Mae Enga luluai in traditional dress, carrying stone axe

Robert M. Glasse

glancing arrows. They leave the shirts unfastened so they can slip free from an enemy's grasp. Even so, older and more experienced fighters deplore the practice as dangerous.

The Mae armory of offensive weapons is limited, comprising primarily the axe, the spear, and the bow—and in a sense the torch.

Men know of the pointed daggers made from cassowary femurs common among the Ipili and Huli farther west; but although some of these have reached the Mae in trade, they are not considered serviceable weapons. The knife in everyday domestic use, made from a strip of bamboo, is similarly disregarded in warfare, even though it takes a keen edge.[5] Again, whereas men caught up in intraclan brawls use fence palings or pieces of firewood with telling effect, they do not manufacture clubs for military purposes.[6]

Bows are usually made from the strong wood of the black palm, whose dense fibers are naturally laminated. The wood, which grows only in other, lower areas, may be imported in the form of rough billets or as

Mae Enga man repairing a stone axe

the finished article. In either case it is a scarce and highly valued commodity among the Mae, who depend on extended chains of exchange and trade partners to obtain it. Nowadays, Enga who travel to work in other parts of Papua New Guinea make a point of bringing such bows home with them, and once again almost every Enga man has at least one in his house. The bow itself is about five feet long, with a single arc in the general western highlands' style. The "bowstring" is a narrow strap of flexible bamboo or rattan. The whole is, for the novice, very difficult to bend. In the hands of an Enga it discharges an arrow with tremendous initial force, and at close range can drive the arrow three or four inches into a pandanus trunk or through a half-inch pine plank.

Arrows, which are about four feet long, are generally undecorated and are not fletched. The untapered shaft is fire-hardened cane grass. The points used in fighting are of several kinds. Mae men greatly prize barbed heads made from black palm, because these do severe damage and are difficult to withdraw. However, given the local scarcity of this and other

55

suitable wood, until recently such points were rarely seen. Nowadays men import them in quantity from peoples farther east.

Similarly, only a few Mae obtained in trade the carved and slightly barbed points made from human armbones that are popular among some Fringe Enga and other peoples to the south and west who, unlike the Mae, expose their dead in elevated coffins and keep the dry bones as mementos. These arrows are thought to have the advantage not only of being hard to remove but also of carrying in their grooves a cargo of decaying detritus that ensures infection of wounds. Some Mae manufacture a homologous form of arrow from a slender bamboo tube, which is sharpened and given a longitudinal channel with keen edges. They may also, as I have seen them do, stud the channel with slivers of broken glass.

A more common fighting arrow among the Mae is one whose head is a leaf-shaped blade of bamboo. The edges are razor-sharp and, when they encounter bone, tend to explode into their component fibers and spread out to cause infection. A modern version of this arrow has appeared in several recent battles. Here the point is the finely honed steel blade of the small paring knife sold in European trade stores.[7]

Perhaps the most widely used fighting arrow is one with a plain needle point of tough local wood, which is smoke-blackened to make it almost invisible against dark backgrounds and hence difficult to dodge. Sometimes the point is sheathed with the long claw of the cassowary; as the arrow is withdrawn from the victim, the claw remains embedded in his body, there to fester and, it is hoped, cause a lingering death.

The Enga do not use quivers. A man usually enters a fight with one arrow notched in readiness and another six or seven held in his left hand, together with and parallel to the bow. He may also have two or three spare bowstraps tied along the bow. Before going into action an archer generally bites each arrow shaft near its junction with the point in order to weaken the missile, so that it breaks on impact and cannot be re-used by the enemy. Moreover, if it snaps on striking home, removing the point is that much harder.

Although Enga bows are powerful, the arrows, because they are not feathered, waver in the air and quickly lose both velocity and accuracy. Accordingly, an alert and agile man who is more than about thirty to forty yards from his opponent has a good chance of evading the latter's arrows. The real danger in battle lies in the number of arrows simultaneously in the air, for a man cannot concentrate on more than one at a time. Most arrow wounds occur when a man loses sight of the arrow against the trees or moves into the path of an unnoticed arrow fired at an angle to him. Although some archers are obviously stronger and more experienced than others, the inherent limitations of the Mae arrow and the almost universal basic expertise in archery tend to level out differences between bowmen.

The Mae spear is generally made of black palm, again imported in the rough or ready-made. It is of one piece, quite plain, about ten to eleven feet long and one to one and a half inches in diameter, with a conical needle point that is sometimes sheathed with a cassowary claw. Men who cannot obtain black palm spears may make substitutes, regarded as inferior, from the tough wood of the Dodonea tree (which is also favored for axe handles). When thrown in the Enga overarm fashion, the spear has an extreme range of about fifty yards, but it can be thrown accurately only about thirty yards. The Enga know nothing of the spear-thrower.

Men may go into battle carrying a spear in the right hand and bow and arrows in the left, in which case they quickly hurl the spear at the end of a darting, weaving run, then drop back as they fire arrows. More often the spear is employed as a stabbing weapon at close quarters, especially in ambushes. In battle, spearmen, who usually number only about a tenth of the force, carry shields and move together as a tight front line, keeping close to protect one another's flanks. Their archers fire over and around them. Each spearman engages a similarly armed opponent and tries, by means of feints and lunges, to open up the other's guard for a fatal thrust.

Archers, needing both hands to manage their bows, do not usually carry shields. The Enga shield is made of plates of light but tough bark secured to a rectangular wooden frame measuring about forty by 15 inches. Whereas it is not likely to halt an arrow fired at short range or to stop an axe blow, it is an effective defense against arrows shot at a distance. When not in use, shields are stored in the rafters of the men's houses, where constant exposure to the fire's heat and smoke preserves, hardens, and thoroughly blackens them.

Recently some men experimented with shields made of galvanized iron nailed to wooden frames, but soon found that in crowded combat these caused arrows to ricochet so erratically that they endangered their own supporters. In consequence they have adopted shields made from single stout planks of pit-sawn timber, in which arrows stick fast. By and large, however, the shield has not occupied an important place in Enga fighting techniques.

Until the recent passage of local ordinances against the practice, no Enga man moved anywhere without an axe tucked in his belt. Even now a man feels naked without his axe and only travels without one when he is likely to be seen by Administration officers and police. Formerly, axe blades were made of stone, most of them imported from the Jimi River area to the northeast (see Chappell & Strathern 1966), but a few were mined and shaped in eastern Enga country. Like most western highlanders, the Enga had their own local manner of hafting axes, and they also distinguished between the two main categories of working axe and display axe, within which they recognized further subtypes on the basis of the kind of stone employed. Both working and display axes, despite differences in size and conformation, were used to considerable effect in fighting and, of course, were suitable weapons for ambush and murder.

By the early 1950's steel axes, either disbursed by the Administration and the missions in payment for labor and commodities or bought at trade stores, had everywhere replaced stone working axes (see Meggitt 1971). Men continued, however, for a few more years to value stone display axes to include in payments of brideprice and also to wear on ceremonial occasions. Lately, since 1972–73, the eastern Enga have located new quarries of stone suitable for ceremonial axes, and there has been a noticeable resurgence in their manufacture. Nevertheless, men still prefer the steel axe for everyday work and for fighting.

The Mae, like other Enga, do not fancy the heavy (four-pound) steel axe that Europeans use for serious work. Instead, they demand the light (one-and-a-half- to two-pound) tomahawk head, which they mount on their traditional "reverse-curved" haft. The axe is kept finely honed (indeed, I have seen a man shave with one) and altogether is an effective weapon for in-fighting. With it a skilled man can decapitate or dismember an opponent, or can inflict deep puncture wounds in the head and chest.[8]

Formerly some men also carried in action the "fight pick," a spear point of black palm, sheathed with a cassowary claw and hafted like an axe—a weapon more common in the west. I have not seen one among the Mae for years.

The weapons I have described are the only ones the Mae today employ in intergroup fighting. Although a few of the wealthier and more acculturated men own shotguns (perhaps two or three in a clan of average size), to date they have confined their use to occasional hunting in the high forests. I know of only one case where a man, incensed by the killing and mutilation of a clan "brother" in battle, returned to the fray with his shotgun and went looking for the killer. To the great relief of his own clansmen, he missed his target at close range, and an ally persuaded him to relinquish the gun.

As far as I can discover, the agreement among the people not to employ firearms on one another has been tacit, and it appears to stem from two considerations. One is the clear recognition that to do so within the existing patterns of Mae warfare and residence would lead to slaughter on such a scale that there would be few victors left to enjoy the land thus won. The other is the belief (not supported by the evidence) that, as long as the Mae keep their warfare within traditional bounds, it should remain their own business and the authorities will have less warrant to intervene vigorously to halt it. However, given the increasing ferocity and spread of fighting since the late 1960's, I wonder how much longer the Mae can restrain hotheads among them from turning to shotguns to settle their quarrels.

58

Weapons and "supernatural" aid

The effect of the supernatural on weaponry is a subject about which Mae men have obvious differences of opinion. In general, although there is a common belief that some magical rituals and extrahuman agencies may on occasion enhance the efficacy of military weapons, there is also considerable uncertainty over the mechanisms by which this improvement is achieved, and by and large men emphasize more the role of their learned skills in ensuring effectiveness in combat. Indeed, some men have assured me that recourse to extraordinary devices is unnecessary for the expert warrior. His very competence, acquired through experience, so sustains his self-confidence that he takes many risks on the battlefield. This hardihood demoralizes his opponents, who in consequence are the more easily overcome; and such triumphs, depending on the man's own assumptions, confirm his belief either in his personal prowess and "strong skin" or in the effectiveness of the spells applied to his weapons.

Further evidence of the relatively pragmatic view Mae take of these matters is their assertion that axes in any case need no bespelling, because they are wielded at close quarters where only an incompetent can fail to do the maximum damage. Bows and arrows, on the other hand, are less certain to kill, so that there is some point in aiding their action with magic. Appropriately enough, opinions are divided over the utility of bespelling spears.

Weapon magic, which falls into the general category of wealth and welfare magic, comprises spell and "medicine," the former being given primacy. The materials include various leaves, stones, ochres, and spatulas made from the wingbones of bats. The mere presence of the medicine may reinforce the spell as it is intoned over the bow, or in addition some of the ochre may be applied either to the bow or to its owner.

Individual men privately procure such magic, usually in exchange for locally made salt, from trade partners among the Saui or the Maramuni Enga, both of whom are considered the specialists in this field. The buyer subsequently has the right freely to bequeath or sell the spell and the materials to any kinsman or friend, and the magic of a former renowned warrior finds a ready buyer if his son has not already acquired it. Most weapon magic among the Mae, however, is probably in the hands of Big Men and other prosperous men, and they pass it on to their sons. Even during prolonged warfare the current owner of such magic is under no obligation to share it with his clansmen, but he could scarcely refuse if a close agnate asked him to bespell a bow or spear.

Most men agree that magic serves primarily to ensure that the slightest wound from a treated weapon will fester and eventually incapacitate the victim. Others say the magic also makes the weapon more accurate, so that all the wounds it inflicts are more likely to be fatal. But still other men argue that such "accuracy" is factitious—what really happens is that the magic somehow enlists the aid of a malicious ghost of the enemy clan, who at the critical moment seizes the spirit of the intended victim and prevents him from evading the arrow. In this manner the ghost settles an old grudge with his own clansmen. It is all very complicated and uncertain.

At any rate there is no doubt that men believe ghosts can in some circumstances "strengthen" weapons. Thus, when a man falls in battle, his close agnates should try to recover his weapons as well as his corpse, for his angry ghost will make these weapons doubly dangerous when used against the killer.

Similarly, a weapon (axe, spear, or bow) that has killed somebody is thought to acquire in some obscure fashion a potentially lethal charge from the victim's ghost, a charge that will recoil on the user, causing him a fatal accident, if he tries to employ the weapon in a peaceful activity such as wood-chopping or hunting. Fortunately, a "killer" weapon warns the unwary of its condition by becoming exceptionally heavy or by vibrating and buzzing when placed indoors. It must then be taken to a specialist, a spell man, who for a fee exorcises the offending ghost and drives it back to its natal territory.

Two other conditions affect weapons deleteriously. If a mature woman—that is, one old enough to menstruate—steps over a weapon, its efficiency is forever impaired. The owner would be foolish to depend on it in combat, and generally he should give it to a youth to keep for show or for casual use. Similarly, a man and his newborn child (of either sex) should not see each other for two to three months after the birth, while the infant is still polluted by contact with its mother's blood. If father and child were to meet, the man and his weapons would be so weakened that he would be a casualty next time he fought, and at the same time the child might well die under the impact of his father's "man-killing" gaze.[9] For these reasons a sensible man keeps his idle weapons in his men's house and not in that of his wife.

Military education and competence

The pervasive apprehension among males over the harmfulness of excessive intimacy with women is a significant determinant of the residence pattern.[10] In particular men encourage their sons to curtail their contacts with female relatives, so that by the time a boy is about eight years old he generally spends most nights in his father's house, and passes his days in the company of men or ranging the clan territory with other lads. A common admonition is: "If you stay always with women, you must

60

Cooking a pig in the owner's house yard

expect to become as weak as they are, and you will never become a killer of men."

The boys' main task is to tend the family pigs when these are grazing away from home, to ensure that they do not stray or get stolen. By and large Mae children indulge in little organized play, for their parents believe they should early acquire useful skills and contribute to the domestic work force. Nevertheless, boys find time to scuffle and brawl among themselves, and their fathers are content to see them exhibit the aggressiveness that will be useful to them later. One of their pastimes is especially appropriate. Two teams form (sometimes but not necessarily on subclan lines), and each makes a "house" and marks out "gardens." Then, armed with sticks and "spears" of cane grass, the two groups engage violently and noisily, each trying to overrun and destroy the other's domain as the small warriors act out what they know of military tactics. When the battle is over and "casualties" are tallied, the combatants assemble to pay elaborate compensations of "pigs" and "pork" (sticks and stones) for the "deaths."

More important, of course, is the boy's constant exposure to men's talk and attitudes after he moves into his father's house. Night after night he hears the interminable discussions of political disputes and past battles, the minute dissection of successful and unsuccessful strategies and tactics. In this way he not only learns something of the practice of warfare and the history of his clan's relations with friends and enemies, he also absorbs martial values: he grows up expecting and wanting to be a warrior.

Although the moral, disciplinary, and practical training of boys is not nearly as public or formalized among the Mae as among, for instance, Australian Aborigines or some African peoples, it is relatively effective. Generally the fathers (and the elder brothers) are responsible for teaching the lads, by both precept and example; a man should be quick to punish his young son for laziness, inattention, or infractions of the rules.[11] At the same time he should teach his son to use the weapons that he will later depend on. Accordingly, the man makes a scaled-down spear and a bow for the boy, gives him old arrows, and takes him on short hunting trips. At home the boy practices assiduously with these weapons, and his elders correct his faults.

The instructions the lad now receives are quite specifically military and include advice such as the following:

Never waste arrows on a difficult target, such as your enemy's head; always aim at his body.

Never fire all your arrows in action; always keep one to draw as you drop back to where the old men are bringing up fresh supplies of arrows.

Never turn your back on the enemy, or you will surely be killed.

Single out an opponent and watch him carefully, but at the same time try to be aware of everything that is happening around you.

Do not start to dodge until your adversary draws his bow to the point of release, for then he will have difficulty in aiming anew; if you move too soon, he can more easily follow you.

Note how many arrows your opponent fires and be ready to dart in with axe or spear when he has only one left.

An archer usually holds the bow in the left hand and draws with the right; this pulls the bow to his left, so be ready to dodge to *your* left.

Spearmen tend to thrust or throw across their bodies to their left, so move to *your* left; but be alert to the left-handed archer or spearman.

If you can see the pale shaft of your enemy's arrow in flight, remain still, for that arrow will miss you; but if you see only the point approaching you "like a black insect," duck or dodge!

If a house is burning, especially your own, do not watch it lest you are dazzled by the glare or miss seeing an enemy on your flank.

If an arrow hits you and you cannot pull it right out, keep your eyes on the enemy as you drop back through your own lines to safety; do not ask the man beside you to help you, lest you distract and endanger him.

If you are wounded and have to withdraw, warn the men on either side of you, lest you leave them with their flanks unprotected.

Listen for the signals of the older men and the fight leaders, and go at once where they direct you.

When boys take up residence with their fathers, they receive their first taste of sentry duty. When a clan is at war with another or an attack is expected, men patrol the borders and vulnerable areas by night. An hour or so before dawn, fathers wake their young sons and send them to keep watch in the relatively safe environs of the men's house. A boy who cries or shows reluctance to venture outdoors is beaten until he goes. After a few such episodes the boys wake and take up their posts without being told to do so.

Moreover, during fighting that is not critical or perilous, boys are encouraged by day to take up safe vantage points and to watch carefully, marking everything their fathers do. They are admonished to keep alert and to be ready to flee if the combat moves toward them, for an irate enemy would not hesitate to fire at them. Some men go farther during minor fights or the more or less predictable interphratry tourneys and tell their young sons to join the reserves in the rear, where they can stay fairly close behind their fathers and observe their techniques. If in these circumstances a boy is wounded, he is simply pulled to safety and the arrow is removed. Nobody makes a fuss over him. Instead, he is told: "This is what pain is all about. Sooner or later everyone suffers minor wounds; it is fate [='the work of the sun']. Pay no attention to them but learn how to avoid serious injury."

When the lad is about fifteen or sixteen years old he formally joins the bachelors' association attached to his subclan or clan (see Meggitt 1964a). Now for the first time he is entitled to wear a man's dress and decorations, and his father and other close agnates equip him with a full complement of real weapons—axe, spear, and bow. Although the bachelor's ritual activities are directed primarily toward protection from female pollution, entry into the association also marks the youth's acquisition of the status of potential warrior. Outside the recurrent periods of seclusion and cleansing, the bachelors spend much time together (often in tasks set by their elders), and the older ones share in training the younger in the use of weapons.

Mae Enga bachelors, armed and decorated, attend an interclan distribution of food

After the youth has participated in about two rituals of seclusion, that is, when he is about eighteen years old, his elders have him do his share of patroling and take part in the clan's battles. His limited capacity is recognized; he is not allocated duties beyond his competence, and nobody expects him to fight in the front line. At the same time, however, especially if his own clan has been enjoying a prolonged peace, he is urged to take every opportunity to participate in the wars of related or friendly clans so that he can gain experience and overcome the fear of being wounded. In this way he will the sooner become militarily useful to his own group, a man who can be depended on under fire—for, as the Mae say, "A man who has never fought is always afraid of dying when an attack threatens."

"Man-killers" and fight leaders

Presumably as a consequence of social training and cultural expectations, most Mae men, today as in the past, are tolerably competent warriors,

64

both able and willing to fight when the occasion demands. Overtly at least, they express in various stylized ways their self-confidence both in times of peace and when danger threatens.

Nevertheless, the unfortunate fact of personal cowardice is recognized, albeit men believe with reason that few of their fellows will display or acknowledge fear in the face of an impending attack. A youth who falters in these circumstances is generally excused his trepidation; the older men try to rally his spirits by making light of the hazards and assuring him that as long as he remains alert and keeps moving, he will perform creditably once the action begins. If this approach is ineffective, they remind him that the manner of every man's death is ordained ("it is the work of the sun") and that hiding from the enemy is no guarantee of longevity (see Meggitt 1965b).

A frightened youth may also be publicly shamed. Thus, in a recent conflict one clan had invaded another without warning. As the men of the latter were hastily arming and counterattacking, a visiting matrilateral cross-cousin aged about twenty said he was going home before he got hurt. At that an old firebrand of at least seventy, who was on his way to the front drew his bow and threatened to shoot the poltroon there and then. Other clansmen dissuaded the elder, and the young visitor, stung by their biting comparisons, stayed and fought for the four days—although, I was told, none too enthusiastically.

Should an older man try to evade his military obligations either by hanging back or by actually running away, his "brothers" revile him as a coward ("one who flees in fear") and tell him to stay with the women where he belongs. They may also beat him. During the action the combatants gather their battle rations from his gardens and afterward use his crops to sustain themselves if their own gardens are destroyed. When the offender returns they merely say: "You fled when we needed you. Now tell us where you and your children propose to obtain food!" The coward then has no choice but to take his family for an extended visit to relatives elsewhere, depending on their generosity for the necessary sweet potatoes. Later he is obliged to repay his hosts for their hospitality.

Eventually the recreant comes home, to face no other sanctions than the scathing remarks of his fellows and a loss of reputation and influence in public affairs. He can redeem his name, at least in part, by contributing more than his share of pigs to whatever homicide compensations his clan now has to pay and by fighting bravely in the next battle. An able-bodied man who constantly avoids combat, a rarity indeed, is considered beneath contempt. His clansmen simply ignore him when making their plans for war or exchanges, and sooner or later his position becomes so uncomfortable that he has to beg residential privileges with his wife's or his mother's group.

The Mae do not point to any particular category of men as more likely than others to display cowardice, but rather see this failing as an expression of individual personality. Interestingly enough, members of that limited class defined as "rubbish men"—poor, landless protégés of Big Men, are frequently among the most resolute of warriors. Some men have suggested to me (most unfairly) that these dependents fight well because their unremitting toil has left them with strong arms and thick heads.

Within the great majority of men who do fight, there are of course individual differences in both bravery and skill. Indeed, the two characteristics seem to be highly correlated, and bravery in turn interacts with self-confidence. Among the Mae no one goes berserk or runs amok under fire. Men do not go into battle determined to die facing suicidal odds, either to prove a point of honor or to shame their clansmen. On the contrary, every man hopes to survive to fight another day, and the competent warrior is he who inflicts maximum injury on the enemy at minimum cost to himself.

Nevertheless, there are those men who from adolescence are confident of possessing such a strong skin that they can outface any opponent, in argument or in combat. Such a man, who is not necessarily physically stronger or bigger than others, brooks no insults to himself or his clan, nor does he lie to escape the consequences of his own actions. Thus, if he sees an opportunity to steal and eat the pigs of an enemy clansman, he takes them and shares the pork with his "brothers." He does not deny the theft when the owners challenge him, no matter how powerful their group may be, for he believes that should he do so, in the fighting that will probably ensue their arrows will follow the "track" both of the pork and of his denials and pierce him in the throat and belly. In any case, say the Mae, the bold, generous man survives wounds that would kill the mean and cautious dissembler. When the latter is injured or falls ill, few people care enough to worry over his misfortune, so that his spirit fails him and he dies; whereas the condition of the "strong" man excites public concern and therefore he recovers. Moreover, when the strong man confronts an opponent in battle, the latter's resolution falters, his arrows and his axe blows go astray, and he is soon overcome.

Small wonder then that the strong man takes the lead in skirmishing, revels in hand-to-hand combat, organizes the dangerous small-scale nocturnal raids into hostile territory, and is the first to climb the palisades or to crawl into the enemy men's house to steal the firestick.[12] Such a hero becomes a member of that select category of warriors known as "constant strikers" or "man-killers," and in time he may also earn the right to wear the insignia of knotted string that serves as a visible reminder of his courage.[13]

The string is not simply the badge of the homicide, for, as the Mae say, any man can kill another without risk to himself in ambush or by deceit. Nor can a man assume the string merely because he has dispatched an enemy in battle; it is thought that every man should be able to achieve this at some time in his life. Rather, a triumph is defined as an occasion on which a man fights with such reckless vigor that single-handed he slays or seriously wounds three or four opponents and in doing so determines the outcome of the combat. After such an achievement the hero may wear the string, containing a single knot, and he may add another knot for each comparable exploit in the future.

There is no public ceremony or decision to confer the decoration; the man himself decides if he is worthy of the honor. But one who was foolish enough to flaunt the string to mark a lesser feat would be jeered at by his fellows and would soon have to remove it.[14] Although a man may inherit the weapons and ornaments of his late father, he obviously cannot take over the latter's string. Instead, he may hang it in the men's house as a memento of his parent's valor and then set out to earn his own.

The rightful wearing of such an insignia on public occasions carries with it a certain danger. Man-killers of other clans, especially those whose members have fallen to the wearer, view his appearance as a direct challenge to their own strength. As they say, "Although he has a beard, I too have a beard; I am as strong as he is"; and each of them may seek an opportunity to ambush and kill the hero.

At the time a redoubtable warrior assumes the knotted string or adds another knot to it, he may also establish a "tally tree." For this he selects a large tree that stands beside his clan or subclan dance ground, frequently an old casuarina thought to have been planted by one of his direct agnatic forebears, and he removes a vertical strip of bark from the trunk. Across the bare patch he makes horizontal axe cuts (one for each of his victims), into which he rubs soot or red ochre. Ostensibly these marks are to serve as mnemonic aids in connection with the payment of death compensations, but in fact they magnify not only the hero's name but also the reputation of his clan. No visitor to the dance ground can fail to see the signs and be aware of their meaning.[15]

From among the limited ranks of the man-killers emerge the small number of fight leaders (= "belly-stirrers") to be found in each clan. Whereas a man who is a hero, a wearer of the knotted string, is likely also to be a fight leader, the correlation between the two statuses is not perfect. The Mae recognize that the bravery, self-confidence, and skill in fighting which distinguish the hero are not always accompanied by the intelligence and experience requisite to the successful deployment of armed forces. That is to say, for a man to be accepted and followed in battle as a fight leader, his own confidence in his ability to kill opponents does not suffice; his clansmen must be confident that his commands will be the right ones, that he can use the terrain and the available warriors to the best advantage, that he can perceive and capitalize on changing

67

circumstances in the flow of combat, and that he can assess the morale of the enemy group. Accordingly, a fight leader is more than his vernacular title suggests. He is not there simply to urge his own clansmen with calculated metaphors of praise or insult (although this is an important aspect of his role); rather, his task is to employ his forces effectively to produce a material victory. To this end, then, the fight leader divides his time during a battle between performing exemplary actions in the front line and assessing the total situation from the rear. In the latter activity the fight leader may well be aided by the Big Man (or Big Men) of the clan. What then is the relationship between these two statuses?

In general, at each level in a local hierarchy of agnatic descent groups, there is in every group—lineage, subclan, or clan, but not always the phratry—at least one Big Man, who is in effect the business manager of that unit and its main representative in political, economic, and ceremonial dealings with other corporate groups. The position is one the incumbent achieves largely through his native wit and his ability to manipulate people and situations with such finesse that the fellow members of his descent group believe he is advancing or at least adequately protecting their interests, both individual and joint (see Meggitt 1967, 1974).

By and large the contexts in which a Big Man makes, maintains, and enlarges his reputation ("makes his name known throughout the valley") are not specifically military. Of course a proclaimed coward could not become a Big Man, and many Big Men of my acquaintance are said to have been "man-killers" in earlier days (although I suspect retrospective halo effect in some cases). But as a rule a Big Man is so regarded primarily because of his skillful dealing in the arena of intergroup ceremonial exchanges. Big Men take the lead in (and to a degree "finance") religious rituals to benefit their groups, in settling disputes within their own groups and with friendly groups, and in exploiting the political climate within which their groups interact with others.

Given the perspicacity needed to succeed in these multifarious ventures, it is not surprising that some Big Men are also fight leaders, noted for their grasp of tactics; and those who can play both parts obviously command additional respect from followers and neighbors, and may translate this into increased influence. Nevertheless, the Mae regard two statuses as analytically distinct. The Big Man, especially the leader of the clan, "the man for all seasons," in a real sense consistently outranks the fight leader, whose military abilities are called on only in more narrowly defined circumstances.

Thus, in peacetime the fight leader *per se* is hardly to be distinguished from his fellows as he goes about his daily business, and he is held to be as amenable to the social rules governing daily life as is any other respectable member of the community. True, some well-known fight leaders and man-killers are given to displays of temper and threats of violence when crossed by their clansmen; but the latter generally refuse to be intimidated by these tantrums, which normally blow over without incident. In short, most of the fight leaders of my acquaintance, who are not also Big Men are well-disposed men who do not put themselves forward on peaceful public occasions.

In times of war the difference between "true" Big Men and fight leaders is also apparent. As I shall describe in more detail later, the decision to initiate military action is usually taken by the men of a clan meeting together in council, during which all have the right (indeed, the obligation) to express opinions and to furnish relevant information. If the group decides on an attack or invasion, both the Big Men and the fight leaders determine the overall strategy to be followed and instruct the others accordingly. In this context the views of both are given roughly equal weight, but if, as is rare, they differ seriously in their assessments of the situation, the fight leaders are likely to prevail.

Once the clan's forces are in the field, even before action is joined, the fight leaders, including of course those who are also Big Men, assume command and thenceforth make the immediate tactical decisions.[16] As I have noted, this responsibility entails constant movement as they hurry back and forth between the front line, where they fight vigorously, and the rear, where they take stock of the current situation and dispatch reserves. The Big Men who are not fight leaders, especially the most important ones, should remain in the rear. There they keep up a constant flow of exhortations, praise, and insults intended to stimulate combatants to greater efforts; assist the old men in maintaining a supply of arrows for the warriors; and from time to time discuss the course of the battle and the incidence of casualties with the fight leaders.

Repeatedly, in response to my questions about this division of functions, I have been told that it is entirely proper for Big Men to remain aloof from combat, and always the same reasons have been given me. First, these observers are expected to restrain the exuberance of the fight leaders or of any hotheads whose enthusiasm is endangering the clan's forces. In particular, if the group's casualties are mounting and victory is not in sight, the Big Men should urge a tactical withdrawal from the field despite the desires of angry clansmen wishing to fight on to avenge their dead.

Second and more important, however, the Big Men should remain in relative safety at the rear because they are much too valuable to be exposed to enemy arrows. Whatever the outcome of the current hostilities, the Big Men are needed afterward for the complex negotiations that lead to the large-scale payments of homicide compensations by both sides. But beyond this immediate preoccupation is the wider recognition that the major Big Men are at all times among the clan's most significant assets. That is, they are the repository of the knowledge, experience, and expertise necessary for the clan's future economic and political well-being. In short, if the Big Men were killed, the clan's future would indeed be dim, and a battle won at the cost of their lives would be a Pyrrhic victory.[17]

This protective attitude toward "true" Big Men is not confined to those of one's own clan. On occasion, at least, it is proper to avoid injuring the Big Men of the enemy group who remain in the rear. The reason given is purely pragmatic: "If we kill those Big Men, who then will fire the bellies of our enemies afterward so they will feel impelled to meet their obligations and pay compensation for our dead?" The implication is that the Big Men on both sides, because of their long-term, mutually profitable relations in the Te and other exchanges, will work hard together to secure prompt payment of homicide compensation, which will be to their own advantage as well as to that of their clans (cf. Meggitt 1974). On the other hand, no such tenderness need be shown those Big Men who fight in the front line; they must take their chances like any other warriors.

Such are the ideal views of the situation, and it appears that in warfare between fraternal groups, at least as long as the constraints of "brotherhood" are recognized, as well as in interphratry tourneys, the contestants generally honor these maxims and accord noncombatant Big Men a degree of respect and inviolability. This treatment indicates, at a minimum, the importance opponents in such fights place on the ability to achieve a truce before casualties get out of hand, but beyond that it says something about the position of Big Men in Mae society. In the all-out warfare in which non-fraternal clans engage, however, especially if the control of land is at issue, such restrictions crumble in the face of the desire, indeed the need, to rout the enemy and do him as much damage as possible. And what better way is there of jeopardizing the prospects of an enemy clan than to kill the men who have hitherto steered its fortunes?

The decision to fight

In Table 1 (p. 13) I have listed the reasons Mae have given for outbreaks of intergroup warfare occurring in the sample neighborhood before about 1950. These conflicts arose, in order of frequency, over encroachments on other people's land, thefts of pigs, homicides, failure to pay homicide compensation, stealing pandanus nuts, felling the trees of another group, theft of garden produce, rape, and the jilting of a suitor. In addition, men told me that disputes occasioning violence between groups could also stem from the destruction of crops by another group's pigs; the theft of dogs and fowl; failure to meet brideprice obligations, to make death compensations to matrilateral kin, or to pay debts owing to the Te exchange; the removal or destruction of magical plants used in bachelors' purification rituals; and accusations of sorcery. In short, if two groups are

70

of a mind to fight, there appears to be virtually no limit to the situations that can be interpreted as provocation.

Nevertheless, none of these offenses automatically evokes an immediate violent response. A clan's decision to defend its interests by military action is not taken lightly, for people are well aware of the discomfort and domestic dislocation that accompany mobilization, of the penalties that follow defeat, and of the risk, win or lose, of significant casualties. Accordingly, if time and circumstances allow, the men of an aggrieved clan endeavor in closed conference to analyze carefully the current situation, especially the relative strength of the opponents, and the probable consequences of a determination to fight.[18]

Given the realistic caution prevalent among the Mae, it is not surprising that, even in the face of repeated affronts, a clan doubtful of its present ability to withstand a full-scale attack by its neighbor may refrain for some time from resorting to violence to protect its rights and instead retaliate by engaging in similarly "illegal" activities. Meanwhile, the offending group, also unsure of its capacity at that time to bring off a successful invasion at small cost to itself, welcomes the breathing space, which it uses to continue harrying the other with low-key depredations.

Thus, an extended series of thefts and counterthefts of pigs, pandanus nuts, and the like may ensue, in a manner still to be observed today. Indeed, a brief description of recent events of this kind provides an illuminating picture of such political robbery in the traditional style.

During the 1930's clan A of phratry I was on friendly terms with a neighbor, clan B of phratry II; and the two helped each other substantially in a number of battles, mainly over land, with clans of phratries II and III. Eventually A and B fell out over a division of spoils and by the late 1940's had fought several times over land they had jointly seized from an adjacent clan. Throughout the period of Administration-imposed peace in the 1950's and 1960's their relations continued to sour. Intermarriage declined appreciably, ordinary social intercourse was at a minimum, and large-scale brawls frequently erupted at the disputed border.

Tensions came to a head in 1971 when, without warning, clan B invaded the territory of clan A, aiming to occupy the several acres of arable land in question. Allies poured in on both sides, and some 500 men fought for four days before the Administration officers and hastily summoned riot police could halt them. By then clan A had regained its land; the common border remained unchanged. In reaching this stalemate clan A lost 16 houses burned and (with its allies) two dead and at least 65 wounded; clan B lost 19 houses burned and (with its allies) two dead and an unknown but large number wounded. Feelings continued to run high, and in 1973 both clans remained semi-mobilized.

Meanwhile, some months after the battle, a large pig belonging to a man of clan B wandered into the disputed area of clan A. Three men of clan A who were patrolling there recognized the beast and promptly speared it, later sharing the meat with clansmen who lived nearby. When the men of clan B discovered their loss, they followed the pig's tracks to the border and satisfied themselves that their enemies had seized it. Naturally, they did not care to risk entering the territory of clan A to demand the return of the animal or the payment of compensation. Instead, they prevailed upon affines from another phratry to act for them. These men went to clan A and announced that they had lost a pig they had had on agistment with clan B. It might have strayed here—could they look for it? The men of clan A replied that they had seen no strange pigs around but that the visitors were welcome to search. So prompt and free an invitation at once informed the inquirers that the pig had been consumed, and so, after making a perfunctory examination for appearance's sake, they carried the sad news to clan B.

Months later in 1972 three pigs belonging to two men of clan A disappeared. The owners followed the tracks to another part of the border between clans A and B. Soon afterward friends told them that three men of clan B had killed the beasts and shared the meat with their clansmen. The aggrieved men shouted their complaint across the border but merely received the same response they had made earlier to the visiting affines of clan B. Although some of the men of clan A saw the joke, the owners of the pigs were not amused and resolved to retaliate when the chance arose.

One night early in 1973 these two men stealthily and at considerable personal hazard entered the territory of clan B and made for a corral containing pigs belonging to one of the men who had killed their beasts. They opened the fence and, with the aid of scraped pig bones tied to pig ropes (apparently an infallible lure) removed the two largest pigs, which followed them home. The men cooked the pigs and shared the pork with their clansmen.

It happened, however, that men of another adjacent clan had seen the thieves as they were approaching the corral, and these later reported their observations to relatives in clan B.[19] The owner of the pigs thereupon "made a court" with a neutral Local Government Councillor, charging the two men with theft. The latter, supported by their clansmen, flatly denied the accusation and, in the absence of clear evidence, the plaintiff was thwarted.

Subsequently the owner's sister, who was married to a man of another clan with strong connections to clan A, came to the men of clan A and complained that the missing pigs belonged to her husband, who had been agisting them with clan B. Therefore, she argued, the men of clan A should compensate her husband for his loss. Their answer was: "We are sorry for your husband but your brother will have to recompense him. Your brother's clansmen have stolen three of our pigs, and in return we have taken three of theirs. Now we are even and that's that!"

The next move followed soon after. Men of clan A making a routine patrol along the disputed border observed that the tracks of some pigs of clan A led to the boundary fence, which had been opened to let the animals into clan B's territory. An immediate check by the men of clan A revealed that one of them was missing three pigs, which were known to have been grazing in the area earlier that day. The incensed owner of the pigs, who had been given them in a distribution by his wife's father, a Big Man of another clan, at once enlisted the latter to demand their return from clan B on the grounds that they were his property, merely on agistment with his affines in clan A. Because the wife's father as a Big Man had important exchange connections with men of clan B, the latter, who were on the point of killing and cooking the beasts, somewhat reluctantly gave them up to him, and he afterward brought them back to his son-in-law in clan A. At that point I left the field, so I do not know the latest episodes in this series.

The events just recounted, which typify the relations between clans at enmity, have interesting implications. The difficulty, if not the impossibility, for two clans thus opposed to negotiate directly, means that in many cases they must rely on relatives in other clans to act as go-betweens. Obviously, though, if the aggrieved group is not then ready to use force to recover its property, it cannot expect to secure "justice." All it can do is act toward its opponents in the same illicit manner when the opportunity arises.

Moreover, it is clear that in such cases the actions of the offenders, be they thieves or trespassers, have the full support of their own clansmen. That is, the latter regard them as entirely proper expressions of their clan's policy toward an enemy, as non-sanguinary tactics of harassment in a continuing, albeit undeclared war, one that will be actively resumed when the time is ripe for overt violence. In this respect the view of the Mae on what constitutes war appear to approximate those of Hobbes.[20]

Although such a condition of theft and countertheft may persist for some time, it is, of course, inherently unstable. Sooner or later one group is persuaded that it is strong enough not only to carry off a major attack on the other but also to retain any land it may overrun. If the intended target is a fraternal clan, the would-be invaders may try to manipulate circumstances to disguise their aggression. Thus, they step up their depredations and insults, not only continuing their thefts of pigs, pandanus nuts, etc., but also by constantly shifting their garden boundaries and asserting ownership of the opponents' fallow land near the common border, and by passing over the latter's rightful claims in public presentations.

The victims, also convinced of the aggressors' superior strength, may for a while lie low and allow the aggressors to secure small areas of land at no cost; but eventually the loss of property and reputation becomes

intolerable. In desperation the victims respond with violence. Fully prepared for this, the other clan quickly converts what has begun as a limited protest action into its own full-scale attack, meanwhile announcing
to the world that the fault lies with its opponents, for they initiated the
overt hostilities. Other clans of the phratry cannot know until the combat is concluded whether or not the real aggressors will retire to their
own territory or will remain in possession of some of the victims' land.
In any case there is little they can do when presented with a *fait accompli.*

  • If the opposed clans are of different phratries, the group that believes
itself the stronger generally acts much more directly and mounts an invasion quickly in order to achieve maximum surprise. However, should
this group feel really confident of its ability, it may dispense with secrecy
and open the hostilities with a series of nocturnal raids intended to pick
off notable warriors, thus demoralizing the enemy and weakening them
for the subsequent engagement. If the incursions stampede the victims
into attacking first, so much the better. Not only do the real aggressors
score some propaganda points, but also, being thoroughly prepared, they
can cut up the attackers at the border and then go on to invade their
territory in force.

These raids merit a brief description, not only because their success
can significantly affect the outcome of later fighting but also because,
being extremely hazardous, they reveal a reckless side of Mae character
not apparent in ordinary life.

For obvious reasons of secrecy and mobility a raiding party is small—
usually less than ten men. Normally the enterprise is suggested and directed by an experienced fight leader who invites certain of the bolder
"man-killers" to accompany him. The group must be able to function with
few commands, and in the event of unexpected difficulties, each member
must know he can rely implicitly on the others' steadiness. The men first
pool any information they have about the enemy's current residential
arrangements and decide which of the accessible men's houses has the
most numerous and important occupants.

Some days beforehand one of the party commonly will reconnoiter
the border region for enemy sentries or patrols. He may also spy out a feasible route through the intervening bush or cane grass, which he carefully
marks with a few leaves. He returns several times by night to ensure that
the enemy has not discovered the path and set an ambush. If all appears
safe, the raiders set out during the moonless hours and stealthily make
their way to the chosen men's house.

Once they reach the outer defenses of the house, one man silently
scales the palisade and opens the gateway for the others (the heavy planks
can be removed only from inside the wall). It takes a brave man to climb
the barrier, for he cannot know whether or not a sentry waits within to
pick him off as he is silhouetted against the sky. The hero crawls onto the

shallow houseporch and touches the sets of rump leaves hanging there to signal to his mates how many men are sleeping inside. He then attempts with infinite caution to remove the planks securing the small (thirty inches square) entrance to the house itself. Should he perceive that he cannot shift them noiselessly, he retreats and the raiders move off to another house nearby.

Once the doorway is cleared, one man edges inside on his belly to abstract a brand from the banked fire, while two others hold his legs, ready to haul him out if the sleepers stir. The firestick is handed back to a colleague, who blows it into flame as he applies it first to the thatch over the porch. Should the occupants wake now, the man inside the door lays about him with his axe before withdrawing to allow his partners to fire arrows indiscriminately into the sleeping area. Some men stand ready with axes to cut down anyone who tries to break out, and they may also watch the rear of the house for escape hatches or tunnels.

Naturally the raiders hope the sleepers will not rouse until the roof is well ablaze. Then the besieged have to choose between being asphyxiated and incinerated or crawling outside to meet the waiting axes. In any case, the longer the raiders can stay by the house, the more certain they are of destroying all the residents—but the greater opportunity they give other enemies to find and surround them. The fight leader must therefore choose the right moment to order his men to run for home, and he is responsible for covering their rear by halting from time to time to fire at pursuers.

Once safely across the border the raiders announce their success with victory yells, and their clansmen join in chanting insults at the dismayed enemy. This is the time when the victims, ill-prepared but enraged beyond endurance, may attempt a retaliatory attack and be badly mauled by the already mobilized and confident aggressors.

This, then, is the ideal raid—and I have been told (but can scarcely credit it) that in such a foray, properly planned and executed, as many as ten men have been killed in one house. Two or three dead seems to be the more usual tally. However, in ventures of this kind many things can go wrong, especially if the intended victims expect trouble and have posted sentries around their houses. At the first sign of such preparedness the raiders have no choice but to turn back. Even so they are unlikely to regain their own territory without suffering casualties. I have noticed that men prefer not to talk about these unsuccessful sorties.

There are variants of this style of raiding. In one, which is obviously more dangerous and apparently is rare, a man chooses a time when most of the enemy clan are attending a ceremony or festival elsewhere, and enters a men's house that is accessible and empty. There he notes the positions of the bed planks and neckrests, which usually adjoin and parallel the heavy side walls of the house, then inconspicuously tucks small pale leaves under the eaves outside to indicate the locations of the beds. When the raiders arrive at night, each man, guided by the markers, stands beside the low eaves and carefully slides his spear down through the thatch above a sleeper. At a signal the spears are plunged home, while another man tears open the door to seize a brand with which to ignite the thatch. General slaughter should follow. However, it is difficult to believe that so complicated a stratagem could be carried off without alerting the occupants of the house.[21]

A simpler kind of foray is that in which the raiders select a house not far from the common border and, before first light, take up positions covering the doorway, ready to shoot and cut down the first sleep-dazed man who crawls outside to relieve himself. The killers may also hastily mutilate the corpse (for instance, by cutting off the genitals and cramming them in the owner's mouth—a refinement still employed on occasion nowadays) and prop it up in front of the entrance as an insult before they run for safety. Such incursions, in which the killing is largely random, appear to be intended simply to terrify and demoralize the enemy.

As we have seen, although the intermittent incursions and depredations undertaken by individuals or small parties from a clan during a period of undeclared war will eventually involve that group in overt warfare, they generally take place with the approval of the perpetrators' clansmen, who regard them as legitimate expressions of clan policy. This is not to say that on each occasion the whole clan assembles to approve a particular enterprise. Nevertheless, throughout times of increasing tension the men of the clan meet relatively often to assess the trend of events and their probable consequences, and in this way the climate of opinion within the clan is made apparent to all. Those men who go forth to steal the enemy's pigs or to raid his men's houses are confident that, in the face of reprisals, their own clansmen will offer physical support.

When, however, a substantial number of clansmen, especially if Big Men or fight leaders are included, believe the time has come for positive military action, they call a meeting of all clansmen to consider the issue. Indeed such assemblies, which follow a fairly regular pattern, should, and generally do, ratify by consensus any significant decisions the clan makes concerning warfare (and nowadays also litigation over land), the payment of homicide compensations, the performance of major ancestral rituals, and participation in the Te exchange. Members of the constituent subclans and lineages also engage in analogous but separate conferences to discuss payments of death compensation to matrilateral kin, the arrangement of funerary feasts, and the distribution of bride-price, as well as to clarify their opinions about the larger problems with which clan convocations deal.[22]

The men who convene a clan meeting to debate military matters do so quietly, and the participants proceed unobtrusively to the designated

Mae Enga men attending a clan meeting

men's house in the hope that neighboring groups do not perceive that something important is afoot. The house may be chosen simply because it is the largest or most secluded; it may, however, be the house of the most important convener or of the clan's major Big Man. If, as is likely, it cannot accommodate all the participants, much of the business is transacted in the porch yard. Women and children may not attend, although wives should bring food to the houseyard for the men. All resident clansmen, that is, putative agnates, who have entered or have passed through the bachelors' association are entitled to be present. They reserve the right to exclude any other men who are currently living in the clan, on the grounds that the latter are liable to potential conflicts of interests. Nevertheless, non-agnates who have long resided with the clan parish and have in other ways unequivocally demonstrated their political reliability may be specifically invited—even if, or perhaps because, they are former members of the clan with which the host group is contending. It is thought that such men can sometimes take a wider view of the situation. Although no man who has the right to be at a clan assembly is forced to appear, only a man who was profoundly indifferent to his clan's welfare would voluntarily absent himself.

The men who initiated the conference, or their spokesmen, briefly indicate their view of the clan's position and the action they favor. Thus, they may argue that now is the time to launch a full-scale attack on the neighboring clan with the aim of occupying a specific section of its territory. The major Big Man then solicits responses from the audience. Ideally, everyone present has a voice and, being among his own clansmen, can speak with complete freedom. Moreover, anyone who possesses pertinent information has a moral obligation to contribute so that the group may reach the best possible decision in the circumstances. Most men in fact are ready to make their points at length and with elaborate oratorical flourishes. Only young bachelors and some very old men are likely to hold back and say little unless directly questioned. The task of the Big Man at this stage is to ensure that all have a chance to offer their opinions and facts in full, and hence he makes no attempt to cut off any but obviously irrelevant speeches.

Only in this way, it is believed, can each clansman truly ascertain the thoughts of his fellows and the evidence behind them. So instructed, he can cleave to or modify his own ideas, and his reactions in turn affect those of others. Naturally, the Big Men and fight leaders have their own opinions of an appropriate outcome of the discussion; but none of them, especially in the early sessions, reveals much of his hand or tries patently to push for the acceptance of his suggestions. Not until hours of argument have clarified the issues and carefully dissected the facts are these men likely to signal unequivocally their own positions, and even then those, including the major Big Man, who perceive that tide running strongly against them may well go along with the emerging majority view. Thus, step by step the slow process of constant feedback inches toward the possibility of general agreement on a correct course of action. Then, when the Big Man believes that consensus is close at hand and that further talk will add nothing of value, he incisively summarizes the main arguments, indicates which have been rejected, and finally announces the decision reached by the clan.

Sometimes, of course, given the gravity of the issues and the likelihood of deep but honest differences over the interpretation of inherently ambiguous evidence, real consensus is impossible to achieve. For instance, although most of the assembly, including Big Men, agree that, on the basis of available information, war is the only feasible choice, a significant minority may hold out against this view. When it is clear that no amount of exhortation will change their opinion, the Big Man states that the pro-war majority will proceed with preparations for an attack; but he also warns the bellicose faction that, having overruled the opposition, they must be ready to pay most of the costs—in particular, the burden of the subsequent compensation for allied and enemy deaths will fall mainly on them. At the same time he reminds the cautious minority that those who do not fight in support of the clan's interests cannot expect to enjoy the fruits of victory—that is, they will not share in enemy land the clan may seize or receive any homicide pigs coming to the clan. The dissidents acknowledge the force of the warning, while emphasizing their own prerogative of contributing few or no pigs to the homicide compensations.

But even as both parties are making clear their positions, everyone knows that, because the clan's survival may be at stake, once combat begins the doves will almost certainly be in their accustomed places fighting strenuously alongside the hawks. Moreover, many of them will probably join in the payments of homicide compensation, not merely to establish claims to whatever wealth the clan may secure but also, and equally important, to maintain their own reputations and that of the group.

A more difficult situation arises when, in the face of reasoned opposition from an antiwar majority, a group of hotheads remains determined on fighting, that is, on attacking in force and not simply on raiding. The difficulty is compounded if fight leaders support the activists, although one should not assume that experienced fight leaders always want to go to war—they, too, can recognize hopeless odds. Then the Big Men can only voice the disapproval of the majority and warn the others that, if they go ahead, they must bear the costs. Again, everyone realizes that, should these men provoke a major counterattack by their opponents, the whole clan had no alternative but to fight, both to extricate the hotheads (who, after all, are clansmen) and to defend the home territory. Much depends on the identity of the clan that is the intended target; if it is one regarded as an inveterate enemy, the hawks by persistent argument, exhortation, and taunts may eventually win a reluctant majority to their side.

However, should most of the gathering remain unpersuaded, the Big Men can try further to dissuade the reckless minority by stating that the clan will hold them responsible for the deaths of any "brothers" killed coming to their aid. Thus, after the clan makes payments for allied and enemy dead and receives payments from the enemy for its own losses, the hawks' subclans or lineages must give additional homicide compensation to the agnates of any dead doves and must also contribute heavily to the death payments that the latter make to matrilateral kin. This sobering prospect may daunt the activists, who then temporize by continuing small raids on the enemies and by stealing their pigs.

Finally, if the same headstrong few frequently flout public opinion and provoke large-scale fights with other clans, their own careers may be brief. Should men of parallel but unenthusiastic subclans be killed in consequence, their agnates may reject offers of extra homicide pigs and instead try to slay the offenders, an action that can trigger intraclan warfare. If because of this imprudence men of the hotheads' own subclan have died, their agnates are not likely to kill them in retaliation, "for we share the same blood"; but they may publicly revile the culprits, refuse them economic help, and generally make life so unpleasant for them that they are forced to seek shelter with relatives abroad until passions cool. At the least the agnates will demand that these men contribute massively to the matrilateral payments of death compensation.

To conclude, I should emphasize that such deep and irreconcilable divisions of opinion do not emerge often when clansmen assemble to determine whether or not they should go to war. Given the crowding of the compact clan territories along the narrow valleys, the men of any clan are usually quick to agree that the actions of an expanding adjacent group are a serious threat to their security. Only the few really obtuse men must have their attention drawn by Big Men and fight leaders to the growing danger; the rest readily accept the need for a prompt defensive response, which may also be defined to include a preemptive attack on the potential aggressors.

Preparations for war

Once a clan has elected to fight, events usually move quickly. The first step is to ensure that noncombatants are quietly evacuated from the vicinity of the border with the enemy clan. Generally, however, men whose wives occupy houses there have already gauged the situation and for some time have been unobtrusively moving their families, pigs, and other portable wealth to more secure houses of close agnates. The very old and infirm men join them there. From this position, if the fighting goes badly, the women can more readily flee with their children and pigs to the clans of their own parents or other friendly kin.

At the same time the fight leaders select young warriors to patrol the vacated area without being observed (by no means an easy task), and to keep careful watch for signs of untoward activity in the enemy's domain. Other men check their weapons and prepare food, such as sweet potatoes, to carry as battle rations.

While these safety measures are implemented, the Big Men, fight leaders, and experienced warriors remain in conclave to plan strategy and move detailed preparations. Now concern with security intensifies, and outsiders, with rare exceptions, are barred from participation.

The Mae recognize the possibility of treason ("the betrayal of secrets to the enemy"), and they say that occasionally a man who is otherwise an upright member of his clan may be impelled by feelings of obligation or by short-sighted self-interest into action prejudicial to the group safety. The clan to be attacked without warning may include a mother's brother with whom he has strong ties of affection, as well as extensive and personally rewarding exchange connections, and whose wife's house will be in the path of the invaders. Add to this the fact that some of his own pigs are on agistment in that house, and the man's dilemma becomes obvious.

80

Should he not alert his uncle, if only to enable the latter to clear the house in time? But if he does so, his uncle cannot in decency protect his own family from harm and not warn his agnates of their danger.

In real life it seems that a man almost always remains faithful to his clan; he keeps his knowledge to himself and, when the fighting begins, simply takes care not to fire at his relative. Indeed he may go further and, as the battle line sweeps toward his uncle's woman's house, he may risk enemy arrows to climb on the roof and ask his clansmen not to burn it, for his pigs are inside. They are likely to heed his plea, for his is a brave action; but later he may learn that a helpful ally has burned the house in his absence.

Nevertheless, in one case I was told of (and it is presumably not unique), the men of a clan so distrusted a "brother's" attachment to his close kinsmen among the enemy that they not only excluded him from their initial deliberations, but also, once they had decided to fight, kept him under restraint, tied with pig ropes and guarded by the old men, until the attack was launched. Even if this story is exaggerated or untrue, it is widely told. Small wonder, then, that participants in strategy sessions take great care to keep their discussions secret.

During these meetings one or more of the important men customarily contributes several, perhaps three or four, pigs to be killed both for ritual purposes and to provide meat for a celebratory feast. A specialist supervises the clubbing and preparation of the beasts, whose blood and "vital essence" he formally offers as food to the ghosts of men earlier killed by the clan to be attacked. This dedication informs the ghosts that their agnates are about to avenge their deaths and exhorts them to restrain their characteristic domestic malevolence and not lead their "brothers" into danger during the combat. At the same time this ritual is thought to propitiate in a general way all the clan ancestors, to impress upon them that their descendants are not afraid to fight and die for the interests of the clan. Sometimes the specialist also kills a pig on behalf of the ghosts of recently dead men of the enemy clan, hoping to induce these to unleash their malice against their own clansmen.[23]

The participants later share the cooked pork with all the clansmen, who without ceremony eat their small portions, accompanied by sweet potatoes, taro, bananas, etc., which the women bring to the men's house-yard and the men cook in large earth ovens. They take care to heat the oval stones indoors so neighboring groups do not observe an unusual amount of smoke.[24]

Some men at this time may engage in oven-divination. Various signs, such as the emergence of particular insects from the oven mound, foretell success and indicate the number of men the enemy will lose. Others, such as the presence of earthworms in the oven pit or the breaking of tubers in the cooking, point to deaths among their own clansmen. Ordinarily, nobody pays much attention to these omens, for the decision to go to war has already been taken and everyone knows that casualties will follow. But if the portents are numerous and uniformly disastrous, the Big Men and fight leaders may call off the attack.

One of the first decisions the important men must make concerns the use of allies. Whereas clansmen rarely reject the services of relatives and friends who come as individuals to help them once combat is joined, there is considerable reluctance to issue formal invitations beforehand to other groups (except perhaps fraternal clans). In part this stems from the rational fear of jeopardizing the secret preliminary plans, for it is always possible that someone in the allied group has such close ties with men of the target group that he cannot leave them in ignorance of the proposed attack. Allies, moreover, are difficult to control in battle, especially in large numbers, for they are not all amenable to the commands of another clan's fight leaders. Further, allies join a fight for different reasons and cannot really be relied on in precarious situations. Thus, men of clan A are willing to aid clan B against clan C, not because they have any pressing quarrel with clan C but because they know their own current enemies in clan D will probably help clan C, and they welcome the chance to injure clan D. But once they have evened the score with clan D, they are quite likely to go home, leaving clan B unsupported at a critical moment. Worse, some of them, as I have known happen, may even change sides in mid-fight if they decide that friends or relatives in clan C are in imminent danger of total defeat.

Even if the allies continue fighting beside their hosts, it is not their own land they are defending, and they are not wholly willing to risk their lives if the situation becomes desperate. Being ready to withdraw under heavy fire, they may leave the flanks of their hosts' skirmishers unprotected—a situation every experienced Mae warrior dreads. In many cases allies are poorly acquainted with the particular terrain on which they are engaged; this makes them uneasy and more concerned to protect themselves than to attack boldly. When men fight in a place they know well, such as the territory of a fraternal clan, they charge with great confidence, saying: "I know this ground well, it is like my own—fighting here is food for me!"

Finally, a formally invited group of allies participates in the reasonable expectation of sharing the spoils, and everyone is well-aware that postwar arguments over their division are usually acrimonious and likely to lead to further bloodshed.

On the face of it, then, a clan planning an attack has good reason to go it alone and not imperil its security or autonomy by relying on others. On the other hand, a clan whose invasion is coordinated with a flanking or rear attack by an allied group knows that the odds are very much in its favor, that its chances are improved for a quick victory with fewer casualties. Thus, the decision whether or not to seek allies beforehand is not one to be taken lightly, and indeed opinions among the planners can be sharply divided. My sample of intergroup conflicts shows no clear pattern in these decisions. Whether or not a clan launching an attack invites allies depends on how it perceives the prevailing circumstances.

At any rate, if the consensus is to secure allies, representatives of the initiating clan go quickly and unobtrusively to the Big Men of the other group with their invitation, and the latter promptly convene a clan meeting to take a decision. Should they agree to help, the allies' Big Men and fight leaders visit the host clan to join in the high-level planning and to share in the accompanying feast.

Obviously the strategy a clan adopts for its invasion depends not only on whether it has persuaded another clan to join in the venture, but also on the form this aid is to take. Thus, depending on the location of the allies' home territory, they may be able to make a direct, simultaneous, but independent attack on the enemy's flank or rear, or they may have to fight alongside the host group on a single front. In addition the invaders planning group must make some estimate, however crude, of the strength of their own forces relative to that of the opponents, including any allies the latter may enlist. When these "facts" are at hand, the high command can make more specific plans, where the opinions of fight leaders carry much weight.

Accounts of actual invasions and discussions with experienced Mae warriors suggest that in general the overall strategy intended is informed by principles common to all successful military campaigns—speed, secrecy, and the propitious concentration of strength. With these requirements in mind, the organizers make the critical strategic decision, namely, on which section of enemy territory their warriors will converge. That choice, together with the number of men they have at their command, governs subsequent decisions on the size and disposition of units, the manner of their entering the combat area, and the action they take once there. Nevertheless, as the Mae well know, strategy planned by one side in the privacy of the men's house does not always prove appropriate once the battle begins. Then the fight leaders' experience and personal bravery are crucial, for these men must make constant tactical judgments to meet the rapidly changing circumstances of combat, as well as provide the steadying influence that heartens men confused by sudden shifts of fortune in the field.

When the clan leaders are agreed on such matters as the point of attack, the division of the forces, and the routes to be taken to the battle-ground, they summon the warriors and explain in careful detail what is to be done. Every clansman attends this important briefing (even sentries and patrols are called in turn to hear it), so that each can ask questions and be sure he understands what is required of him.

By now it is likely to be late at night. Assuming that all the men have prepared their weapons and food, they are given an hour or two to rest and take a final snack of sweet potatoes before setting off in groups for the border. There they assemble at designated locations to await first light. Then, shortly before dawn, they attack.

Aspects of Combat

5

Before examining the tactics Mae warriors employ in sudden incursions and in prolonged wars, I shall briefly describe a typical campaign that occurred in the 1940's. I do so not merely to indicate the broader strategy that informs Mae warfare and establishes the context for specific engagements. I am also concerned to emphasize that two clans do not confront each other in isolation: each of the contending groups must anticipate the responses of its neighbors, be they "brothers" or enemies.

A typical campaign

The populous clan A of phratry I, hungry for more land, had been probing the border it shared with the smaller clan E of phratry II to its west. At that time clan E II was also on strained terms with its own western neighbor and nearest fraternal clan, the large group F II, which, too, was nibbling at the territory of E II. Moreover, the next closest fraternal clan of E II, the smallish group G II situated across the river to the north, was currently in dispute over land and trees with yet another big clan of that phratry, H II, farther to the north. Clan G II, assisted by its eastern neighbor, clan C of phratry I (also quarreling over boundaries with clan H II), had been caught up in sporadic raids and counterraids against H II.

The Big Men of clan A I decided the time was ripe for a surprise attack on clan E II. They believed with reason that clans F II, G II, and H II would be slow in coming to the aid of their "brothers," and that they (A I) could expect to occupy a substantial piece of E II's territory before more distant fraternal allies from phratry II could help the victims. However, to make the outcome more certain, clan A I secretly solicited the assistance of its fraternal clan C I, which also lay north of the river and had been intermittently supporting clan G II against clan H II. During a quiet nocturnal feast of pork held in clan A I's domain, the Big Men of A I and C I agreed on their overall strategy.

While most of the forces of A I prepared to strike at dawn across the eastern border of clan E II, other warriors of A I, together with those of C I, slipped unobtrusively through the territory of their fraternal clan B I to the east, then crossed the river north into that of C I. Thence they passed unchallenged through the southern section of G II, the western neighbor and current friend of C I, to reach the river again at the northern

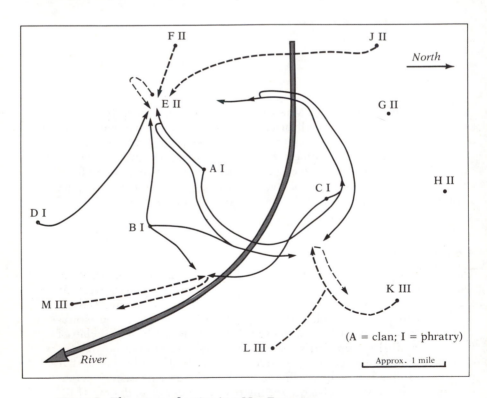

Figure 5   The course of action in a Mae Enga war

86

border of clan E II. They could do this largely because the men of G II were massed on their own northern marches, guarding against incursions by clan H II. Moreover, such men of G II who observed this movement shut their eyes to it because clan C I had earlier reinforced them against pressures from their common antagonist, clan H II.

When the glare of burning houses signaled that the main body of clan A I had begun its assault on clan E II from the east, the other units of A I and C I forded the river and entered the gardens of E II from the north to take the defenders' flank. Outnumbered but resisting stubbornly, the men of E II slowly retreated to the southwest, calling on their "brothers" for help as they did so.

Warriors from the more distant fraternal clan J II set off at once to assist E II, but those of F II nearby did not join the battle until it was obvious that E II faced serious defeat and that the forces of A I might drive right to the border of F II. Few men of the fraternal clans G II and H II came to help at that time; neither clan would risk leaving its domain undefended and open to the other's raids.

Meanwhile, clans A I and C I, attacking from east and north, were pushing deeper into the territory of E II, burning houses as they advanced. In desperation, the men of E II called for aid from clans K and L of phratry III, their "mother's brothers," who lived to the north and east of the territory of clan C I. A contingent from each of these groups, long-term enemies of C I, quickly combined to lay waste the eastern part of the latter's domain.

At once men of clan B I, who had been mobilizing to help their "brothers" of A I and C I, shouted warnings to the latter. The warriors of C I immediately disengaged from the main action with E II and hastened to meet the threat to their own families. Recrossing the river, they ran through the territory of G II and swung south to hit the invaders on their northern flank. Simultaneously, a detachment of A I men hurried through the territory of their fraternal clan B I, picking up reinforcements as they did so, and drove north across the river to assault the other flank of the party from clans K III and L III. This two-pronged attack caught the intruders in a heavy crossfire, and they were forced to withdraw into their own domains.

Leaving the men of C I to patrol their borders with clans K III and L III, the units from A I and B I returned to the battle with E II and the allies who had now joined them. The latter, relieved of the earlier pressure by the diversion, had been able not only to halt the advance of the main body of clan A I but also to regain some ground. As a result, this engagement settled into the typical prolonged war, by the end of which clan A I, assisted mainly by its fraternal clans B I and D I (latecomers from a distance) succeeded in retaining only a small part of E II's land near the common boundary—which they hold to this day.

The warriors of clan C I, however, having cleared the invading clans K III and L III from their own eastern borders, found that a company of M III clansmen, "brothers" of K III and L III and old enemies of C I, had seized on the confusion to occupy a small and always vulnerable piece of C I's domain situated south of the river. It cost C I, together with allies from B I, some hard fighting to recover this. The main reason why the much larger clan M III did not press the confrontation with C I at this time was that all the fraternal clans A I, B I, C I, and D I were by then alerted and fully mobilized, ready to engage M III on three fronts simultaneously. Much later, after the opponents of M III had relaxed their vigilance and clan C I was embroiled in fresh disputes with clan H II, a strong force of M III warriors pushed the C I residents from that tract and occupied it permanently.

This compressed history points up the impediments facing would-be aggressors who try for a quick victory. The varying and not wholly predictable reactions of neighboring groups often deflect what begins as a surprise attack and convert it into a protracted war in which the original invaders have no hope of making great gains cheaply.

Invasion

Obviously, the strength of the forces engaged in any armed conflict reflects several related factors, some of them virtual imponderables but nonetheless critical, such as the perceived gravity of the issue, which in turn is at least partly conditioned by the asserted genealogical connections between contending groups and their recent mutual dealings. A more measurable determinant is the number of clansmen that each of the contending groups comprises, and the number of allies who join each side—two variables likely to be connected, because a clan's size is in general correlated with its resources and wealth, and the latter have a bearing on its exchange relationships and hence on how many allies it can attract in warfare.

Let us take first the simplest case of a clan, initially without allies, that invades its neighbor's territory without warning. Given that the mean population of a Mae clan parish is around 300–400, and that all men capable of bearing arms usually do so, we can estimate that the average attacking force at the start comprises about 100 warriors, and the defenders about the same or perhaps twenty or so fewer.[1]

Such figures have a bearing on how the aggressor mounts a surprise attack, as distinct from simply charging in a skirmishing line at already mobilized adversaries. An unannounced assault or invasion is, of course, different in intention—and surprise is the significant term. For such operations the strategists prefer to split their force into two or preferably, three compact columns when entering enemy territory, provided they have enough men to do this without leaving the component sections too small to be effective in either attack or self-defense. Thus, if the total force comprised no more than fifty men, their leaders would be inclined to keep it entire (albeit as a loose phalanx) to conserve its striking power.

Whatever the number of attackers, however, initially they are usually divided into two or three smaller groups to facilitate their silent movement in the darkness to the clan border, where they take up their stations in readiness for the predawn onslaught. This is necessary because of the local terrain, whose slopes not only tend to be naturally uneven but also are encumbered with deep garden ditches, sturdy fences, and groves of trees. For a force to try to move as one through these obstacles at night could be disastrous. To get into position for the assault quietly, rapidly, and more or less simultaneously, the bodies of men keep to tracks carefully chosen by the fight leaders to converge on the appropriate place of assembly.

Obviously, the point or points at which the aggressors break into the victims' domain depends largely on which part of it is the prime target. The invaders try to avoid entering enemy territory through dense forest or stands of cane grass. It is difficult enough for small raiding parties to negotiate these in the dark without alarming their foes prematurely; it is almost impossible for large groups to do so. And if the enemy is thus alerted, the invaders are at a serious disadvantage. They have to advance in single file and, as they debouch from cover, the waiting line of opponents may pick them off one by one before they can bring all their own bows to bear.

Ideally, then, an invading force wishes to strike where it can quickly cross the border in two or three compact columns, each with a specified leader, and move freely into an area where several enemy houses stand close together—houses whose occupants are too few to repel the attacks of the central unit yet numerous enough for their destruction or rout to demoralize the remaining defenders, who by now are aroused and mobilizing. As the men of the central column quickly deal with the initial targets (forcing doors, shooting arrows into the houses, and burning the thatch), the men of the other units cover their flanks, standing ready to cut down fugitives.[2] Even so, some of the latter may well escape in the half-light and the confusion.

Then all the columns converge to form a shallow phalanx, four or five ranks deep (of which the first may comprise men armed with spears and shields), and, firing arrows as they go, charge the oncoming defenders, preferably downhill for impetus. If they are able to overrun the opposing line, the invaders split up again into tight columns, each of which mops up the small, disorganized enemy clusters, using axes to dispatch any wounded they overtake. Less experienced or skillful warriors drop behind to burn houses, fell pandanus trees (a matter of a few quick blows with an axe), and shoot at frantic pigs.

Should the initial collapse of the defense become a true rout, in which individual warriors simply break and flee without attempting further to check the enemy, the invaders' columns may spread out, if the terrain permits, into a loose skirmishing line to try to bring down escaping men before they escape from arrow range. However, the scattered defenders may try to reform into groups large enough to harry the attackers and to fight delaying actions in order to give their allies (alerted by the noise and the fires) time to come to their aid. At this the invaders again regroup to create a shock force, protected by small flanking units, to break up such moving pockets of resistance. This practice of attackers alternately dividing and combining their resources to deal with the enemy's varying strength (and they may repeat this several times during an invasion) appears to be a basic element in Mae military tactics.[3]

The invaders press their assault, pursuing and killing any opponent they see, and they try to sweep across the clan domain to force the survivors to flee severally into the forest or the territories of neighboring clans. If the assailants can achieve this goal on the first day, they have won a complete victory, and there is little to prevent their holding most or all of their opponents' land. It is unlikely that the latter, having been widely dispersed, can reassemble in one location quickly enough to launch effective counterattacks or to induce many allies to help them undo this impressive *fait accompli*.[4]

So much for the perfect assault that succeeds fully, rapidly, and at minimal cost to the instigators. Given the many Clausewitzian "frictions" inherent in the prosecution of warfare at any level of elaboration, it is not surprising that actual performance often falls well short of intent.

Defense

The ideal response to such an incursion, assuming that the defenders can at once mobilize a substantial body of warriors, is for them to get to the invaders before these can complete their initial killing and arson, and to try to pin them down and surround them. Then the defenders can with their arrows inflict heavy casualties as their enemies attempt to break through the cordon in order to reach their own territory and regroup before the defenders attack over the border. The invading columns, however, put out flanking units precisely to guard against encirclement. And in any case the odds are against the defenders' mustering enough men in time to form a circle sufficiently strong or deep to hold their opponents.

A more feasible and more common tactic is for enough defenders to reach the invasion point before the invaders are ready to make their concerted rush deep into the victims' territory, or at least before that charge has gained momentum. Here the defenders oppose the enemy phalanx with their own, albeit one shallower and less numerous, which then, fighting strenuously against superior strength, drops back as slowly as possible to allow the remaining clansmen (as well as allies) time to join the combat. The main danger now facing the defenders is that the longer the delaying action continues, the more opportunities the larger invading force has to break their front or to outflank them. Accordingly, when the fight leaders in the retreating group believe they have sufficient reinforcements and the terrain and cover are suitable, they attempt, by "refusing" their own center, to trap the invaders.

At its simplest this maneuver merely requires that, as both wings of the defenders' company withdraw slowly, the men in the center drop back more quickly, as if the enemy center is too much for them. As the overconfident attackers press forward to exploit their apparent advantage and push into the concavity created by the yielding defenders, their own men, first at the center and then on the wings, are increasingly exposed to heavy crossfire from archers on the defenders' wings. The attackers, moreover, are too crowded to deploy freely their greater numbers and fire power. If the defenders' wings can hold steady and maintain the pressure, they have a chance to close the trap and subsequently to take the invaders in the rear.[5]

Sometimes the retreating defenders employ a further refinement in attempting to encircle the enemy force. As reinforcements stream in, the defenders' leaders instruct some of these men to fall away unobtrusively into concealment on both sides of the track or gardens along which the small armies are fighting. The newcomers remain hidden until the invaders have passed them and are being drawn into the defenders' refused center. Then, as the archers on the defenders' wings are firing into their opponents' flanks, the fight leaders order the concealed men to attack from the rear.[6]

Properly carried out (and with a liberal helping of good fortune), such tactics can radically and relatively quickly change the course of battle, enabling the defenders to switch to the attack as the invaders, in order to keep down their casualties, are impelled to break through the groups harassing their flanks or rear and retire in some semblance of order to the safety of their own territory. Even if mistiming or lack of discipline prevents the defending force from wholly exploiting its advantage, partial success may still blunt or turn the thrust of the invasion and create the necessary breathing space during which large numbers of allies can make their way to the field. It is then apparent to both sides that there will be no swift victory that day, and that the likelihood of a protracted war is great.

Protracted warfare

When, as is commonly the case, a surprise attack does not achieve decisive results by nightfall of the first day, the invaders withdraw to safe positions and throw out patrols. The Big Men and the fight leaders (including those of any contingents of allies who have joined them) then weigh the alternatives open to them.

If the intended victims have put up an unexpectedly vigorous resistance and kept the attacking forces from penetrating any distance into the disputed territory, and especially if numerous allies have come to the defenders' aid, counsels of caution may prevail. The aggressors retire inside their own border and partially demobilize, while maintaining strong scouting parties and posting sentries at the border to detect and delay any counterattack or retaliatory raids that the now emboldened enemy may be tempted to mount. Then, if within the next few weeks neither group initiates further large-scale military action, all parties (including neutral bystanders) assume the war is, for the time being at least, ended, a state of affairs that receives public, almost formal, confirmation when the Big Men of both sides open negotiations over compensation to be paid for deaths incurred in the fighting.

A more likely outcome, however, given Mae intransigence and the aggressors' explicit desire for more land, is for their leaders to press for a continuation of overt hostilities, arguing that, since they have already occupied some of the enemy's territory, it is worth pursuing the struggle and risking more deaths in the reasonable hope of retaining possession of their present gains.[7] Moreover, as experienced warriors know, if from a vantage point within the enemy domain they maintain pressure on their opponents, they are in a better position to exploit any weakness in the defense and thus to seize more of the coveted land.

Such a unilateral decision pushes both groups into a war of attrition that, depending both on their relative strength and on the extent of the initial incursion, may continue for weeks, even months. Whatever the duration, the course of events is much the same—periods of comparative inaction punctuated by sporadic raids intended to unsettle the opponents and by larger engagements aimed at forcing them to give ground. The situation also becomes very much a war of nerves. In general, the clan that can better bear the casualties and the destruction of property is the more likely to achieve its goals.

Significant in this respect is not only the number of warriors a clan can muster but also the extent of its domain (the two variables are not perfectly correlated). A group whose territory is relatively large can more easily afford to let part of it stand idle temporarily as a battleground while the noncombatants, especially the women with their pigs, move to another section and there, under the protection of armed patrols, get on with the daily round of food production. Also, during quiet intervals between engagements, heads of household may take turns to leave the front in order to prepare new gardens in the secure areas.

People tending crops in wartime depend not only on their patrols for security but also, and less reliably, on the warnings of neighboring clans in the event enemy raiders approach from unexpected directions. On these occasions the youths and old men who from the start of hostilities have remained with the women are expected to fight, however inefficiently, to cover their escape or in their defense until enough warriors can get back from the front to drive off the assailants.

When actions involving the entire forces of each side are in progress, the noncombatants may observe the conflict unobtrusively and from a safe distance, having been commanded not to shout encouragement to their own warriors lest this draw the attention of roving parties of enemy scouts. The women watch anxiously in order to judge the course of the battle and to determine when to flee with their children and pigs. The males, especially the old men, hold themselves ready to bring up supplies of arrows when ordered, or to remove and undertake emergency surgery on seriously wounded warriors.

In any protracted war between two clans, the periods of quiet and limited raiding far exceed those in which large-scale actions are fought. Whether the two groups confront each other across the original border or whether the initial combat has enabled one force to establish itself in the other's territory, the precautions that each subsequently takes are much the same.

Thus, neither side confines its energies solely to standing guard over the area that forms the obvious battlefront. Fight leaders well know that enemy raiders will attempt by night to skirt the front line and strike at the clan's houses from various directions, sometimes passing stealthily through the domains of neutral or friendly neighbors. Accordingly, they place sentries at vantage points along much of their own borders, especially beside the entrances to major tracks and at bridges and fords.

If numbers permit, sentries are posted each night in pairs, one to watch while the other dozes. The need for complete concealment and silence is stressed; inexperienced men are instructed beforehand not to smoke or even to slap at stinging insects lest the noise reveal their positions. Sentries usually take cover behind trees and fences, or in garden ditches. They may also construct temporary hiding places in patches of cane grass. Sometimes a sentry makes a fairly obvious shelter and then settles down some distance away, hoping that an enemy scout will discover the empty shelter and wait to ambush the sentry as he returns to his station. The latter then tries to stalk and kill the scout.

When the sentinels at a border post detect the approach of a raiding party, they shout warnings, including information about the numbers and location of the intruders, to the rest of their clansmen, some of whom are making plans or are sleeping fitfully in men's houses deep in their own territory, while others are watching at the front. The outmatched sentries then attempt to drop back to safety, sniping as they go. Once discovered, the raiders may try before turning back to overtake and cut down the sentries, on the assumption that half a loaf is better than none; but they dare not advance too far lest their aroused opponents encircle them. Such nocturnal alarms and excursions are characteristic of the "quiet" periods.

It usually happens that early in the war, as a result of pitched battles or selective raids, a belt of several hundred yards on either side of the antagonists' common border is laid waste. All the houses there are burned, fences destroyed, pandanus and other valuable trees felled, and gardens torn up or trampled into mud. This area becomes the main field of combat. By day small parties of scouts (with about four to six men), exploiting what cover remains, patrol there to keep a constant watch for any untoward activity among the foe and, most important, to detect the arrival of potential enemy allies, because this may presage a renewed attack. Similarly, the men who are not guarding the borders but discussing military and political plans do so in shelters set high on the slopes, from which they can observe the enemy's movements and oversee their own women who are working in the gardens.

Meanwhile, the parties at the front remain ready to snipe at warriors who incautiously emerge from cover and approach too closely. If numbers favor them, they may strike suddenly across the border to cut off careless stragglers from an enemy scouting unit. Occasionally, when their opponents have temporarily withdrawn some of their sentinels, four or five of the more adventurous slip deeper into enemy territory to set an ambush beside a track that they believe an enemy patrol will follow on returning to its task.[8]

There, if the others' scouts do not discover them, they may be able to dispatch one or two men and escape unscathed to their own fastness. Once home, the raiders utter the "killers' victory shout" to announce their success to the entire neighborhood and to tell the foe to collect its dead. At this their own clansmen mass on a hillside and caper, as they chant rude, exultant songs. Such a provocation may easily trigger another major engagement as the enraged enemy charges across the border, bent on avenging its loss.

Days, sometimes weeks, may pass in this manner, with increasingly tired and edgy warriors taking turns patrolling by day and standing sentry by night. Even when those who are temporarily off-duty gather in one of the men's houses, they sleep little. They cannot be sure this is not the night the enemy and his allies have chosen for a full-scale predawn incursion. The slightest unexpected noise (or indeed a prolonged silence) sends the armed men out into the darkness to scour the paths leading to the disputed area or to the borders with unfriendly clans to check on their sentinels. In

94

these circumstances, as they know, an attack can come from almost any direction. Then, when the apprehensive warriors reassemble and agree that it was only a false alarm, they count heads to ensure that nobody is missing,[9] after which they sit around until first light, endlessly analyzing the situation.

During these times of inaction many of the allies who came to help in the early fighting drift away. As heads of household and the military support of their own clans, they cannot afford to absent themselves from home for long. At best the young bachelors among the allies, who do have fewer domestic and public responsibilities, remain to share in the tasks of watch-keeping and patrolling. And these, of course, are usually the less experienced warriors, who cannot be expected to carry out their duties efficiently without supervision or to be wholly relied upon in an emergency.

All of which means that the relatively limited manpower of the host group must bear an onerous burden as it has to ensure simultaneously the security of its domain, the continuity of supplies, and the maintenance of political and social relations, however exiguous, with current and potential allies abroad. It is small wonder that Mae men speak with real feeling of the great strain they undergo at such times, of the combination of anxious boredom and physical exhaustion that oppresses them, and of the frequent overwhelming urge that seizes them to do something to stimulate action, however ill-advised.

It is then that the more restless and hardy warriors, especially the "man-killers," plan risky nocturnal raids deep into enemy territory, hoping to burn houses in the "safe" areas and so intimidate their opponents, as well as to relieve their own frustrations. Such forays, if they succeed, may provoke the incensed enemy to counterattack in force in an attempt to avenge the casualties. Accordingly, when a raid is mounted all the clansmen stand to arms that night, not only in readiness for retaliation but also to provide support quickly should the raiders get into serious difficulties.

The Big Men and fight leaders are aware that the psychological pressures of inaction can have violent consequences, and they carefully gauge the situation to determine how and when it can best be exploited. Thus, they are concerned to head off, without obviously depressing the general morale, manifestly foolhardy calls to action, and to encourage properly organized raids by experienced warriors that promise to foment disquiet among the enemy. Indeed, a well-executed foray by a fairly numerous party may so dislocate the opponents' defensive measures that the waiting fight leaders, apprised by the raiders' shouts, immediately throw in the whole of their force to capitalize on the confusion, trusting to the tumult and the burning houses to call up their own allies.

On the other hand, the clan leaders may decide that further inaction will simply erode the morale of their warriors, especially the younger men, and endanger whatever gains they have already made. Accordingly, they wait no longer for obvious advantages or provocations but forthwith send covert messages to their allies to join them in a major attack. Indeed, they may launch an assault even as the messengers are calling on the allies.

The course of large-scale combat that occurs within a protracted war is markedly affected by the impossibility of a true surprise attack, for both sides are at all times mobilized. Thus, defenders against a sudden incursion generally have enough sentries and scouts in the field not only to give ample notice of the aggressors' approach but also to harry and delay them while already armed reinforcements assemble quickly at the front before the invasion gathers momentum.

The invaders therefore have little opportunity to implement the preferred tactic of striking alternately with columns and phalanx. Instead, they attack in small columns, protected by flanking scouts, in order to sustain mobility as they engage in turn the rapidly converging units of the defenders. Given that the intruders' companies at this point do not greatly outnumber the enemy's, the battle may break up into a shifting, confused scramble of lesser actions, with the fight leaders on each side judging where they can throw in reserves (especially of incoming allies) to gain temporary advantages.

The tactics of these smaller units are not elaborate. Some strike where there are houses to burn, while opposing groups try to intercept and head them off. Other columns or bands of scouts attempt to use the cover in order to get behind an enemy unit and take it in the rear. If a company with flanking scouts in support is attacked by a stronger group, its leaders may employ a variant of the refused center to draw on the enemy—retiring in pretended panic while sending its wing men into concealment to wait for the opponents to pass before emerging to encircle them.

If the terrain permits, both sides may form extended skirmishing lines, each trying to outflank and roll up the other. Or one line may employ the technique of "striking alternately," continually rushing the other only to fall back quickly when the opponents stiffen their resistance and charge in turn. The men keep this up until their leaders judge that the enemy is tiring and losing coordination, while at the same time enough of their own warriors or allies have come up to exploit this weakness. Then they direct this fresh reserve group at the center of the enemy's slowing line in the hope of shattering it and leaving the disorganized and unprotected individuals vulnerable to heavy crossfire, a situation that shakes the bravest warrior's nerve.

Fight leaders are aware, however, that when their darting, weaving men spread out into a skirmishing line, this can soon become too thin to withstand shocks and may be pushed into broken or obstructed terrain where it crumbles completely. Hence, if the enemy concentrates reinforcements at any point on this overextended front, the leaders try quickly to reform their shallow line into small columns to meet the threat.

Combat may continue in this fluid and highly mobile fashion for four or five days. Each evening the increasingly weary men break off the action as the light fails and occupy secure positions as close as possible to the often highly disjointed battlefront. They spend the nights taking turns to patrol, to doze, and to eat sparingly—consuming enough sweet potatoes to give them strength for the next day but not so much as to make their limbs feel heavy and endanger their agility.[10] Men also visit in relays the wife's house of any warrior killed that day, there to mourn briefly with the women keeping vigil over the corpse and to reaffirm their determination to avenge his death. Meanwhile, the Big Men and fight leaders (including those of the allies) take stock and plan for the next day's fighting, which resumes at dawn.

Given the fragmented and opportunistic nature of this kind of battle, the fact that each side may have secured an advantage and won ground in one place only to have lost it in another, it is clear that military planning alone, no matter how well-informed or careful, is unlikely to achieve a decisive outcome if the groups are fairly evenly matched. The very mode of combat, with its heavy demands on the physical endurance of the antagonists, almost ensures that the longer the action continues, the less chance there is that the exhausted men of either force can do more than hold onto small gains made early in the encounter. The only factor that can tilt the balance at this juncture is marked numerical superiority, especially if it is represented by the appearance of a contingent of enthusiastic and ably led allies who can coordinate their tactics with their hosts'.

Ordinarily, military direction at these times remains in the hands of the home force. Its fight leaders know the terrain intimately, they have previously fought the enemy (usually a neighboring group) and thus understand his strengths and weaknesses, and in any case their participation from the start of the fighting should give them a better overall view of the circumstances. It is recognized, however, that allies may refuse to take orders from leaders of other clans. If, therefore, reinforcements (particularly from a fraternal clan) include well-known fight leaders, the hosts may not only agree to these commanding the visitors in the field but also may place some of their own men at their disposal. This is the more likely if the home leaders have failed to make substantial gains or, especially, if their situation is desperate. Then common sense directs them to accept the advice, even the orders, of outsiders in the hope of defending their patrimony.

Thus, when a large and capably led party of allies arrives in the heat of battle to find their "brothers" tired and hard pressed, they may tell them to fall back in apparent confusion, drawing the confident enemy with them, and then quickly to open their ranks so that the body of fresh warriors can charge through to surprise and scatter the opponents. On occasion this maneuver can sharply change the flow of combat and enable the rested home force to rally sufficiently to take the enemy's flank and so make a decisive push that ends the conflict.

Similarly, if the host group has already pressed the enemy onto the defensive and is winning ground, the allies who join the aggressors at this juncture may suggest that they should utilize the cover to make a sudden assault on the opponents' flank or rear. Their well-founded assumption is that simultaneous heavy blows from two directions will disorganize and demoralize the enemy, opening the way for a drive deep into his territory.

In short, in a protracted struggle between two evenly matched clans, the advent on one side of substantial numbers of competent allies late in the action can decide the outcome. Faced with an influx of fresh adversaries, the tired and disheartened warriors believe they now have little chance of fending off continuing vigorous attacks, especially if they cannot summon more aid. Their Big Men and fight leaders prefer to concede partial defeat then, rather than to fight on and risk losing more territory.

The ways contending groups call a halt to hostilities, in terms either of a temporary truce or of a more lasting peace, are bound up with the deaths that each side incurs and the compensation to be paid for them. In consequence, I shall postpone discussion of this topic until after I have treated the matter of casualties.

Women and warfare

Mae women are wholly excluded from the meetings in which men decide whether or not to go to war, just as they take no part in the deliberations that precede Te distributions or ancestral rituals. Their only role on these occasions is to prepare and bring vegetable food to the male participants, who say nothing significant in their presence. This restriction prevents women from learning the details of battle plans, and it is meant to do so. In this way a woman married in from another clan (and almost all are) is not faced with a difficult conflict of interests if, as may well be the case, her natal group is the intended target.

Nevertheless, although men recognize the possibility that a wife could feel impelled to warn her parents if an invasion of their territory is planned, clansmen do not, at least in conversation, appear greatly worried that this will occur. They seem to assume, unlike men in some other parts of Melanesia, that once she is married a woman's allegiance is basically to the group of her husband and, especially, of her sons, rather than to that of her birth. My own observations support this view. Thus, the care men

98

take to keep women in ignorance of the clan's military intentions is not posited so much on an imputation of female treachery as on a more general opinion that women (and children) are so careless they may inadvertently disclose to outsiders information (whether concerning war or pig exchanges) better kept secret—an attitude I consider unwarranted.

The refusal of men to take their wives into their confidence at such times accords with their apparently total disregard of women's opinions about warfare in general. When Joan Meggitt talked to Mae women about these matters, all of her acquaintances, without exception, said they detested the frequent clashes, no matter how just the cause. As one woman phrased it: "Men are killed but the land remains. The land is there in its own right, and it does not command people to fight for it."

Not only do women fear for the lives of their husbands and sons in these conflicts; they also dislike the prospect of being widowed, of being left to bring up their children relatively unaided or, to avoid this fate, of being pressed into leviratic marriage with men they dislike. In addition, they feel no pleasure when, during periods of war or of prewar tension, they have to bear even more of the burden of food production, working in the shadow of armed guards in exposed gardens. Finally, the women dread the constant threat of a clan rout, in which they must hurry their children and pigs to refuge with their parents or other friendly relatives. It is not merely the obvious danger of death or injury that distresses them, but also the dislocation of living for a long time on charity in another person's house.

Indeed, some women say that when they perceive their men are thinking in terms of attack or invasion, they use these arguments to try to dissuade them from fighting—but to no avail. "Although we tend the gardens and feed the children and pigs, we are only women, and the men never listen to us!" Men with whom I have raised these points clearly cannot understand my wanting to discuss them. "Yes," they say, "women generally do not like their menfolk to go to war, but we take no notice of their fears. These matters do not concern them; they must do as they are told." And the men quickly turn the conversation to the subject of counteracting the dastardly plots that enemy clans are no doubt hatching.

Battle Casualties

6

Casualties resulting from Mae warfare can be discussed under three headings: wounds received in action, deaths that occur in combat or follow from war wounds, and illnesses and deaths, mainly of noncombatants, attributable to the social dislocation war brings.

Wounds

When I first visited the Mae I was struck both by the number of men who bore scars of battle and by the matter-of-fact way they regarded them, as a nuisance that sooner or later every man expects to endure—an attitude toward wounding much like that of the desert Aborigines. Hence, it is not surprising that normally a clan gives no compensation to enemies whom its members have merely wounded. Only if close kinship ties bind the victim to men of the assailant's clan will the latter consider a token offering. On recovering from a battle wound, a man should take the initiative in paying to his close matrilateral kinsmen the kind of compensation that any personal injury or illness requires (see Meggitt 1965a:ch. 7 for the rationale underlying these payments). Yet some Mae assert that, because a warrior voluntarily risks combat wounds in a good cause, he need not feel impelled to compensate his mother's relatives.

The scars I saw were almost all made by arrows, and men would guide my fingers to protruberances on their bodies under which I could readily detect pieces of arrow points. Few carried the marks of axe cuts or spear thrusts because such blows are usually fatal. This prevalence of arrow wounds is related both to the modes of Enga fighting and to the characteristics of the weapons. Although the black palm bow is tremendously powerful, the unfletched arrows are inaccurate and lose velocity over a fairly short distance. An alert and experienced warrior, if he can keep his adversary directly in front of him, stands a good chance of evading the missile. This is not so easily done when men are rushing hither and thither and firing in a confused action. Even if the combat is clearly structured, as when extended lines face each other in open country, there can be so many errant shafts in flight that a combatant cannot hope to watch them all.

Nevertheless, it is assumed that, even at close range, an old hand should be able to escape most arrows. Consequently, when he is seriously or fatally wounded in battle, his "brothers" are quick to attribute his misfortune to a malevolent ghost of his own or of the enemy clan, which at the critical moment impaired his judgment and impelled him to move into the arrow's path.[1] At the same time Mae recognize that the more experienced and hardy "man-killers" who occupy the front ranks in an attack, whether as archers or as spearmen (who also carry shields for protection), enjoy an advantage in being able to observe the actions of the enemy bowmen most carefully and so dodge at the right time; on the other hand, the vision of the lesser warriors in the rear is often obstructed by the movements of the men ahead of them and they are more likely to be wounded by unnoticed arrows. Thus, bravery reaps its own rewards.

Not only the number of their scars but also the men's descriptions of combat attest to the high rates of wounding in warfare. It is not feasible to extract statistical frequencies from accounts of earlier engagements. However, analysis of an interclan war that lasted for four days in 1971 and involved the clan with which I reside gives a good picture of the rates and kinds of wounds. The fighting was in wholly traditional style and was typical of the serious warfare I have described earlier.

Our clan and a non-fraternal neighbor have for years disputed ownership of a small tract of land on their common border and have fought over it several times. When the other clan invaded our territory without warning, of the 116 of our clansmen who were above about sixteen years, 25 were absent on various kinds of employment. Twelve of these were at work in places such as Lae and Bougainville Island, too far for them to return to join in the fighting. The remaining 13 were employed in other parts of the highlands; four of these men came home as soon as they received word of the conflict but arrived too late to participate. Three young bachelors who were at the time in Wabag nearby made no attempt to aid their embattled "brothers"; these were the only clansmen who clearly evaded their responsibility and were later severely chastised by their elders. Of the other 88 clansmen, three were simply too old to do anything, five were physically incapacitated by illness, and ten were still attending school and therefore were "too young" to fight.

Seventy men of the clan did fight, and of these 27 (39 percent) were wounded, some several times, and one other was killed. At one time or another at least 173 allies (perhaps 200 in all) supported our clan, and at least 39 of these were wounded (certainly there were more injured—say about 25 percent), and one other ally was killed. These rates of wounding seem to me to be substantial, but clansmen asserted most emphatically that they were in no way unusual, an opinion confirmed by estimates of casualty rates in other recent interclan battles.

Also of interest is the small number of immediate deaths relative to the number wounded—two men on each side. There is of course no way of telling how many of the more seriously wounded eventually succumbed. Of the four men killed, two were brought down with arrows and then dismembered with axes, and the others were killed outright by arrows (one by a glass-studded horror received in the groin). Naturally, I could not make an accurate count of the wounds received in the engagement by the enemy clan and their allies; it would have been impolitic to visit them to make inquiries.

Table 4 shows the bodily locations of 61 of the wounds received by our clansmen and our allies. The pattern revealed is instructive. The disproportionate number of wounds on the left side of the body and limbs is noteworthy. This, Mae told me, is simply the consequence of most men's being right-handed; when they halt to discharge their arrows (at which time they are more obvious targets), they present their left sides to their opponents. The small number of non-frontal wounds in the sample suggests that most warriors take seriously the injunction "Never turn your back on the enemy!" Indeed, some wounds in the back and shoulders are incurred not when a man is turning away from his adversary, but when, instead of moving to the side, he attempts to drop underneath the arrow so that he can continue to observe his enemy and fire quickly in return.[2] This is a dangerous maneuver because the man risks taking the arrow inside his collar bone, with fatal results. However, a cool-headed warrior who is merely hit in the back or shoulder when ducking may feign serious injury and briefly lie there in the hope that an inexperienced opponent will rush forward to finish him off and so be vulnerable to crossfire. The decoy, of course, must judge when to scramble backward to safety before other enemies take advantage of his immobility.

The arrow wounds that warriors most fear, apart from the shaft near the collar bone, are frontal hits in the chest, belly, or groin, and, above all, an arrow in the armpit "fired by the enemy you did not see."

Table 4 Location of arrow wounds received in Mae warfare

Location	Left side	Right side	Not applicable	Total
Limbs				
lower leg	10	2	—	12
thigh	12	1	—	13
forearm	4	1	—	5
upper arm	5	—	—	5
Body				
buttock	1	1	—	2
belly	—	—	2	2
ribs	1[a]	1	—	2
chest	2	1	—	3
shoulder	6	2	—	8
back	3[b]	2	—	5
Head				
face	1	2	—	3
head	—	—	1	1
Total	45	13	3	61

[a] Fatal.   [b] One fatal.

The last is the wound typically incurred in an extended line of battle when a frightened or uncertain companion drops back without warning and leaves uncovered the flank of his neighbor, who, concentrating his attention on the enemy in front of him, is now open to the angled shooting of the opponent whom his partner should have been engaging. It is this kind of unreliable behavior the Mae impute, perhaps unfairly, to unenthusiastic allies.

If a warrior is so seriously wounded that he is staggering helplessly, his comrades close round and push him back behind them into the next rank, where someone can steer him farther to the rear. If he has been brought down by an arrow, a comrade tries to drag him away under covering fire before the enemy can get to him with axes. However, the opponents' momentary success is likely to inspire them to greater efforts, so that the victim's clansmen may be forced to give ground. Then the man removing him is in a precarious position and may have to abandon his charge and run to safety. At best he may attempt to conceal the other in cane grass or a thicket and hope that the enemy will not find and dismember him before his companions can counterattack.

Other arrow wounds, especially those in the limbs, a warrior takes in stride. Without taking his eyes off the enemy, he simply pulls out an arrow that is lightly lodged and, if the shaft is intact, uses it himself. If the arrow is deeply embedded but the man can still move about, he breaks off the shaft and goes on fighting. If his mobility is impaired, he falls back through the lines to the rear, where the arrow is removed so he can return to the fray. Men who have suffered lesser wounds, sometimes two or three in the first day's combat, tend on subsequent days, they say, to be less agile and rather more cautious as their limbs tighten and the pain increases. Nevertheless, they continue to fight, not only to support their own clansmen but also to stiffen their allies' resolve. The latter, they assert, are often all too ready to go home when wounded.

Mae Enga medical therapy, whether aimed at coping with illness or with injury, is rudimentary and, especially with respect to illness, shades into what can only be regarded as ritual practices, ranging from manipulation of "magical" spells and substances to the elaborate propitiation of ghosts. The treatment of wounds is perhaps the more "empirical" of these modes but is nonetheless severely limited in scope. A man's recovery from serious injury is primarily a tribute to his hardy constitution.

As a rule minor combat wounds, which almost by definition are those caused by arrows with simple needle points, receive no more than hasty first aid in the field. The arrow is merely pulled out or, if the point has broken off and is readily palpable, an incision is made with a keen bamboo knife and the piece is removed, sometimes with rough tweezers. A dressing of leaves, some thought to have healing virtues, is then tightly strapped over the wound. If the wound (for instance, a puncture) is small and cannot easily be bandaged, it is covered with a quantity of the viscous white sap of the shrub *Ficus dammaropsis*, which congeals with the application of a hot coal.

Usually experienced men, often those too aged to fight, undertake or direct these tasks. If the wound is more serious, as when a bamboo-bladed arrow strikes bone and disintegrates, or a needle point deeply penetrates the torso and breaks off, the expert is unlikely then to attempt surgery. The hole is dressed and left to heal, in the hope the victim will regain his strength and the wood will in time work its way to the surface. In the event a man has received in a limb a barbed arrow, an exotic item imported by Mae with trade connections abroad, a special and singularly painful treatment is attempted. The patient takes to his bed and a strong cord is tied to the arrow shaft and to a rafter above him. As the wound suppurates and the flesh weakens, a friend twists the arrow a fraction each day and the steady tension on the cord gradually pulls it free. It is recognized that the patient may die (of infection) before the arrow is removed. Little or nothing can be done for a man wounded in the body by a barbed arrow.

A surprising number of men in whose bodies deep-seated arrow points remain embedded survive to resume a more or less active, albeit

104

probably shortened, life. Others, however, merely linger, incapacitated, for a few agonizing weeks or months. The Mae believe the basic cause of death in such cases to be that the victim's blood turns rotten, becoming pus. Accordingly, when a man is in these straits, whether shortly after being wounded or much later after an apparent remission, his kinsmen resort to somewhat desperate measures to try to evacuate this bad blood before it spreads throughout his body.

A specialist, usually an elderly man, is called in to attempt a cure. Such accepted experts are few, there being probably no more than one or two in any neighborhood of ten to twenty clans. Although the victim's agnates pay generously in pork, salt, and lesser valuables for the services of the specialist, he is not expected to be infallible and faces no penalties other than a potential loss of reputation if his patient dies during or immediately after the operation.[3] Such men may also act as coroners, performing autopsies in the case of puzzling deaths, again for handsome fees.

The basic treatment is simple. With a bamboo knife the expert makes an incision below the man's armpit (left or right) and then, either by forcing the ribs apart or by breaking one with a wedge, creates an aperture large enough for him to insert two fingers into the thorax. The intrusion, although the Mae are unaware of this, apparently causes a partial and temporary collapse of the lung. The specialist pours bespelled water from a narrow-necked gourd into the cavity, agitates the patient to make certain the water mixes with the potentially or actually bad blood, and then rolls him over to drain out the liquid. Finally, he dresses the incision with a poultice of leaves that resemble those of the Anthurium plant and are thought to promote rapid healing. Then he collects his payment and departs. What seems remarkable about this practice is that there are men who have survived for years both the treatment and the wounds that occasioned it.

Combat deaths

I turn now to a discussion of the somewhat complex matter of deaths incurred in, or as a consequence of, combat. I begin with a brief account of the manner of disposing of those killed in such circumstances (see Meggitt 1965:a182 *et seq*. for a general treatment of Mae funerary arrangements).

As we have seen, there is great concern to retrieve quickly the corpse of a fallen comrade. In part this is because his "brothers" wish to spare him the ignominy of mutilation. Such a grisly insult, aimed also at humiliating the victim's clansmen, is always a possibility when the contending groups are long-term opponents of different phratries.

But equally important here is the popular attitude that men should be buried in their natal (which normally means paternal) territory. The practice not only ensures that the deceased's clansmen and their wives can readily gather to mourn his passing; it also facilitates the ultimate merging of his ghost with the collectivity of clan ancestral spirits, who continue to intervene intermittently in the affairs of the living (see Meggitt 1965b). A woman is usually buried in the land of her husband's clan, not in that of her father's, a custom underlining the extent to which marriage incorporates her into her husband's group.

The propriety of interring a dead man in his home territory is further emphasized by the belief that those who kill a man in an ambush or raid should out of courtesy call out or sing to notify his clansmen of the whereabouts of his corpse, so that they may recover the body for mourning. If circumstances—for instance, the risk of another assault—prevent his clansmen from doing this, extraclan relatives of the victim may return his remains to his "brothers." Later, when conditions allow the agnates to mount the necessary funerary feast and distribution of pork to his matrilateral kin, his agnates may reward the bearers for their service with extra portions of meat and other minor valuables.

In the event that a clan is so decisively defeated that it must flee from its domain and abandon its dead, relatives from other groups, especially men from clans in the same phratry, should collect the corpses and take them for mourning and burial in the territory of a fraternal clan. If any of the survivors of the rout are able, from their place of refuge, to make the customary funeral distributions for the deceased, they should repay their phratry brothers for their kind gesture.

Violent death at the hands of another clan tends to confer on the dead man (although apparently not on a woman) an importance in his own clansmen's eyes that, as an ordinary man, he would not necessarily have received had he died peacefully or from ghostly interference. Indeed, public reaction to his demise may approach that normally reserved for the passing of a Big Man. At the least his decorated corpse is prominently displayed for two or three days, either on a platform or lashed to a crossbar erected on a danceground in a safe area. Women gather there to keen, while men who can be spared from military duties assemble in turn to pay their respects. They hear emotional harangues by Big Men and fight leaders, who not only exhort their followers to fight on with redoubled vigor but also promise the ghost of the deceased, as well as the clan ancestors, that they will avenge the death. If the dead man was socially prominent, the orators may vow to kill five of the enemy in retaliation—one for his head and one for each of his limbs.

At the same time a victim's close clansmen may publicly refuse to don the armlets of grey Coix seeds, usually worn by male mourners, until his loss is balanced by an enemy death. Similarly, his widow, in addition to assuming ordinary mourning regalia and lopping off a finger tip, should smear her head and body lavishly with gray clay, and she may place a

106

broad clay stripe on the head of each of his pre-adolescent sons. This should be renewed until homicide compensation is received for the father, whether or not his killing has been avenged. Such gestures serve to remind the survivors of their obligation to clear their clan's reputation.

Meanwhile, without ceremony, a small party of men takes the body for rapid burial in a convenient location. If the deceased is an important man, his grave may be made beside the danceground and elaborately fenced with palings and living Cordyline shrubs, both to magnify his name and constantly to "heat the bellies" of his clansmen so that they will avenge the loss. Sometimes the victim's clansmen may have made such territorial gains in the war that they can bury him where he fell, thus doing him greater honor.

When a prominent man or an experienced warrior is killed in battle, his clansmen especially his close agnates, may wish to delve further into the reasons for his death. Did he die simply because his own carelessness or inattention left him open to the enemy's weapons? Or did an offended agnatic ghost settle an old score and push him into danger? Or, and here is the crux of the inquiry, was one of his own living clansmen responsible? Did someone bear the dead man such ill-will that he secretly induced a ghost to make him vulnerable? Or had this man, contrary to the demands of group solidarity, engaged in covert self-interested dealings with the enemy that in some way encouraged them to attack without warning and thus "cause" his brother's death? The last, although it may appear to be a convoluted and unlikely reason, was indeed a burning issue during a recent interclan war.

Mae men believe they can answer such questions with the aid of the dead man's ghost. Within a few days of his burial, the deceased's closest agnates enlist the services of a diviner to direct the appropriate ritual at the grave. Two young men, chosen because of their supposed naïveté, stand facing outward at the head and foot of the grave. Each holds an end of a slender branch of a species of Commersonia, which the specialist has be-spelled and to which he has attached fronds of a fern, bracken, and an edible plant. Several witnesses (agnates) watch while the diviner sharply raps the branch with an arrow shaft as aloud he puts each question to the ghost. "We have come here to find out how you died. Was it merely an arrow of clan X that killed you? Did an enemy ghost kill you? Did a ghost of our clan kill you? Was he incited to do so? Was a man of our clan the killer?" And so on—until in response to a particular question the branch becomes heavy and swings back and forth along the grave.[4] Then the identity of the culprit is sought, the diviner pronouncing names in turn until the branch moves again.

At this the party leaves, to decide what action to take. If a particular agnatic ghost alone was responsible, a domestic propitiation is called for to dissuade it from attacking anyone else. If an enemy ghost acting of its own volition is the "cause," nothing can be done. But if a living clansman is in any way implicated, the investigators may quietly present their evidence to a Big Man for his consideration, although they do nothing publicly for the time being; wartime is no time to foment dissension within the clan. Should the culprit come from a different subclan from that of the deceased man and his "brother" investigators, they may perhaps plan to kill him later in revenge. They are more likely, however, merely to wait until the deceased's subclan initiates the usual compensation of his maternal kin for his death, as they would also do were the culprit a member of their own subclan. Then, supported by the Big Man, they publicly accuse the culprit and demand that he, helped by his close agnates, make the major contribution of pigs and pork to the compensation being paid the subclan of the dead man's mother's brother.

Whatever the circumstances that are thought to have occasioned the loss of a "brother" in battle, his clansmen will in due course claim homicide compensation from the enemy group held to be one of the "owners of the quarrel." As the discharge of these payments is intimately bound up with the cessation of overt hostilities, I shall deal with them in the context of peace negotiations.

Meanwhile I turn to the subject of mortality rates in Mae warfare: how many people die in battle, who are they, what are some of the larger consequences of these losses? These are not questions to which simple, unambiguous answers can be given.

Mortality and population

I have referred in passing to the numbers of combat deaths incurred between about 1900 and 1950 in the neighborhood of clans that largely constitutes the basis for my account. These figures are brought together in Tables 5a and 5b. I remind the reader that, having been abstracted from descriptions of past conflicts, they are at best rough estimates—and probably underestimates at that. Nevertheless, treated circumspectly, they are illuminating. Over all, the statistics in this sample indicate that on the average about two men are killed on each side in such intergroup hostilities.[5] At first sight this may suggest that Mae warfare does not take an unduly high toll. When, however, we note both the mean size of a clan parish (350–400 members—that is, at most about 100 men), the frequency with which a clan goes to war, and the higher losses it may suffer, the figures assume a different complexion. On the one hand there is the immediate impact that the deaths of five to ten active warriors in an engagement have on a clan—a couple of such encounters and the group is in serious trouble *vis-à-vis* rapacious neighbors. On the other hand, one must consider the consequences over a period of time of the steady drain on manpower that even lower casualty rates may have.

108

Table 5a   Frequencies of Mae combat deaths, c.1900–1950

Number of men killed	"Owners of the quarrel"			
	Subclans of same clan	Clans of same phratry	Clans of different phratries	All
1	3	5	8	16
2	2	1	5	8
3	—	1	1	2
4	—	—	—	—
5	—	—	1	1
6	1	—	—	1
7	—	—	—	—
8	—	1	—	1
9	—	1	1	2
10	—	—	1	1
•				
16	1	—	—	1
•				
24	—	—	1	1
Total deaths	29	27	69	125
Mean deaths	4.1	3.0	3.8	3.7

Table 5b   Frequencies of Mae combat deaths, c.1900–1950, in relation to the ostensible cause of conflict

Ostensible reasons for conflict	Number of conflicts	Total deaths	Mean number of deaths
Land disputes	17	79	4.6
Other disputes	17	46	2.7
All disputes	34	125	3.7

Whatever the direct political implications, the cumulative gross effects of frequent warfare on the male population are apparent when individual genealogies are examined. Table 6 summarizes a sample of genealogies drawn in 1955–57 from the neighborhood of clans with reference to the stated causes of death of men before 1950.

The categories employed in Table 6 deserve comment. By and large the Mae attribution of certain deaths to old age means no more than that, a recognition of "natural causes," although this explanation may perhaps be utilized more often for the passing of unimportant elderly men (and women). Mae usually ascribe deaths from illness or accident to ghostly

109

Table 6   Stated causes of death (pre-1950) for a sample of Mae men

Stated cause of death

Status of victim	Old age	Illness or accident	Killed or died of wounds	Insufficient information	Total
Married	38	50	66	68	222
%	17.1	22.5	29.7	30.6	100
Bachelor	—	14	25	—	39
%	—	35.9	64.1	—	100
All men	38	64	91	68	261
%	14.5	24.5	34.8	26.1	100

malice (rarely to sorcery or to the intervention of the sky people), and they may include here the demise of old but formerly prominent men. Occasionally deaths in battle or subsequently from wounds may also involve the imputation of ghostly attacks, but this plays a minor part. What is critical is the later payment of homicide compensation by the appropriate group, and, if necessary, an autopsy is performed to verify the identity of those responsible.[7]

Given the obvious concern of the Mae to secure compensation for killings, it seems unlikely that in the sample many battle-induced deaths are conflated with the category of deaths about which I have insufficient information.[8] By the same token, the circumstances of deaths occurring in, or because of, battle may be better or longer recalled than those defining other deaths, thus distorting the statistics. Be that as it may, the ratio of male deaths attributable over time to warfare is substantial—at the least of the order of 25 percent of all male fatalities.[9] In short, the frequency of overt hostilities among Mae groups significantly determines the pattern of male mortality.

A further noteworthy feature of the distribution of deaths in the sample is the disproportionately high loss of bachelors in warfare. With almost all men in this society wed by the age of about thirty, bachelors are by definition young men—that is, still in the process of acquiring military expertise. Discussions with older Mae made it clear that they are aware of the differential chances of dying in battle between married and unmarried warriors. They simply assert that rash and inexperienced youths are usually at a disadvantage when they face wily and cautious old fighters, and that a novice has to suffer through several engagements before he gains the knowledge, skill, and self-confidence necessary for his continuing survival. I suspect that another, albeit minor, factor contributing to the higher casualty rate among apprentice warriors is the practice of posting

110

them in the middle or rear ranks of fighting forces, where they are more likely to be vulnerable to unseen arrows. But on balance there seems to be no reason to dispute the veterans' view of the situation. In battle experience is all-important.

To summarize, it appears that traditional modes of Mae warfare, both in their nature and in their frequency, take a relatively high toll of men's lives, whether in a clan through time or in the region as a whole, and many of the victims are bachelors, cut off before they have children. In addition these death rates have direct political repercussions in that they can quickly and radically erode the fighting strength of a clan and leave it open to the incursions of more fortunate neighbors.

Granted all this, can it be argued that Mae warfare has larger or long-term effects on the population as a whole? Does it, for instance, act to keep the total population in some kind of balance with material resources, especially the limited amount of arable land and the crops it produces? Indeed, some Enga believe that warfare in some way serves to restrict their numbers. Thus, men in the sparsely settled Kandepe area to the south of the Central Enga have told me that hostilities among their small clans rarely halt before about five men have been killed on each side, which seems to be the case. They compare this situation with what they take to occur among the Mae who, they say, stop fighting when each force has lost a couple of men. The higher casualty rate among the Kandepe groups, they assert, accounts for the visibly smaller population there.

The matter, of course, is much less simple. In all Enga societies polygyny traditionally not only has been the ideal but also has been widely practiced in fact. Thus, in a sample (drawn in 1955–57) of 413 Mae men who were then married, 17.2 percent had more than one wife (the mean number of simultaneous unions per husband being 1.2); of 89 married men then dead, 23.6 percent had been polygynists (the mean number of simultaneous unions per husband being 1.3). Moreover, at that time 28.5 percent of a sample of 117 Mae widows had remarried (some of them twice), and a number of the remainder would also do so in due course. Indeed, on the average, only about 16 percent of the women of a clan parish were either young spinsters or widows who had not yet remarried. All of which strongly suggests that many more Mae men would have to fall in combat before there would be a significant number of women in the society unable to marry and reproduce.

Clearly the rates of male combat deaths are unlikely in themselves to have imposed any appreciable check on Mae population growth in general. The critical question is what are the direct effects of fighting on female mortality, and here the evidence is ambiguous.

Enga men speak as though, in raids or invasions against non-fraternal clans who are long-term enemies, the opponents' women and children are no less appropriate targets than the opposing warriors. It is

111

deliberate policy, they say, to burn women's houses on these occasions and to incinerate the occupants in the hope of demoralizing the opponents. If the women are spared, their husbands will fight on stoutly to protect them. Indeed, among some western Enga, warriors wear special plumes to mark their killing of women, and reports of early Administration patrols in these areas (and my own limited inquiries) indicate that there a substantial number of the women have died violently.

For some time I thought the same held true for the Mae. The explicit statements of many men supported this view. It was not until I analyzed more closely both the histories of intergroup wars in my neighborhood and the genealogies I had collected that I came to doubt the validity of these assertions. In fact, after careful examination of my data, I found clear evidence for the killing of no more than six women and one child, and one attempt to burn a house containing women and children.[10] Faced with these findings men of my acquaintance later conceded that, although it is proper to attack enemy noncombatants, they generally did not try too strenuously to do so lest the enraged menfolk of the victims retaliate in kind. The houses of men and women in accessible areas were and are indeed burned with great frequency, for this is a recognized and valued tactic, but usually the buildings have been evacuated well in advance.[11]

In short, the casualty rates among women and children immediately attributable to Mae warfare (and probably also among the Central Laiapu Enga) are very low. It is scarcely conceivable that, even in the long run, their cumulative effect is such that the traditional patterns of war in themselves directly impose significant limitations on population growth in this region.[12]

What of the indirect influence on population size of the physical dislocations that accompany serious or prolonged fighting? In the absence of any quantifiable data I can here only point to consequences that I believe take a toll of clan strength. I refer in particular to the circumstances of the sudden and forced movements of women and children, the elderly and the ill, over difficult terrain in bleak and often wet weather. We simply do not know how many infants and old people succumb to pneumonia in these flights, how many refugees are drowned when trying to cross boulder-strewn torrents, how many already sick and weak people die because food supplies are interrupted. These less obvious costs of war, I believe, accumulate significantly through time and, in conjunction with other "non-military" conditions such as endemic and epidemic illness, female deaths in childbirth, infant mortality, weather-induced garden failures, have played their part in effecting a relatively low rate of population growth in the recent past.

112

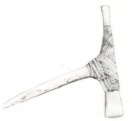

Peace-making and Homicide Compensations

7

Ways of ending hostilities

We have seen that Mae clans do not wage wars in a vacuum, that we cannot treat such collisions as self-contained events simply erupting from the immediately conflicting interests of two local groups. Similarly, we cannot talk of peace-making ("fastening the weapons with speech") as a unitary, disjunct phenomenon. When and how hostilities are halted depend on the kind of warfare that has taken place, the casualty rates, the military outcome, and the kinship connections among opponents and allies. Moreover, these factors are themselves interrelated in varying degree.

Thus, the status of the combat's originators, the "owners of the quarrel," is significant. Are they subgroups of one clan, clans of the same phratry, or clans of different phratries? Even if they have been disputing fiercely over an issue as important as the control of land, opponents in the first two categories may from the start encounter constant urging by fraternal groups (who may also be allies) to end the violence lest the lives of too many "brothers" be lost and the phratry be unduly weakened. Such appeals to morality and group interest, which the contenders may welcome as an excuse to cut their losses, are of course pointless when non-fraternal groups are at war.

Cutting across these considerations is another scale of assessment, namely, each group's perception of its position as the fighting continues and of its immediate prospects. This balance sheet does not concern only the land taken or lost but also the casualties suffered, and, very important, the compensation due for these deaths. Obviously, the interested parties cannot mount the elaborate assemblies at which homicide pigs are disbursed while they are at war, even if no battles are actually in progress.

The Mae, like other Central Enga, meet this problem by trying to equate, in both intention and effect, the complex negotiations that precede the presentations with the beginning of a truce and the disbursement of pigs with a declaration of peace, however brief and fragile it may prove. But whether the contending forces can terminate a confrontation promptly in this way in turn depends importantly on what has happened in the combat.

Thus, in the case of a rout, the victors may see no need to make immediate concessions, even to a fraternal clan. They occupy the territory of the losers who, being dispersed, are in no condition to recover their land. Nor are the vanquished likely to persuade allies to counterattack on their behalf. Indeed, were a neighboring clan confident of evicting the usurpers, it might well seize the area for itself. Clearly, after a complete victory, the winning group is under little pressure to negotiate an immediate peace. Consequently, any decision to pay homicide compensation to the losers turns on other considerations. For instance, the victors may have lost a number of men, including allies, in the war. In the process of compensating their allies, which they should do without delay, they may also offer homicide pigs to the appropriate subgroups of the scattered enemy, especially if these are members of their phratry. In this way the winners attempt to impress uneasy neighbors with their magnanimity as a first step in justifying their illicit occupation of another's territory. At the same time they hope the losers, having accepted the compensating pigs, will subsequently agree, with the aid of their several host groups, to pay reciprocal compensation for the victors' dead.

The defeated in turn are likely to take the offered pigs, partly because they owe compensation for deaths among their own allies and also to their own maternal kin, and partly because they will need to discharge debts to their hosts. Moreover, especially if the winners and losers are phratry "brothers," the losers may want to give homicide pigs for at least some of the winner's dead with an eye to opening the way for invitations from the deceased's satisfied agnates to reoccupy portions of their lost land. Should all these payments and counterpayments of homicide compensation take place over a period of months or years (and they may well not occur at all when the adversaries are of different phratries), their consummation defines, at least for the victors and other neighboring units, an apparent peace which in effect is also a statement that the losing clan (or subclan) no longer exists as a viable autonomous group.

A somewhat different situation may arise when a clan that has seized part of a neighbor's territory decides it has nothing to gain by pressing the struggle further. It may be that the invaders were concerned only to retrieve a tract of land which, they assert, was formerly theirs. Or they may judge that topographical obstacles, stiffening enemy resistance, or the arrival of fresh allies of their opponents will prevent their overrunning and, more important, holding more land, even at a high cost in lives. Or they may have already suffered so many casualties that their resolve is ebbing. Indeed, if fraternal clans are opposed, the attackers may shrink from killing more of their "brothers" on the other side in order to make further advances. Other clans of their phratry may influence their decision here.

At this point both owners of the quarrel may be prepared to suspend the fighting and to negotiate payments of homicide compensation. The present victors, though they may hope to secure more land in the future, offer indemnification now to buy time to consolidate their existing gains. The longer they can occupy this area and so establish gardens, fences, and houses on it, the more difficult will it be for the enemy to make a case for owning the land that will induce allies to support attempts to recover it.

By the same token the losers may welcome a respite from warfare that has gone against them. They can employ the period of peace to reorganize men and supplies, to plan for a counterstroke, and to furbish their extraclan exchange connections in order to attract sufficient allies when they do make their move. This is not to say that a group which yields ground in this way accepts the hiatus cheerfully. On the contrary, the men may go into mourning for their lost estates as for a dead brother, holding a "death house" feast, lopping fingers, and slashing ear lobes— all of which serve as stimuli to eventual retaliation. It is small wonder in these circumstances not only can the negotiations preceding homicide payments easily founder, but also the formal prestations themselves may explode in a pitched battle. Even if pigs are disbursed, the peace that follows is likely to be tenuous and short-lived.

Finally, there is the common situation of stalemate, when neither side has made appreciable gains, and continuation of the war merely ensures the loss of more lives to no obvious advantage. Both owners of the quarrel have the same interest in ending the conflict, and the two can in effect negotiate from positions of equal strength. Accordingly, rational appreciation of longer-term self-interest can here emerge early and, I believe, have a continuing effect in steering the interchanges to a successful conclusion. The way this is achieved is worth examining in some detail.

The first pressures to end a stalemate in which casualties are rising are likely to come from allies in each force. This, it seems to me, is not simply a consequence of the allies' less wholehearted commitment to the struggle. We are in addition dealing here with an accepted convention designed not only to save face for the instigators of the conflict, but also to allow them to shift onto the allies the responsibility for suing for peace

115

and thus to mollify the ancestral spirits who would otherwise be angered by their descendants' apparent cowardice.

To take a typical case: Most of the men of clan A (and others) are aiding their neighbor, clan X of another phratry, in a protracted and so far fruitless struggle over land boundaries with clan Y (and allies) of that phratry. Because the territory of clan Y is near that of clan A, the latter cannot simply withdraw from the conflict whenever it chooses; as long as the others continue the war, the borders of clan A are vulnerable to raids by men of clan Y.

Eventually the Big Men and elders of clan A, after discussion with their own fight leaders, announce to the Big Men of clan X: "The two sides have reached an impasse. The casualties are about equal. Of these, we in clan A have lost three men killed and one seriously wounded and likely to die. We want you to stop fighting clan Y so that you can receive homicide compensation from those people and in turn give us the ally compensation due for our dead. If the war continues and your Big Men are killed, who then will give us our compensation? So do something, for we are ready to go home; we will not help you further."

The notables of clan X themselves are by then well aware that the contending groups, together with their supporters from other clans, are too evenly matched for either to have much chance of a decisive victory. Moreover, they also know from information brought by visiting neutral men who have connections in both camps that allies of clan Y are becoming restive and are urging an end to hostilities. Accordingly, they agree that this is an opportune moment to initiate peace negotiations. But first they need to secure unanimity among their own clansmen. In particular, they must dissuade the hotheads among them, whether self-confident fight leaders or overenthusiastic young bachelors, from continuing the action. In this task they use much the same arguments their allies have, especially the proposition that more fighting will only result in more deaths, which may well include those of important men among the enemy. "Then who will push the members of clan Y to pay the homicide compensation owed us? Without pressure from their Big Men, nothing will be organized! So let us stop fighting now, secure these reparations, and give homicide pigs to our allies. Then we can plan ways of avenging any outstanding deaths." A more or less balanced number of fatalities in the two forces makes the exhortations of the doves that much more persuasive, but as always it is by no means easy to restrain the hawks.

Once a consensus is reached, the Big Men of clan X ask men of substance, exchange partners from neutral clans, to carry their message to the Big Men of clan Y. "Tell them that if they are willing to call a halt and to talk about payments of homicide compensation, we are ready to do the same." When the dignitaries of clan Y receive the communication, they closely question the emissaries on their opinion of its worth. "Do the

116

men of clan X really mean what they say, or is this just a ruse to induce us to lower our guard and be left open to a surprise attack?" Once they are reasonably satisfied that clan X does indeed want peace, the Big Men of clan Y must persuade the militants in their own ranks that, in the light of the stalemate already reached, nothing will be lost by taking up the negotiations. To this end they have recourse to the kinds of arguments employed by the important men of clan X.[1]

The messengers return to clan X with the news that clan Y also desires peace and the exchange of homicide compensations. Then follows a difficult period as the go-betweens travel back and forth with proposals and counterproposals concerning the composition of the negotiating parties, where and when they will meet, and how they will initiate the exchanges of valuables. Given that some men on each side still do not wholeheartedly favor a truce and given that others understandably fear the enemy may be laying the groundwork for an ambush, it is not surprising that each group tries to get its own conditions accepted for the meeting.

At this point negotiations may well founder on the rocks of stubbornness and suspicion. If this appears likely and if the notables in each clan genuinely want the discussion to proceed, they may take matters into their own hands and communicate directly by yodeling offers and counteroffers to each other. In particular, each team may promise to bring to the first meeting a quantity of valuables (perhaps some pigs but mainly pork, pearl shells, and axes) as proof of good faith. The Big Men, helped by close kinsmen and supporters, may provide most of these goods.

Such gestures serve a multiple function. Valuables offered are an admission of responsibility for the killing of specific men, a partial payment of homicide compensation, and a promise to provide the balance promptly. Acceptance of valuables in this context means the recipients acknowledge their liability for deaths among the donors and are promising homicide compensation in full for them. Obviously a reciprocal exchange of valuables publicly commits each group to fulfill its obligations toward the agnates of the other's dead.

If the Big Men of both owners of the quarrel undertake to initiate this transaction at the proposed meeting, there is a better chance that it will take place, that skeptics will be disarmed, and that contacts between the clans will continue. In short, by means of this ploy the Big Men are on the way to establishing an interim truce, which may perhaps flow into a more lasting period of peace—although in any given situation nobody can be sure of this. Not the least of the obstacles in the way of an enduring peace is, as we shall see, the readiness with which clans later try to evade paying agreed-upon homicide compensations, especially to non-fraternal groups.

A problem facing the Big Men in arranging this first and crucial encounter is to ensure that their parties are of controllable size and compo-

Armed Mae Enga clansmen making their formal entry onto a ceremonial ground to attend an interclan distribution of valuables

sition. On the one hand, some men, such as senior agnates of those whose deaths are to be discussed, have the right to present their case. On the other, the Big Men are concerned to exclude, if they can, hotheads (who may be close kinsmen of the deceased) whose anger or grief may drive them to attack the enemy negotiators. It is no easy task in these circumstances to create a setting for reasonable discourse, one that will not disintegrate into bloody violence. Naturally the Big Men strive to select as representatives of the subclans concerned the older and more level-headed men, and they try to persuade their more intransigent followers to remain at home (or at least in the background) to guard the clan against treachery or surprise raids. In addition, they invite the Big Men of their allies to attend, as well as those reliable men who have acted as go-betweens. In this way they attempt to provide a balance of calm judgment against overwrought emotions.

On the appointed day the two small groups meet at the place agreed upon. This may be a danceground close to the border, or, if suspicion still runs deep, they may gather on a convenient clearing at the border itself—one from which they can readily retreat if fighting erupts during the discussions. Each party assumes, of course, that hidden somewhere in the vicinity are warriors of the other clan, awaiting the negotiations' outcome.

The armed men in each team stay close together as they carefully watch their opponents across the clearing. Behind them are the valuables they intend to offer in the initial transactions. The Big Men, including those of the allies and those among the former emissaries, stand between the two groups of tense warriors, ready to berate followers who voice insults or challenges. As a further show of good faith, the leaders may

118

ostentatiously lay down their bows and spears (never their axes)—but not out of ready reach.

It is common for Big Men among the go-betweens or the allies to open the proceedings with relatively bland speeches that touch lightly on the circumstances of the conflict and the reasons for the present assembly, both to give the uneasy audience time to settle down and to pave the way for the Big Men among the warring clans to take up specific issues. Ideally, the protracted, florid oratory that follows should be confined to Big Men. And indeed they are quick to choke off supporters whose anger or indignation impels them to interrupt, lest the latter's comments call up an uncontrollable response from their opponents.

This is not to say that the utterances of the Big Men are low-keyed or conciliatory. On the contrary, they are (and should be) aggressive and ostensibly unyielding; and the speakers, using a wealth of metaphor and sardonic humor, score points with references to the many victories and the impeccable motives of their own clans, and to the losses and humiliations they have inflicted on their double-dealing adversaries. But this "fighting with words," as practiced by experts, remains within conventional bounds and can be parried or exploited by the opposing orators, who have also learned to mask their feelings with the thin, wolfish smile that an irate Mae man affects. At the same time, whenever tempers appear to be fraying and an explosion seems imminent, the neutral Big Men intervene with innocuous, irrelevant, or mildly amusing speeches that give the others time to regain their composure.

Eventually, as the parties agree on the circumstances of the deaths in question, the oratory shifts from mere verbal combat to argument during which offers to pay fairly specific homicide compensations are advanced, criticized, and rephrased. The disputants also attempt to determine the future sequence of the prestations. Normally this should reflect the order in which the fatalities occurred, but considerations of the victims' social importance, marital status, and sex may take precedence.

Throughout these interchanges the Big Men are alert to their followers' reactions, and they constantly take aside individual men to seek their opinions or try to change them, to cajole or to press the stubborn. Close agnates of the deceased are in a somewhat equivocal position on these occasions. Convention, as well as real grief, prompts them to reject all offers of compensation, largely on the ground that only blood can assuage their loss. On the other hand, they stand to benefit substantially in such transactions. If then their comrades support the Big Men's plea for peace, and if their own reluctance causes the negotiations to collapse, not only will they let slip highly prized pigs but in addition they may suffer the odium of other clansmen who had expected to gain materially.

Should both parties still be slow to come to terms, or should the discussions run aground in the face of unreasonable demands, the Big Men among the owners of the quarrel may seize the moment to promise handsome compensations for their allies who were killed, and they may even suggest that their own clan will contribute to payments for the dead among the enemy's allies. The latter offer, of course, goes beyond the ordinary requirements and in many cases is no more than a ploy unlikely to be honored when the time comes, unless the groups concerned are fraternal clans.[2] Nevertheless, at this point in the negotiations such proposals encourage the Big Men among the allies to argue even more vigorously for a settlement.

When the Big Men of the opposed clans believe they have most of the audience on their side, they try to nail down the agreements quickly by producing the valuables on hand and designating various items as partial reparation for particular deaths. They hope to bustle the intended recipients into accepting the objects, for once they do so, each group has committed itself, however doubtfully, to two courses of action—one, to trust the other to hand over later the balance of its indemnification, and two, to meet its own obligations in compensating for the other's dead. Obviously, this is a delicate and crucial stage in the confrontation. None of the recipients is ever really satisfied with the offering, and the Big Men have to exert every ounce of their influence to persuade disgruntled men to accept what has been presented and to withdraw peacefully. Moreover, even if the Big Men manage to steer the reciprocal distributions to a relatively quiet conclusion, considerations of clan prestige require that they close the proceedings with vainglorious oratory that in itself can jeopardize the agreements. Thus, each group feels bound to threaten renewed attacks or raids should the other delay in paying full compensation. Men find it difficult to listen to such speeches without wanting to humble their opponents there and then.[3]

If, however, as may easily happen, the interim valuables are too few to provide more than token offerings to the representatives of the deceased's subclans, or if some men appear to be favored over others, a brawl may erupt as outraged warriors hurl the goods at the donors and charge them with drawn weapons. All the Big Men try to interpose themselves between the combatants and disarm them before serious injuries ensue. They may succeed in this and in more or less calming their followers. Then they hurry through the distributions again and attempt to draw the restless men away from the arena before insults and blows provoke another outbreak. Sometimes the melée, although bloodless, is too violent for transactions to continue, and the groups seize their own valuables and depart, as the Big Men shout to each other that they will try to arrange another meeting when tempers have cooled. Should blood be spilled in the affray or, worse, someone be killed, the parties retreat quickly to their own territories, calling to their clansmen to arm for more fighting. Warfare is resumed, albeit with less enthusiasm, and may continue until more casualties and another stalemate lead to a repetition of the whole precarious round of communication and negotiation.

Clearly, many potential obstacles impede a prompt or easy decision to end hostilities and to make reciprocal payments of homicide compensation. Even when the interested parties circumvent these difficulties and the warriors are prepared, at least for the time being, to put up their weapons and to re-establish social contacts between the clans, no simple or unequivocal timetable can be imposed for the promised prestations.

As with warfare and peace, the actual payment of the agreed-upon compensations does not occur without reference to other events or processes. When, to what extent, and indeed whether a clan will meet its commitments depend on its present political and economic status relative to its neighbors, both friends and enemies.

The nature of homicide compensations

Before describing the distributions of homicide compensation and the complications that may attend them, I shall briefly indicate their place in the total system of Mae prestations, as well as the distinctions made within the general category of homicide compensation. Without some knowledge of the functional and conceptual relations among these transactions, one cannot appreciate either the aims of the individual participants or the maneuvering of the groups to which they belong.

The structural hierarchy of descent groups among the Mae is paralleled by a ranking both of the kinds of public prestations in which the social units should participate and of the valuables appropriate to each occasion (Meggitt 1971, 1974). Not only does this gradation govern the magnitude of the distributions (see Meggitt 1965a:Table 43), it also defines their order of precedence. These interconnections are summarized in Tables 7 and 8.

Thus, the freedom of individual clansmen to augment their wealth through dealings with others is constrained not merely by obligations to the descent groups they belong to, but also by the structure governing situations in which prestations are made and the commodities appropriate to them. Within these limits a man tries judiciously to handle his domestic economy and his participation in larger transactions so that over time, through complex incomings and outgoings, he builds up his holdings (whether actual or in the form of credits) of the more highly prized valuables, especially pigs.[4] At the same time and by the same means, he aims to build his social reputation, notably by improving his standing in the great ceremonial cycle of Te exchanges. Not all men, of course, succeed in this, and only a very few manage to manipulate the system so effectively that they win recognition as true Big Men (see Meggitt 1967).

121

Table 7 The traditional Mae hierarchy of commodities

1. Pigs, cassowaries.
2. Pearl-shell pendants, pork sides, stone axes, cassowary-plume headdresses, cowrie-shell headbands, tree kangaroos, dogs.
3. Cowrie-shell necklets, bailer-shell pendants, gourds of tree oil, packages of salt, net bags and aprons, bird-of-paradise plumes, bows, spears, hand drums, possums.
4. Conus-shell discs, woven armlets and belts, bone head-scratchers, water gourds, rattan, bark fiber, tobacco, etc.
5. Vegetable foods: *luxuries:* pandanus nuts, taro, yams, ginger, sugarcane, setaria, etc., and *staples:* sweet potatoes, beans, relishes, etc.

Table 8 Relationships among Mae groups, prestations, and valuables

Group	Appropriate prestation	Appropriate category of valuables
Phratry	—	—
Clan	main phases of Te exchange cycle; homicide compensation	1, 5
Subclan	death compensation of maternal relatives	1, 2, 5
Patrilineage	illness compensation of maternal relatives; brideprice and return gift	1, 2, 3, 5
Individual	insult compensation of maternal relatives; compensation for broken betrothal	2, 3, 4, 5

The way the notion of precedence diverts the flow of valuables from one set of intended recipients to another deserves comment. The basic assumption is that normally the commitments of higher-order units override those of their constituent elements. For instance, a man whose wig has been violently disarranged in a quarrel with a neighbor may feel impelled to erase this insult to his person by offering compensation in the form of minor valuables to his mother's close agnates. He should do this because he shares his blood and therefore his corporeal (as distinct from spiritual) vitality with her natal lineage. Accordingly, he calls on a few close friends and kinsmen, who may include men who belonged to the bachelors' association in his time, to help him amass the goods needed for this purpose.

But before the offended man can hand over the items, senior men of his lineage may intervene to solicit his contribution to the brideprice the group is gathering for one of its young men. The man must meet this request, even at the cost of postponing indefinitely his own distribution.

122

However, another member of his subclan may then die suddenly, in which case the wedding preparations are suspended and the valuables collected for the brideprice added instead to the larger amount of pigs, pork, etc., that the subclan requires for the death house feast and for the compensation due the deceased's matrilateral subclan.

Now it may happen that Big Men of the clan, especially those of other subclans, have recently decided that this is the appropriate time for the clan to pay an outstanding homicide compensation to another group—perhaps in the hope of inducing the group to deliver an even larger reparation promised earlier. Such a conflict of interests between the subclan and the larger clan can lead to bitter altercations; but ideally the lesser unit should simply stage its funerary feast and devote the other pigs to the more important transaction, on the understanding that fellow clansmen will afterward help it make the appropriate death payment to the deceased's maternal kin.[5]

In short, just as individual Mae attempt to exploit for their own ends all levels of distributions, so also do descent groups up and down the hierarchy try to turn them to their corporate advantage. Clans in particular, largely through the expertise of their Big Men, strive to utilize prestations to sustain their own political and economic autonomy and to magnify their reputations, while at the same time placing their rivals at a disadvantage. Naturally enough, the manipulation of homicide compensation payments, themselves a consequence of overt political competition, plays an important part in this ceaseless struggle.

The Mae term for homicide compensation in general, "cause of origin settling," refers to the material reparations for any death by violence, whether or not it is war-related. This is to say, malice, if not premeditation, is imputed to the act, and the killer *and* his clansmen are held accountable. As the "cause of origin" of the fatality, they should "settle" the imbalance they have produced by making appropriate payments to the deceased's agnates. However, as I noted earlier, the aggrieved parties, if it suits their ends, reserve the right to avenge the homicide in kind, even after accepting the killers' pigs. This means that every killing (or later death from wounds), except perhaps the obviously domestic murders of spouses, is potentially a political issue. For this reason the Mae tend to assimilate all deaths to the basic category "death in combat" and handle them accordingly.

The inclusive definition of homicide compensation has a number of subsidiary and supplementary concepts. Thus, there are the two preliminary transactions that we have seen figure importantly in the negotiating of a truce between warring groups—namely, the interim payment of pork and valuables to the victim's agnates, by which the killer's group admits culpability and the obligation to make full reparations later, and the offering by the deceased's group of valuables to the killer's agnates, acceptance of which is also a public admission of the latter's liability.

A somewhat different partial payment of homicide compensation may occur when a clan has unduly postponed meeting such an obligation. Then some men of the killer's group may make a small-scale offering of pigs to the deceased's close agnates, either because the latter are relatives or exchange partners whose goodwill they value, or because they fear that further delay will provoke a military attack for which their clan is unprepared. By acting independently in this way, the men wish to reaffirm their clan's intention to pay and so assuage the other clan's indignation, to maintain profitable exchange connections with that group, and to shame their own clansmen into behaving properly. Sometimes the decision of the small group of donors is triggered when a visitor who is a close "brother" of the deceased touches a large pig belonging to one of them and states formally: "This pig will eat the head of our dead man!" The owner accedes to the claim and may cut off one of the beast's ears, ostensibly as an indication that it is reserved for this purpose, but in fact also as a public criticism of his clansmen's dilatoriness. Occasionally a donor will on his own initiative mark one of his pigs in this way. By and large such actions of individual clansmen, especially if they include Big Men, tend to hasten the ultimate payment by their fellows of the outstanding compensation.

Another explicitly defined situation is that in which two (or more) clans agree to mount simultaneously (or almost so) reciprocal distributions of homicide compensation in order to settle at one stroke all the "debts" stemming from a war and so clear the way for a resumption of mutually advantageous intercourse. Such an arrangement, naturally enough, demands careful planning and obvious good faith; it can easily break down at the first suggestion of double-dealing or reluctance on either side.

We have already seen that a group's indemnification of its allies for their losses in battle is an important and common form of homicide compensation. Whether or not the responsible clan makes the payment at the same time as it compensates the enemy depends in part on the number of pigs it has on hand or can call in from debtors in other groups. Sometimes, indeed, the host clan for various political reasons may prefer to compensate its allies first, while delaying for as long as it dares the obligatory payments to its opponents.

An additional but apparently rarely implemented transaction may attend the compensation of allies when two clans have deliberately joined forces to attack a third. The group that initiated the assault, the owner of the quarrel, instead of sharing the spoils of war (be they land, gardening privileges, or trees) with the supporting clan, may offer the latter a large number of pigs over and above the usual homicide reparation to an ally.

124

Acceptance of these beasts, which are distinguished by having their eyes marked with red pigment, is a public statement by the allied group that it relinquishes any rights to the enemy's possessions. Men say, however, that even if the allies, seduced by the sight of so many pigs, agree at the time to these terms, later they are likely to press claims to a share in the enemy's land, arguing that the extra beasts were simply part of the homicide compensation owed them. Accordingly, there is little point in proposing such pacts; they are almost certain to be followed by recriminations and violence.

The remaining form of homicide compensation to be noted is that offered by a group for fatalities suffered by the enemy's allies. It will be recalled that an owner of the quarrel is not bound to make such payments. Whether or not these reparations are even suggested, let alone actually handed over, depends on such factors as the strength of the donor clan's desire to secure a truce and the importance of its kin and exchange connections with the other groups.

Finally, brief mention should be made of several lesser prestations that commonly accompany the discharge of homicide compensations. Although these may be regarded as an acknowledgment of services rendered, they may also be considered gifts of goodwill. Usually they are interpersonal rather than intergroup transfers of pork and minor valuables. One is the "burial payment," made by the deceased's close kinsmen to those non-clansmen who retrieved his corpse when his own clansmen were unable to do so, and either interred it in their own territory or returned it to the dead man's clan for disposal. The second is the reimbursement by clansmen of those extraclan relatives who have cared for the clansmen's dependents when they took temporary refuge abroad during hostilities. The third kind of prestation involves donations of pork by individual men among the owners of the quarrel to various allies who aided them. These are specifically called "free or voluntary gifts," and my impression is that they are seen as tokens of personal esteem rather than as measured wages for military assistance.

Perhaps the most striking aspect of homicide compensations is the great variety of factors that influence how, when, or if the prestation will be effected, even after the contending groups have agreed to make reparations and have halted overt warfare. It is well-nigh impossible to predict the outcome of any given situation without an intimate knowledge of circumstances that range from a clan's actual holdings of pigs through its perceptions of its current and future political commitments and needs, the significance of the kin and exchange connections linking the adversaries and other interested parties, the way the victim died, to random events such as the unexpected demise of pigs or the individual reactions of angry men. The one reliable conclusion to be drawn is that even when a disgruntled enemy or allied clan threatens a dilatory group with violence or actually engages in murder or ambush, the latter is still disposed to wait until the last possible moment before meeting its obligations. The reluctant donors engage in real brinksmanship as they take into account the elements mentioned above.

Thus, a clan that owes homicide compensation to another may assert, truthfully or not, that it simply does not have enough pigs on hand to make more than a small interim payment. The disappointed creditors accept the animals, albeit with heated protests and threats of retaliation, for they prefer not to forego the bird in the hand. Nevertheless they fear, with reason, that the debtor group will use this token offering as an excuse to play for time. If, however, the claimants have themselves recently given homicide or death compensation to the other clan, or have materially aided it in battle, or may be required as allies in the near future, they stand a better chance of securing the rest of the pigs without undue delay. It may happen that some of the defaulters' pigs sicken or die, a misfortune they may interpret as a sign that their niggardliness has angered and shamed the clan's ancestral spirits, who see it as detracting from the group's reputation. To avoid further attacks the clan is likely to hand over the stricken pigs as a partial payment and to hasten to arrange the distribution of the balance.

Usually the agnates of a man slain in battle try to postpone making the conventional death payment to his maternal relatives until his own clan has received homicide compensation. This is sound economics because as a rule the latter sum is larger. If, however, the deceased's clansmen procrastinate, his maternal kinsmen may apply pressure by threatening to break off valued exchange dealings until the death prestation is made. Should the dead man's agnates themselves owe homicide pigs to the killer's clan, the matrilateral pressure may move them to discharge a part, if not the whole of this obligation, which in turn may persuade the killer's group to meet its commitment to them in the hope of quickly securing the remainder of the reparations due. At the same time those maternal kin who have relatives in the killer's clan do not hesitate to exploit exchange connections there to induce these men to act. They argue that not only will much of the homicide payment given to the deceased's agnates reach the maternal kinsmen, but also this will enable the latter to engage in other exchanges to the ultimate benefit of their partners among the killer's group.

To conclude this account of the ramifications and complications of these transactions I shall summarily describe several actual situations in order to indicate how clans maneuver within the explicit requirements of compensation payments.

Clan A of phratry I fought clan B of phratry II over the division of spoils secured when both attacked a third clan of phratry III. A man of clan D of phratry III, who was a father's sister's son of clan A, was killed

126

helping clan A. Clan A made an interim ally payment of pork to clan D. One man of clan A who contributed to this distribution designated his donation for a particular relative X of clan D, but the Big Men diverted the pork to another member of D. The man X was furious and, to relieve his feelings, fired an arrow into the buttock of another man Y of clan A. The Big Men of both clans smoothed over this unpleasantness, and eventually clan A gave full ally compensation to clan D.

Some time later the man Y of clan A joined with several mother's brothers' sons of clan E of phratry II to steal a pig from another subclan of clan E. Fearing retaliation, man Y moved from his subclan's men's house near the border of clan E to a men's house farther away that belonged to another subclan i of clan A. The men in this house berated Y for his stupidity, pointing out that clans A and E had several times fought over pig thefts and that clan A was not at that time ready to go to war again. In the ensuing argument a man of subclan i shot Y in the other buttock. The men of this group refused to offer Y any compensation, asserting that he richly deserved the injury. The subclan ii of Y did not support him, and the matter was dropped.

About two years afterward Y collapsed and died while tilling his garden. The men of subclan ii thereupon announced that his death had resulted from *both* arrow wounds and claimed homicide compensation from clan D and from subclan i of clan A. Somewhat surprisingly, both groups admitted liability; but the men of subclan i said they would give compensation to subclan ii only on the understanding that the latter would share equally with i any pigs it received from clan D. Subclan ii agreed to this, and subclan i handed over about forty pigs. Clan D sent an interim payment of a few pigs to subclan ii, but did nothing more. Four years later subclan ii gave pork to clan D in an attempt to hasten the latter's discharge of the obligation. But soon after this, both clans A and D were quarreling and then fighting over land boundaries, and clan D never paid the outstanding compensation for Y.

On another occasion a clan A lost a man when helping a fraternal clan B invade clan C of another phratry. Clan B, which suffered several casualties, promptly gave a large ally homicide compensation to clan A, and the latter pronounced itself satisfied. Clan C, which included maternal kinsmen of clan A, stated that it would also hand over compensation to clan A when it made reparations to clan B. However, when the time came, clan C offered only three or four pigs and some pork to a few men of clan A, saying that this was not an interim payment but all that clan A would receive. The men of clan A were angry but, being on enemy soil, took the pigs silently and went home. Months later a noted Big Man and fight leader of clan C on his way to a pandanus feast rather foolishly walked through the territory of a fraternal clan D which abutted that of clan A. Men of clan A saw him pass and waited all night for his return. Early the next morning a girl of clan A observed the traveler and sent up a cry: "Our pig is loose on the northern track!" At once three men of clan A, including the major Big Man, set an ambush and speared the foolhardy man. They hacked up the corpse and called to clansmen of D to take the remains to their fraternal clan C with the compliments of A, and to tell clan C that clan A had no further interest in demanding the unpaid homicide compensation.

The significance of phratry ties is brought out in the following series of conflicts. Men of a clan A of phratry I surprised and killed a man of clan B of phratry II who was stealing pandanus nuts from the forest of A. Large-scale fighting followed, in which clan C of phratry I helped clan A. Clan C lost a man killed, and clan A quickly made an interim payment of ally compensation. But several years afterward, with the remainder of the compensation still outstanding, an angry brother of the dead man killed a man of clan A who was visiting an affine in clan C. Clan A at once launched an attack on clan C, but the Big Men of both began negotiations in an attempt to choke off the fighting before more casualties ensued. They were successful, and clan A without delay handed over full compensation for the original death. Clan C replied simultaneously with an interim payment for the second killing and later discharged the balance of the debt.

Finally, I give an instance of a chain reaction in such transactions that shows clearly how the actions of any one group are importantly affected by the reactions of others, and again indicates the significance of fraternal connections.

In about 1945 a man of a clan A of phratry I was wounded in combat with clan B of phratry II. Early in 1956 he died and clan B II made an interim payment of compensation to clan A I, promising that the rest would soon follow. At the same time clan B II demanded homicide compensation for an old killing from clan C I. Clan B II had given an inducement payment to C I in 1955, and C I had answered with a partial offering of compensation. Clan C I now agreed to give the balance to B II as soon as it received matrilateral compensation from clan D II for the death of a sister's son in that group.

In December 1956, clan D II made the death compensation to C I, which informed clan B II that it was ready to resume negotiations over the payment of homicide compensation. Simultaneously, C I asked clan E I for homicide reparations outstanding from a death C I had incurred in fighting E I in about 1945. The outcome of all this bargaining was that, early one morning in December, clan E I gave substantial homicide compensation to C I. Later that day C I handed over these pigs and others as homicide compensation to B II, which in turn on the same day gave homicide compensation to clan A I.

The homicide compensation as transaction

Whatever the circumstances that may delay or hasten a payment of homicide compensation, once a clan has determined to make an offer the form the transaction takes is much the same on all occasions—no matter that the recipients are allies or enemies, that the distribution is for a man killed in a recent battle or for one who has succumbed to wounds suffered long ago. Indeed, the event displays essentially the same structure as other significant prestations, such as the climactic disbursement of pigs in the Te exchange cycle (see Meggitt 1965a, 1974). First there is prolonged intra-clan discussion, during which the potential donors wrangle over the amounts of their contributions and the identities of individual recipients; then the formal offer is made to the other clan and is accepted; finally, on the next day, the pigs are publicly handed over. I shall briefly describe these stages.

The Mae speak as though a clan acts in a homicide compensation as a unit whose intentions are unequivocally expressed by its Big Men, and the group certainly strives to present this appearance in the presence of others. Nevertheless, this display of unanimity is not achieved without considerable internal argument and occasional ill-feeling, and during the preliminary arrangements some of the component subgroups and members carry more weight than others and push their own interests hard. The Big Men must try to reconcile or override such differences.

Usually the stimulus to undertake the prestation comes from long discussions between the Big Men and the subclan to which the actual killer belongs. On the one hand, the Big Men are concerned for broader or longer-term political reasons to clear away the debt; on the other, both they and the killer's subclan are expected to make the heaviest donations to the reparations. When both are agreed that the matter should go forward and that among them they have the resources to make a good showing, they call a meeting of all the clansmen at one of the men's houses and put their case to them. In addition to advancing arguments based on the clan's political advantages and the need to maintain its prestige, the Big Men point out that a number of men at this time have enough pigs to be able to contribute handsomely, or at least enough to add significantly to the number the initiators intend to give.

The other clansmen know what is afoot, and each comes to the assembly having already decided what he will offer to the common fund. For some poorer men this will perforce be nothing. The Big Men and the men of the killer's subclan indicate the number of pigs they themselves will give, and who will be the recipients, by thrusting rows of twigs in the ground to represent the stakes on the danceground to which the pigs will be tethered on the occasion. Each of the other men then hands twigs to the Big Men, one for every pig he is offering, and also nominates the men in the deceased's clan whom he wants to receive the animals.

In this regard each man tries to protect his own exchange interests insofar as this accords with the good of his clan. Thus he may tell the organizers: "When the clan of the deceased last gave us valuables, I received only two pigs, and these came from certain of my relatives there who owed them to me. Very well, I will provide just two pigs for that clan in return, and I insist that they go to these men." If the Big Men believe he can afford to part with more pigs, they urge him to give them. Or they may try to induce him to let his promised animals go to other recipients—for instance, to close agnates of the dead man whose claims they regard as better, or to Big Men whose goodwill they consider more important to the clan (or, perhaps, important to the Big Men among the donors).

Should the pigs' owners at first reject such proposals (and many do so), the arguments wax furious and men come to blows as they try to promote their own ends. Throughout these confused and noisy altercations the Big Men constantly arrange, rearrange, and count the twigs while they attempt to deploy the maximum number of pigs to what they assert is the greatest advantage of the whole clan. Eventually the counsels of the Big Men, supported by the major contributors among the killer's subclan, prevail, although it may be a day or two before the more resolute dissenters' objections dwindle into surly grumbles. The Big Men make a final summary statement of the clan's commitment, as they tally the twigs (= the pigs) for the last time and definitively nominate each donor and intended recipient.

Then quickly, before disgruntled followers reopen arguments, the Big Men lead the way to a convenient hillside where rows of men face the territory of the deceased's clan and chant in unison. In the stylized language of Enga song they announce that out of their great generosity they are prepared to hand over a handsome compensation for their killing of the brother (or son or father) of so and so, and they invite his agnates to discuss the matter.[6] The men of the other clan sing in response, deprecating the offer but agreeing to hear more. Both sides season their songs with metaphorical boasts and gibes.

The men of the host clan gather in subclan sections on one side of a danceground near the border to await the recipient clan's representatives. To underline their peaceful intentions they place their spears and bows (but not their axes) behind them. Bachelors are dispatched to cut sugarcane for the visitors, a conventional mark of courtesy, and the Big Men may also have clan wives bring cooked vegetable food.[7] Other men, directed by the Big Men, may at this time set up along the middle of the danceground parallel rows of stakes, to each of which a pig will later be tethered. Each row, representing a subclan's contribution to the total compensation, is divided into lineage segments, within which the posts of closely related agnates form smaller units. Usually the stakes of each

130

Mae Enga clansmen gathered for a distribution of homicide pork

subclan's Big Man who is also a major donor are placed at the head of that line.

Vigorous singing heralds the approach of the armed men of the dead man's clan as they halt frequently to chant demands for a large compensation and threats of retaliation if they do not receive it. They utter their last challenge outside the danceground as they mass to make an impressive entrance. At the least the party should comprise Big Men of the clan and the senior members of the deceased's subclan, but typically many men of the clan accompany them, especially those who expect to receive pigs and valuables from relatives or exchange partners in the killer's clan.

Once on the danceground the guests sit together opposite their hosts, whom they watch suspiciously for signs of treachery. At the same time various members of other clans may appear unobtrusively on the scene. These can include Big Men of friendly or neutral groups nearby who want to keep abreast of events, former allies who intend to sue for overdue compensation, and individual creditors of potential recipients who wish to press their debtors for payment.

The Big Men of the host clan command their bachelors to heap food before the visitors. Not only is public meal-sharing a sign of repaired social relationships; the time taken to eat is thought to give the edgy, potentially violent men a space in which to compose their thoughts. Meanwhile other uncommitted visitors drift back and forth between the two groups to exchange greetings and gossip with relatives and friends, and to venture mild witticisms as they try to bridge what otherwise might be an awkward silence.

Mae Enga men arranging twigs in planning an interclan distribution of pork

Then, before either party becomes too restive, the host clan's most important Big Man launches into oratory which, summarized, goes more or less as follows: "Men of clan X, tomorrow we will give you pigs for the death of the brother of so and so. We will do so because we are generous men, always prepared to meet our commitments. True, you did not offer us many pigs when you killed the son of such and such of our clan; but we are prepared to overlook your apparent miserliness, for we know you always lack pigs. We, however, do not try to hide our numerous pigs; rather, we give them freely, scattering them like dust when we are called to do so, just as Big Men should. We have put aside the bows and spears with which we have killed so many men, the weapons that took the life of your brother. Yes, we killed him and we accept our liability in this. We have pigs for you. You may not have given us many before, but no matter, now we shall heap pigs on you, more than you can feed on your poor land. Will you then dare to crow over us? Why, who among you can muster as

132

many pigs as we shall distribute tomorrow? We are all Big Men. You say we killed an important man of your clan—if we did so, we are content. Now we are prepared to indemnify you accordingly with many pigs."

The Big Man who is the chief spokesman for the recipient clan responds appropriately. He reminds the audience of the military successes his own group has enjoyed, of the many adversaries their warriors have dispatched (including, of course, members of the host clan), and of the punctilious, indeed lavish, manner in which he and his brothers have always discharged their obligations when making the concomitant compensation payments—even if the hosts are too petty to recognize such largesse. "And these niggardly men of clan Y now say they will indemnify us handsomely for our brother's death? Given their limited resources, this is unlikely, but they must certainly make us a reasonable offer. They have no choice but to do so, for they well know that if they fail to satisfy us, we shall not hesitate to take by force what is due to us!"

Other Big Men on both sides take up these themes, hurling at their opponents charges and countercharges, boasts and point-scoring gibes, but at the same time taking care not to say anything that would jeopardize the proceedings. These speeches follow no prearranged order. Senior close agnates of the deceased may also speak, and their Big Men stand ready to intervene when their remarks prove too inflammatory. As the verbal skirmishing waxes and wanes, former allies of the hosts take the opportunity to recall unpaid homicide compensations and to demand that these, too, be dealt with on the morrow. At this the Big Men of the hosts and of the recipient clan are likely to join forces to stifle a line of discussion that could prove unprofitable for both of them. The former try to fob off these unwelcome requests with vague promises of future, unspecified payments, while the latter insist that they have first claim on any wealth to be distributed next day. Then the visiting Big Men tell the hosts that they have heard enough generalities; they now want to learn the details of the proposed compensation.

A Big Man or an elder among the hosts loudly counts the pig stakes, tapping them with a spear or an arrow as he walks along the lines.[8] After the total is announced, the hosts' Big Man indicates the number of pigs that each subclan (and sometimes particular lineages) has contributed, and goes on to state how many each subgroup of the deceased's clan will receive. Individual donors and recipients are not singled out; the transaction is between agnatic descent groups. As each share to be handed over is announced, a member of the receiving group should run around the lines of pigs and shout compliments to the donors, before embracing and praising the Big Man to signify acceptance of the offer. If, however, the men of a unit are disappointed by their portion, they remain seated and grumble among themselves.

Orators from satisfied groups discuss the circumstances of the killing, laud the hosts' generosity, and say that, as far as they are concerned, the matter is closed and peaceful intercourse will follow. Disgruntled men, by contrast, deplore the inadequacy of the offering and state that, unless they receive more pigs, they will not recognize the transaction as valid. During these speeches much conversation goes on within each party. Big Men of the host group press followers to contribute extra pigs and valuables to meet the demands. If they are successful, they tell the unhappy recipients that adjustments (unspecified) will be made that night or next day, at which the latter may withdraw their objections. At the same time groups that are satisfied with their shares and wish to see the distribution proceed may attempt to persuade the malcontents that the hosts will indeed make up the differences. In these circumstances much depends on the attitudes of the Big Men of the deceased's clan and of the agnates in his subclan. If these people are clearly content with the offers, their clansmen are likely to go along with them, however reluctantly. The host clan's Big Men and major donors are, of course, well aware of this and aim their speeches accordingly.

If, however, the key figures as well as the majority of the recipients feel slighted, or if the total offer really is derisory, they may say they will accept the pigs only as an interim payment, with a full and proper compensation to be made later. It may suit the hosts ostensibly to agree to this compromise (while privately they hope to evade their obligations), and the transaction continues. But if, in the unlikely event that the donors stand firm and insist they will give no further compensation for the death, the visitors can do no more than reject the offer and stamp off in a rage, threatening future reprisals. In either case, compromise or refusal, trouble looms.

When the recipients are for the time being more or less satisfied with the offer and its allocation among their subgroups, which is the usual situation, Big Men on both sides wind up the proceedings with self-congratulatory speeches. The individual donors seek out the men to whom they will give their pigs and escort them to the women's houses where the beasts are lodged. Each owner brings out the pigs he has reserved for that man and gives him the pig-leads to hold briefly before returning the animals to the house. The visitor thus learns precisely which pigs he is to receive next day. Naturally, he may be dissatisfied with the size, condition, or sex of the animals, and more argument follows.[9] However, as the two men are likely to be relatives or at least former exchange partners, they usually reach some kind of agreement. The donor may substitute larger pigs for smaller, throw in as sweetening valuables such as pearl shells or axes, or promise to give additional pigs on another occasion. Once the two men are wholly in accord, the recipient rejoins his clansmen, and they all go home to talk about the distribution next day.

Meanwhile, the host clan's Big Men, as well as the men of the killer's

134

Mae Enga bachelors at a public distribution of food

Robert M. Glasse

subclan, visit all the men's houses for final discussions of the forthcoming assembly, in particular to ensure that the full number of pigs will be on hand. Early next morning the Big Men command clansmen and their wives to take the pigs and valuables to the danceground, and they may also have the women carry vegetable food there to be cooked in an earth oven and distributed to the visitors. En route the men sing to alert the recipients, who with their wives quickly make their way to the rendezvous. In addition, men of other clans (including those present on the preceding day) who have heard the singing arrive to see what is afoot. Within a surprisingly short time there may be 400 or more adults and swarms of children gathered there in clan groups.

What follows parallels to some degree the proceedings of the day before. Directed by the Big Men, some of the hosts give food to the guests while others check the stakes, adding extra ones as necessary. Then the donors tether their pigs, arranging the animals in linear segments according to the recipients' subclans. They also place any other valuables beside the appropriate animals. Big Men and other senior men of the various groups dart back and forth, brandishing sticks and calling for order. Leaders of the hosts and of the recipients make speeches, shorter this time, in

135

Cooked pork laid out for a Mae Enga distribution of homicide compensation

which they recapitulate the events leading up to this grand occasion. Then the Big Man or an elder of the host group counts the pigs and indicates those promised to the first group of recipients, one of whom circles the animals and shouts the praises of the donors. The Big Man tells him to take the pigs and goes on to allocate the next batch. The wives of the recipients untie their beasts and pick up any valuables due their husbands. At once creditors of these men rush forward and try to drag pigs from the shrieking women. The husbands intervene and loud arguments explode around the danceground. Women throw stones, men scuffle and swing pig stakes. The Big Men and elders intervene to disarm the combatants before blood is shed and the brawling escalates into serious fighting. Other hosts charge into the melée and hustle the quarreling outsiders from the clearing, telling them to settle their disputes elsewhere. People hurry off with their pigs and valuables, anxious to get them home without being intercepted. Within an hour or so the danceground is deserted.

Confused and violent as the scene may appear, both parties are likely to view the encounter as an unqualified success. The donors have discharged a significant obligation and are now free to devote their energies and resources to other interclan activities. The recipients have secured reparations for the loss of their "brother," wealth to invest in other pres-

136

tations. The two groups can resume more or less amicable social and exchange relationships to their mutual benefit, and each now stands as a potential ally of the other in forthcoming conflicts.

The statistics of homicide compensations

The institution of homicide compensation among the Mae is without doubt as complex as it is important, and often the observer cannot readily see beyond the various contingent events that obscure its overall pattern. Accordingly, it is worth presenting, insofar as this is possible, some statistical summaries of fairly general or recurring features of these transactions. As before, the data tabulated here are drawn from my sample neighborhood of Mae clans. The figures in Tables 9–11 refer to intergroup hostilities and casualties that occurred before 1955, although the actual payments that I am able to quantify reliably (as well as some of the deaths from wounds for which they were made) did not take place until 1955 or after.

Table 9   Payments of homicide compensation by category of warfare, pre-1955

| Category of warfare | Compensation paid for: | | | None paid | Total deaths |
	Killer's group	Ally	Both		
Intraclan	14	1	—	—	15
Intraphratry	11	—	—	3	14
Extraphratry	20	8	3	16	47
Total	45	9	3	19	76
Percentage	59.2	11.8	3.9	25.0	100

The distribution of figures in Table 9 shows that, although ideally every homicide should be indemnified by the killer's agnatic group, the culprits often do not meet their obligation, an evasion that frequently provokes further conflict. Thus, reparations are outstanding for no fewer than one-quarter of the 76 killings in this sample. Some of these defalcations the creditors had written off as total losses, seeing no way at that time to bring effective pressure to bear on the offenders. However, they still hold out hopes that others of these debts would be met in the future, as changing political circumstances persuaded the defaulters that it would be to their advantage to do so. Table 9 also confirms what the Mae know well—that failure to make homicide compensation is less likely (three out of 28 cases) when the adversaries are "brothers" than when they are not (16 out of 36 cases). This statistical difference says something

137

about the moral force of fraternal solidarity. Finally, the figures confirm the Mae statements that, even though a clan is not bound to compensate for those allies of its enemy whom it has killed, it may on occasion choose to do so.

Table 10 Payments of homicide compensation by victim's marital status

Marital status	Compensation paid	Compensation not paid	Total deaths
Bachelor	15	3	18
Married man with:			
no children	—	1	1
one child	6	1	7
two children	4	3	7
three children	4	1	5
four children	5	2	7
five children	2	—	2
six children	1	1	2
unspecified number of children	6	3	9
Total, married men	28	12	40
Marital status unknown	14	4	18
Total, men	57	19	76

In many respects bachelors in traditional Mae society occupy a lower social status than do mature married men. They do not control important property and participate in few exchanges; they are military novices; they have little or no say at clan assemblies; they play a minor part in religious rituals; they fetch and carry at their elders' behest. Accordingly, the figures in Table 10 come as something of a surprise. Given that practice falls short of the ideal norm of compensation for all homicides, one might expect the discrepancy to reflect in some degree differences in the social prominence of the deceased, namely, that the killer's group would be more ready to evade payment for the death of a person of little public consequence (especially of one without exchange partners), while the latter's agnates might be inclined not to press their claims on his behalf. The data in Table 10, however, indicate that homicide compensation is secured for bachelors relatively more often than it is for married men. I believe this pattern reflects the indignation of clansmen who see a "younger brother" cut down before he has a chance to fullfil his promise. They feel strongly that the loss cannot be glossed over but should be made good, both by homicide pigs and by retaliation in kind. On the other hand, I suspect that clansmen's passions are not so deeply engaged when the dead

138

man is, despite his married state, a social nonentity of middle age.

This issue of the deceased's status leads naturally to the size of the homicide compensation. When asked, Mae men usually say that a payment should comprise at least forty pigs, plus an unspecified number of lesser valuables depending on the donor's generosity, and that considerations of the victim's age, sex, and social importance should not significantly lower the amount offered or accepted. That is to say, in this context all human lives are considered basically equivalent, and the minimum value to be placed on each one is forty pigs. This figure, incidentally, equals two "full or complete men," a unit of counting based on a normal person's twenty digits. In fact, although the mean number of beasts handed over closely approximates forty in the 16 transactions for which I have reliable data, the range is considerable—from ten to 124.

Mae men are, of course, aware of these differences. They say that in some instances, when the number of pigs presented is markedly below the norm, the men of the killer's clan at the time explicitly describe them as an interim payment, and the recipients accept them as such. The rest of the indemnity may eventually be paid. It can happen, however, that relations between the two groups deteriorate to the point of violence, and the erstwhile donors simply refuse to recognize any further obligation to recompense the other clan, which can do little to retrieve the situation. Similarly, if both clans are already on bad terms, the debtors may offer a small homicide compensation, stating that this is all they propose to give. Fearful of losing these pigs, the deceased's clansmen take them under protest, insisting that they are merely partial payment to be supplemented later with another installment. Once again, the creditors' only recourse is threats of force.

In short, when the compensation is significantly smaller than the rule, this is attributed to the greed, duplicity, or ill-nature of the donors, not to any deficiency in the victim's social status. If the deceased's clansmen asserted or admitted the latter as a consideration, they would impugn their own honor.

On the other hand, there is nothing to prevent a clan from making a larger than expected payment of homicide compensation if it has reason to do so. For instance, the two groups may be fraternal clans whose relations have generally been friendly and who know they will before long require each other's help in warfare. Or the victim may have been a Big Man who had many influential exchange partners in the killer's group, and through him these men have established valuable connections which they wish to keep up, with his clansmen. It is not surprising, therefore, that the largest homicide payment in my sample, 124 pigs, was between two subclans of a large clan that had fought over land and was made for a Big Man killed in that confrontation.

A noteworthy feature of Table 11 is the presence of homicide com-

Table 11   Sample of homicide compensations paid 1955–1962 for deaths incurred in pre-1955 fighting

Status of victim	Number of cases	Valuables disbursed: Pigs	Other items[a]	Cash (shillings)[b]
Men:				
allies	2	42	2	65
mean		21	1	32.5
enemies	11	439	77	280
mean		39.9	7	25.4
Women:	3	167	11	125
mean		55.6	3.6	41.6
Total	16	648	90	470
mean		40.5	5.6	29.4

Notes: These figures overlap with those reported in Meggitt 1965a:Table 43; the present figures are somewhat more reliable.

[a]Other items include, roughly in order of frequency, pearl shells, fowls, steel axes, spades, machetes, and gourds of tree oil. The figures are almost certainly an underestimate.

[b]An Australian shilling was then worth approximately $.10 in United States currency.

pensations paid for women, albeit only three, and the fact that these reparations are on the average larger than those made for men. No women appear in Tables 9 and 10, which refer to payments before 1955. What is the reason for this difference?

Although as we have seen relatively few women are killed during Mae wars, any such deaths ideally should be made good with homicide pigs. Discussion of this matter with Mae men reveals that in this context they are tacitly invoking the pervasive double standard concerning the sexes. Because a clan has access at any time to a limited number of pigs to use in exchanges and compensations, its members have to agree on some order of priorities for prestations. Thus, transactions are ranked in terms of the hierarchical structure of the social units involved, so that the payment of homicide compensations takes precedence, for instance, over the giving of brideprice. But, given the frequency of warfare, a clan is likely always to face a backlog of undischarged homicide debts, which obviously are not met in fixed temporal order. Political and economic considerations hasten some payments and delay others. Accordingly, in the rare cases where indemnification for the killing of a woman is an issue, the groups concerned do not as a rule deny the liability. Rather, they simply keep on postponing the transaction in favor of others whose implementation is more pressing, until the time the matter lapses.

By the late 1950's, however, the peace imposed by the Australian

140

Administration on the Central Enga had been in effect for almost a decade, during which no new deaths in warfare augmented those awaiting compensation. At the same time there was a noticeable increase in local wealth; not only was the pig population recovering from an earlier decline caused by an epidemic of pneumonia, but also government agencies and the Christian missions were pumping large quantities of shells, steel axes, and machetes into the economy. Money, too, was coming into common use (see Meggitt 1971, 1973, for an account of these changes).

Mae clans seized the opportunity to clear away many outstanding homicide debts, doing so with such industry that by the early 1960's they were taking up the few, hitherto ignored, female casualties.[10] Thus, the three deaths of women that appear in Table 11, although they occurred in the 1940's, were paid for between 1959 and 1962. This, moreover, was a period of mounting inflation, with the amounts given in all kinds of prestations generally larger than in 1955. Inflation probably accounts for the size of these "female" reparations.[11]

Nevertheless, despite this demonstrable and recent change in the magnitude of homicide compensations, some Mae in 1955–57 insisted that fewer men were contributing to individual transactions since the Administration imposed peace. They believed that less wealthy clansmen who no longer feared retaliatory attacks by disgruntled neighbors were leaving the burden of meeting these obligations to the Big Men and the close agnates of the killer's family. I lack necessary pre-1955 data to test this assertion, but, the numbers of donors and of recipients for the post-1955 compensations shown in Table 11 support it. In the 16 instances I have analyzed, the mean number of donors is 15 and of recipients 21. Even allowing for the young bachelors and old men who normally do not figure in public exchanges, these figures fall short of the numbers one might expect. Moreover, within the sets of participants, a relatively large proportion of the wealth (53 percent of pigs distributed and 50 percent of those received) initially passes through the hands of a small number of men (20 percent of the donors and 24 percent of the recipients). But this pattern is, of course, compatible with the Big Men's traditional mode of manipulation.

I conclude this discussion of homicide compensation among the Mae with two observations. The first refers to the timing of these transactions which depends heavily on the political and economic relationships, both actual and perceived, of the two clans concerned, not only between themselves but also with neighboring groups. But this is not the whole story— in some situations at least we should also take into account a basic feature of pig husbandry.

It happens from time to time that a clan's herds, which have been increasing naturally because of favorable local conditions, are suddenly and markedly augmented by beasts received from other clans. Thus, in

1962 a clan had at least 335 animals (probably more) on hand, a large number for the extent of territory, and forty or more on agistment with relatives elsewhere. The Big Men, who had been watching this growth, talked in leisurely fashion of discharging some of the group's external obligations. Then, within two weeks and with little warning, the clansmen acquired in marriage and funerary distributions a further 85 pigs, more than could conveniently be farmed out at short notice. Indeed, for a while the place seemed to be overrun by pigs, and at once men began bemoaning the threat of damage to the crops, which would inevitably lead to quarrels, and the work that would be entailed in checking and repairing fences. Strange pigs, before they settle down in new surroundings, are thought to be especially prone to rooting up sweet potatoes. It is noteworthy, in the light of Rappaport's data (1968) for the Maring, that nobody, male or female, complained about the women's having to toil harder to feed the extra pigs; apparently they were expected to take this in stride. The protection of the gardens was without doubt the prime consideration, and, given the density of the local population, this was understandable.

The Big Men quickly convened meetings at which they canvassed opinions concerning the group's options, and several days later the clan gave 44 pigs to a surprised but pleased fraternal clan as compensation for an ally killed 17 years before. This action in turn stimulated the recipients to pay, several months afterward, homicide compensation they had long owed the donors. Meanwhile, the latter disposed of more pigs in various funerary contributions, until they were satisfied that their gardens were no longer in jeopardy. Thus, on occasion an increase in a group's pig herds may in itself impel the owners to act in ways that significantly affect their relations with other clans.

Finally, I want to suggest a possible reason why the institution of homicide compensation is so important to the Mae, who sustain it with great energy and careful planning in the face of considerable obstacles and uncertainties. First, it should be recalled that although disputes over failures to pay, or delays in offering, such indemnities may in themselves induce fighting, nevertheless in most cases (perhaps three-quarters of them) reparations are made. I believe that this emphasis on meeting commitments correlates with the high density of the Central Enga population and with the frequency of military provocations, which arise not only from the constant confrontations over relatively scarce land but also over the deaths occurring in these conflicts. Given that with their traditional fund of knowledge and technology, the Mae can do little about population density, their concern to define a way of discharging more or less peacefully their obligations to idemnify killings does relieve to some extent the bereaved's pressing need for retaliatory violence. Otherwise, life would be an even more grueling round of ambush and raiding, and to that extent it would become well-nigh intolerable.

142

The ease with which the Central Enga at first gave up warfare and turned to litigation at the behest of Australian Administration officers is I think partial evidence for this view. Perhaps a more empirical test would be to compare the frequency and scale of Central Enga homicide compensations with those of the more sparsely settled Fringe Enga. Unfortunately, the evidence for such a comparison has not yet been gathered.

The General Peace

8

So far I have been concerned to depict and to analyze "traditional" patterns of warfare and peacemaking among the Mae Enga—that is, the practices that were common before Europeans came to the area and endured for a short time thereafter.[1] As might be expected, the presence of colonial officers and later of Christian missionaries changed the situation, at first sight radically. At the least, endemic warfare was incompatible with the Government's express aim of bringing British law and order to New Guinea.

I now describe briefly the reactions of the Mae, both to the pacification program instituted by Administration officers (and supported by missionaries) and to the persisting problems arising from a perceived shortage of land, problems the Government's policies left unresolved. This short history reveals two clearly marked stages in the Enga's responses. The first saw the relatively prompt acceptance of the introduced judicial system, the second (discussed in Chapter 9) a reluctant abandoning of the courts as clans found them incapable of protecting their particular interests. With this change in attitude went a resurgent reliance on force.

The first recorded Enga encounters with the Western world occurred in the early 1930's, when several small parties of European gold-prospectors separately entered their country.[2] Of these expeditions only that of the two Leahy brothers in 1934 is known to have penetrated the territory of the Central Enga, including that of the Mae, and their visit

144

was soon terminated. Illness and frequent attacks by large groups of warriors forced them to return to their base camp near Mount Hagen, several days' walk to the east of Enga country. In these confrontations the prospectors' rifles, supported by the arms of their twenty or so "shoot boys," exacted a heavy toll of Enga casualties (see Leahy and Crain 1937:236 *et seq.*)

None of these adventurers found gold in commercially worthwhile quantities in the Enga region, and their reports discouraged others from following them. In 1938, however, the Administration of the Territory of New Guinea established a patrol post and airstrip at Mount Hagen, from which Taylor and Black began long exploratory patrols to the west. These officers, accompanied by some twenty New Guinean policemen and over 200 carriers, cleared a small airstrip at Wabag, in Mae territory, and from there made preliminary aerial surveys to plan feasible walking routes through the difficult terrain (see Taylor 1940). Taylor and Black then set out on separate journeys, leaving the post and supplies at Wabag in charge of a European Medical Assistant (E.M.A.) and a small detachment of police. Next day a dispute over pigs erupted between local Mae clansmen and some of the constables. The Mae attacked in force and in the engagement killed one policeman and wounded two more, as well as wounding four carriers. Eleven Mae were killed and an unknown number wounded. Patrol Officer Downs was dispatched from Mount Hagen to help restore the situation, and subsequent relations between the Mae and the outsiders appear to have been more or less amicable. With the return of Taylor and Black to Wabag in 1939, the Administration closed this base and removed the personnel and equipment to Mount Hagen.

During these months in 1938–39, both Downs and the E.M.A. made several patrols among the Central Enga, as well as among some of the northeastern Fringe Enga. Downs's reports indicate that interclan warfare was then common everywhere.[3] His observations accord well with the account I have given of fighting among the Mae. For instance, the Birip (Laiapu Enga) people blamed a current shortage of food on "tribal fighting. . . . The Gai [Lai] valley between Yarumanda and Li.ink is cut about with tribal disputes which have left a trail of desolation . . . ; the warlike tendency of the people increases as you go west" (toward the Mae and Yandapu Enga). In the Sau valley Downs camped at Tsibamunda, "a former hamlet wiped out by tribal fighting," and he remarks on the "heavily stockaded ridges." Perhaps his most poignant comment is "for reasons of [Administration] prestige it will be necessary for us to forbid tribal fighting on the [Wabag] aerodrome or anywhere in the vicinity of the station."

I do not know if, during the years immediately following the dismantling of the post at Wabag, Administration patrols from Mount Hagen continued in Enga territory. By 1940 Australia was at war with Germany, and the enlistment of Administration officers in the armed forces abroad left the field services seriously understaffed.

The situation changed significantly, however, with the Japanese landings in northern New Guinea. Early in 1942 the Australian Government replaced the Administrations of Papua and of New Guinea with a single military command and set up the Australian New Guinea Administrative Unit to handle civil affairs. Many members of this body were former Administration officers. ANGAU was entrusted with maintaining an east-west communications line through the highlands, based on existing or newly constructed patrol posts and airstrips, whose occupants were to give warning and to offer resistance if Japanese troops penetrated the central mountains in strength. In the event there was no such incursion this highlands line was still important in providing an escape route for the civilians and Australian soldiers cut off near the coast by the Japanese advance. Given the Japanese superiority in the air and at sea, the refugees were driven to make their way on foot inland through the swamps and rain forests to the mountains. For those caught in the Sepik area one feasible route was southeast via the Karawari and Yuat valleys to the Enga area. Accordingly, in 1942 or 1943, ANGAU officers reestablished a base at Wabag and also located posts manned by New Guinean policemen east and west of Wabag. Officers regularly patrolled between Mount Hagen and Wabag to keep open this walking track, in particular to ensure that local "tribal" warfare did not impede the movement of personnel and supplies.[4]

Mae testimony and ANGAU reports I have seen for 1943 to 1946 (when civil administration was resumed) indicate that during this time officers of the undermanned and obviously hard-worked detachment at Wabag imposed their orders on boisterous Enga with a heavy hand. Clansmen who flouted the new law by fighting near the posts and supply routes were summarily arrested for interrupting the "work of the Government," and were sentenced to short terms in the stockade at Wabag.[5] One officer in particular is still remembered for his ready recourse to force. Before his excesses led to his transfer, a number of Mae men and women were killed in armed sorties he headed.

Undoubtedly the reactions of some Enga clans to the strangers' uninvited presence and constraining commands could readily be construed by the ANGAU officers as deliberate provocations. Thus, one of the punitive patrols mounted by the notorious captain was intended to chastise a Mae clan, some of whose men had beheaded a local interpreter employed at the Wabag post when this man had (quite wrongly) tried to use his office to secure land of theirs. In addition, Enga made several substantial attacks on police posts up and down the Lai valley, in all of which the clans involved lost men. In the Sau area persistent assaults drove out

146

permanently a small army radio warning section, some of whose members were wounded. Six Enga were shot in these encounters.

How could a handful of officers and policemen curb the warlike inclinations of the many Enga near the ANGAU bases? As Mae men told me, after a few confrontations they quickly and painfully learned that numerical superiority counted little against police rifle fire. What is noteworthy is that few of these warriors, in referring to those stirring times, expressed any deep or enduring resentment against the outsiders for occasionally taking such repressive measures. Given the traditional Enga view that in intergroup collisions might indeed makes right, it is perhaps not remarkable that they tended to regard the ANGAU detachment as a kind of superclan, and that the attitude toward those Europeans of many Mae I know was largely one of rueful admiration for Big Men who had the power to back up their demands with force.[6] Moreover, in those early days most Enga probably did not believe the intruders were there to stay; rather, they were taken to be "sky people" making a temporary sojourn on earth, a view reinforced by the absence of wives and children among them and by their failure to cultivate gardens and to raise pigs.

Be that as it may, the busy ANGAU officers at Wabag were not then especially concerned to extend their influence far beyond the communications line; their primary task was to keep this road open. From time to time, however, they made survey patrols through the territories of other Enga clans, both Central and Fringe groups, and their reports made frequent reference to the prevalence of warfare over land, and to the local peoples' predeliction for dawn attacks and arson. Their comments parallel those Downs made in 1938–39, and once again accord with my account of traditional fighting.

In 1946, with the war ended and the defeated Japanese troops repatriated, the Australian armed forces were withdrawn from Papua and New Guinea. ANGAU was disbanded, and a unified civil administration was installed to govern the Territories of Papua and New Guinea as one entity. This radical change from two independent prewar administrations was implemented by a Labor government in Australia that explicitly supported the aims of the United Nations Trusteeship Council. In short, the Government was seriously committed to promoting the territories' social and economic "development" (formerly there had been almost total stagnation), with the ultimate, indeed very long-term, goal of securing their independence as a nation-state. The immediate consequence was metropolitan planning for the rapid expansion of Administration services (agricultural, medical, educational, and legal) among the indigenous highlands peoples. In addition, these areas, most of which had scarcely been explored before the war, were to be opened to limited European settlement, not only by missionaries but in particular by planters, in the hope that their capital investment and technical expertise, and the example they set, would facilitate the highlanders' entry into the Western world's primary commodity markets.

The highlands region was redefined as several administrative districts, to each of which the Department of District Services (DDS) appointed a District Commissioner (rather like a provincial governor), who was to coordinate the various public services and to ensure that other settlers, such as missionaries, planters, gold miners, and traders, in no way infringed the highlanders' legally established and customary rights. In the main District Commissioners and their subordinates took their responsibilities to the local peoples very seriously; their actions in protecting the interests of the latter frequently brought them into sharp conflict with other Europeans.

The districts were in turn divided into subdistricts, each with a headquarters and a few satellite patrol posts. All were manned by DDS field officers, who had magisterial powers and commanded small companies of indigenous policemen. These officers had considerable authority over other Administration personnel attached to their stations (for instance, school teachers, medical assistants, agricultural extension officers), and they also kept a watchful eye on the relations between non-official Europeans and the "natives."[7]

To carry out these plans the Government of Australia greatly increased the annual subsidies for Papuan and New Guinean affairs and recruited and trained administrative personnel to staff the rapidly expanding services in the Territory. Nevertheless, for some years the needs of the country consistently outran the resources available to meet them, one consequence being that there were rarely enough field officers to fill all the positions permanently. Personnel were frequently shifted among districts, generally from those currently rated low in the scale of priorities by the Administration in Port Moresby to those whose problems were considered more pressing. Thus, well into the late 1950's the Western Highlands District, where the Enga lived, was constantly short of staff and equipment. Indeed, until 1947 the whole of this district was still "restricted territory," that is, not yet sufficiently controlled or pacified for non-official Europeans to settle there.

In 1948 much of the district east of Mount Hagen was declared open to general settlement, as was a narrow western strip that adjoined the former communications line between Mount Hagen and Wabag, which was then merely a patrol post. In the same year the extensive section of the Western Highlands District that lay west of the Hagen Range became a subdistrict, with Wabag as its headquarters. The field staff was expanded to include two or three officers, and one or two E.M.A.'s set up a hospital at the station. Representatives of three Christian churches, the Roman Catholic Society of the Divine Word, the Lutheran Missouri Synod, and

148

the Seventh Day Adventists, established mission stations along the Lai valley, from which they began proselytizing the Central Enga. In addition, the missionaries provided elementary schooling and some medical and agricultural extension services. They also opened trade stores beside their churches, which were at first the most significant factor in persuading the Enga to accept their new neighbors.

No European planters took up land for development, at that time, in part because the area was so isolated and the limited transport available so costly, in part because these high narrow valleys were less suited to coffee-growing than lower and wider valleys farther east. Moreover, given the density of the Enga population and their continuing disputes over land, the Administration discouraged large-scale alienation of "native" lands that would breed future conflict.

Also in 1948 the Administration granted special leave to several miners (mainly former Government officers) to prospect in the Porgera valley, several days' hard walking west of Wabag. Here, in the territory of the Ipili, a people closely related to western Enga (see Meggitt 1957b, 1973), gold had been discovered, although not sufficient to warrant large-scale commercial exploitation. The "rush" soon collapsed, and only three miners maintained claims there, which they visited occasionally.

In short, during these early years of contact the non-official European population of the Wabag Subdistrict rarely exceeded a few dozen and mainly comprised missionaries and their families, residents whose aims and imported resources made them tolerably self-supporting. Their relations with both the Enga and the Administration officers were generally amicable, and the latter were free to tackle their primary task, which was to "pacify" the clansmen farther afield and to extend the controlled area. This the small number of officers achieved through vigorous patrolling in all parts of the Enga country, as well as among the neighboring Ipili, Iai-era, and Hewa peoples, and through permanent patrol posts set up in strategic localities—at Wapenamanda (Laiapu Enga) in 1951, at Laiagama (Yandapu Enga) in 1952, and at Kompiama (Sau.i Enga) in 1953.[8]

There were two basic elements in this mode of instituting law and order among the Enga, devices which had hardly changed since their introduction in prewar days elsewhere in New Guinea but which, nevertheless, remained relatively effective and economical of Administration manpower. One was the use, more or less within the legally defined limits of the Courts for Native Affairs (CNA) of the magisterial powers of the *kiaps* (DDS field officers), backed by small detachments of policemen.[9] Whether officers were wrestling with paper work at Wabag or making patrol camps in the bush, they could at once convene a CNA to hear disputes over "customary" issues that ranged from adultery through the theft of pigs to encroachment by clans on each other's lands. Not only did they constantly exhort the people to bring their quarrels to court for peaceful settlement, they also promptly arrested anyone whose actions clearly contravened the Administration's explicit policy of maintaining public tranquility. Under the Native Administration Ordinance of 1921 (and its later revisions) the offenders could readily be charged with spreading false reports or with behaving in a riotous manner (specifications that fairly characterized both interpersonal and intergroup confrontations among the Enga) and, if convicted, committed to serve a term in the stockade. Six months in jail was the maximum sentence that a CNA could then hand down.

The other component of the pacification program was the installation by kiaps of Administration representatives at the local level in areas deemed to have had enough contact with the "Government" for their inhabitants to comprehend and, it was hoped, to accept its aims. The general practice in the early days was to try to identify an influential Big Man and to persuade him to be the interim agent *(bosboi)* of the Administration there. His official duties were ostensibly simple. He was to keep the kiaps informed of the clansmen's attitudes and opinions, while at the same time conveying the officers' suggestions, advice, and orders to the clansmen. In addition the bosboi was quietly encouraged to try informally to compose local disputes (though such action was, strictly speaking, a violation of the Territory's legal code) before bringing intransigent opponents to argue their cases before police noncommissioned officers (also technically illegal) or before a CNA magistrate.[10]

Obviously, situations could arise in which the bosboi's official duties conflicted with his private and public concerns as a Big Man of his clan. In consequence some Big Men who had accepted the walking sticks that were the bosbois' badge of office soon resigned them to clansmen who were social nonentities. They preferred to operate in traditional fashion, manipulating the straw men while they themselves avoided the kiap's attention. Other Big Men, perhaps the more clever ones, retained the position of bosboi. Although they perceived the disadvantages of being so visible to the Administration officers, they believed that by suborning policemen and court interpreters, they could both reinforce their own influence at home and advance their clan interests in litigation. Some were markedly successful in this.

The kiaps regarded the appointment of bosbois as a temporary measure that provided a probationary period, during which they could assess the appointees' capabilities and loyalties before appointing any of them (subject to the District Commissioner's approval) to the more prestigious and powerful office of luluai. The luluai was inducted more formally into his position and sported a brass badge, but his responsibilities were basically those of the bosboi. It was expected that a luluai would hold his job

150

for an indefinite period, although he could of course be removed for obvious incompetence or disloyalty. The growing number of these appointments and their distribution closely paralleled the extension of the "controlled" area.

Usually, a relatively populous clan provided both a luluai and a *tultul*. The latter was ordinarily a younger man whose rudimentary knowledge of Melanesian pidgin, the *lingua franca* of New Guinea, enabled him to translate for the often monolingual luluai, whom he also assisted in his new duties.[11] By now an important task of both was to ensure the attendance of their clansmen (and women) once a week at the Government corvée—to build new roads and patrol houses, to maintain existing tracks and airstrips, or to bring firewood and sweet potatoes for sale at the hospital and the jail. Naturally enough, many Enga were unenthusiastic about these imposed obligations, and luluais had to exercise all their authority (backed by the ultimate sanction of police arrest) to ensure that their followers met Government requirements. It says much for the shrewdness with which luluais combined their new powers and their traditional influence as Big Men that most of them managed to satisfy simultaneously the demands both of the Administration officers and of their clansmen.

The expansion of the luluai-tultul network was accompanied by the creation of a small number (at most six or seven) of paramount luluais (*waitpus* or wearer of a silver badge of office). Each was chosen on the basis of his reputation and his apparent ability as a Big Man to coordinate the luluais and tultuls in a neighborhood of clans. Some had the oversight of twenty to thirty clans representing several phratries, that is, of some 9,000–10,000 people. Most of the paramount luluais I knew were exceptionally able men and were so regarded by other Enga, all of whom, even their long-term enemies, tended to view them as larger-than-life Big Men. Naturally, in this novel situation an energetic and ambitious waitpus could exercise much more power than was possible for a traditional Big Man. Administration officers generally were alert to the potential danger of local despotism, and they kept a close watch on the incumbents. The police N.C.Os, too, were vigilant, for they saw the waitpus as a threat to their own covert power structures. Indeed, some Administration officers adeptly manipulated the waitpus and the N.C.Os, so that each served as a check on the other's aspirations. Nevertheless, by astutely playing off the groups under his aegis while retaining the kiaps' goodwill, a percipient waitpus could advance his own fortunes as well as the interests of his clan and even of his whole phratry.[12]

To return to intergroup warfare among the Enga—we see, after the institution of civil administration in 1946, a limited expansion of the Administration field staff, accompanied by a marked increase in the frequency of patrolling, and by the establishment of dispersed patrol posts. Patrol and station reports also proliferated during this period, their content is instructive.

From 1946 through 1948 the scene everywhere in Enga country was much the same. Except for those localities in which Administration officers happened to be, interclan fighting was rife. Kiaps were constantly on the move as they tried to halt what they regarded as the more serious confrontations. Many others they simply had to ignore. Generally, the presence of the kiap and his policemen, as well as a few shots fired in the air, was enough to break up the hostilities, at least temporarily. Not only official reports but also Enga testimony indicate that in those days, although warring groups often made threatening demonstrations against "Government people," they rarely offered them actual violence, and field officers had no occasion to shed blood in their attempts at peace-keeping.[13]

Nevertheless, whether or not the officer arrested some of the combatants or persuaded them to argue their cases in court, if the issue was explicitly a land dispute or avenging a killing, the contestants usually resumed fighting as soon as the patrol had withdrawn. Only in lesser disputes, such as those over the theft of pigs or of pandanus nuts, was a judicial hearing likely to achieve a compromise. Small wonder that those kiaps' reports to headquarters frequently expressed a baffled despair in the face of their wards' smiling intransigence. Their descriptions of the modes of warfare emphasize the features I discussed earlier: the dawn attacks, the burning of houses, the razing of gardens and trees, the prevalence of defensively palisaded and ditched homesteads even within sight of the patrol posts. Their estimates of casualties also accord with the figures I have inferred from clan histories.

It says much for the pertinacity of these field officers that by the end of 1949 the situation was changing, at least among the Central Enga of the Lai valley who resided near the stations and on either side of the track from Wabag to Mount Hagen. The constant presence of the kiaps and police in this area, together with the holding of courts began to have its effect. The incidence of warfare declined sharply. Although there were still sporadic outbreaks of interclan fighting, especially over land, the patrol reports and CNA records now indicate that individual assaults or murders and occasional brawls were the main forms of violence and that men (and groups) were more willing to turn to the courts to settle their quarrels.[14] It is also apparent that in those days a few luluais and bosbois, in their role as Big Men, were still active behind the scenes in inciting their clansmen to attack rivals when they thought the gains warranted the risks. These "stirrers," however, could rarely be brought to trial in the CNA's. Clan solidarity was such that willing scapegoats among the younger men stepped forward to take the blame and to serve the relatively short jail sentences.

152

At any rate, by 1950–51 kiaps could fairly assert that, despite some recurring confrontations over land, the officially designated "controlled area," which now included most of the Central Enga groups, was indeed pacified.[15] Moreover, as the secure region was expanded, the missions (mainly Roman Catholic and Lutheran) were quick to set up new out-stations. Their continuing and restraining influence unquestionably facilitated the imposition of peace.

Nevertheless, to judge from statements of Mae Enga men, what really led to this marked and relatively swift change in their own sentiments and behavior was the ready availability of the courts. From the beginning many Mae were impressed by the exhortations of both kiaps and missionaries that they eschew physical violence and killing in favor of settling disputes by litigation, even though judgments were given essentially in terms of British law and rules of evidence. Of course the punitive sanctions of arrest and jailing also carried weight, but in the main the Mae decision was a victory of enlightened pragmatism. Most of them were willing to put up their axes and bows and to try the new system, which they viewed as a mode of intergroup fighting that could be pursued without weapons. As expressed to me, the opinion of most men was straightforward: litigation appeared to be a speedy and effective way of achieving their individual and clan aims, one that was economical of time, energy, and blood, and that would permit them to get on with their gardening and exchanges without the annoying and painful interruptions posed by military mobilization, the evacuation of noncombatants and pigs, the rebuilding of burned houses and the replanting of ruined gardens.

In any case, the spread of peace among the Central Enga clans is not to be inferred solely from official reports or from the assertions of the people themselves. There were also material consequences, which were at the same time indices, that were becoming apparent by 1955, when I first visited the Enga, and that persisted for some years afterward. Two of the most obvious concerned patterns of mobility and of residence. Thus, there was a noticeable increase in the frequency with which men and women traveled abroad from their clan territories, not only in large groups for public assemblies but also individually for business or social purposes. An important stimulus to this intercourse was the establishment of "highways" linking the three patrol posts of Wapenamanda, Laiagama, and Kompiama with the Subdistrict headquarters at Wabag. These narrow roads and bridges, constructed with great speed and skill by the directed labor of clansfolk, were primarily intended to open the region to the passage of the few Administration and mission vehicles and, hopefully, to hasten the spread of Government control and of "civilization," for instance, by facilitating the access of Enga pedestrians to hospitals, schools, courthouses, and stores. The rugged terrain largely determined the placement of these roads, some sections of which ran along clan borders, while

153

others cut through clan domains or skirted unoccupied stretches of montane forest. Each clan, through its luluai, was responsible for the maintenance of that part of the roadway (and those bridges) on or near its land. The kiaps declared that the highways were wholly public, with no person or group having the right to encroach on them for cultivation or grazing, or to impede the free passage of any traveler. Indeed, Administration officers made it clear that they regarded the roads as extensions of the Government stations and that they would not tolerate any riotous behavior there.

Pacification also stimulated obvious changes in Mae residential arrangements. It was not simply that men no longer needed to expend the labor and the timber for defensive palisades or escape tunnels, or that they could now bring into cultivation land formerly occupied by the stands of cane grass that had served as arrow screens. Now that people did not fear raids by neighboring groups, they were free to build houses for their wives closer to the clan borders or wherever their current gardens were established. Moreover, there was a perceptible movement of all houses down the slopes as they were renewed, to be closer to the new roads and to mission and Government posts.

At the same time the traditional men's houses began to decline in importance and in numbers. This was not only because groups of men had less reason to reside together for military purposes and some men therefore built smaller family houses near their gardens. In addition, the whole complex of masculine attitudes concerning sexual segregation and female pollution was under heavy fire from the missionaries and, later, from Administration school teachers, with one result that more and more men (especially the younger ones) were willing to reside in women's houses with their wives or mothers and thus save themselves the exertion of erecting separate men's houses. Finally, among a growing number of men, such as luluais and tultuls, medical orderlies, mission catechists, and those working for Europeans as domestics, there was a change in architectural tastes. Many of these men drew attention to their new status and interests by adopting the "coastal" style of rectangular, high-roofed house (with flimsy cane walls and large doors and shuttered windows) that the Administration provided for indigenous personnel on the stations, a kind of building that in earlier days would have been an easy target for nocturnal raiders. The innovators generally located these dwellings, which they shared with their wives and children, beside the main roads or close to European settlements, which in turn tended to be in the lower parts of the valleys.

To summarize (at the risk of some distortion), by about 1960 Central Enga society was in many respects markedly different from the one the first European explorers and Administration officers had encountered. In particular, the incessant and destructive warfare that formerly characterized relations among clans had ceased, although on occasion there were still violent confrontations between descent groups over disputed land boundaries—eruptions, no matter how quickly suppressed, whose intensity and bitterness signaled that at some level all was not well. Meanwhile, most people turned to the CNA's or to moots adjudicated by luluais, waitpus, or Police N.C.Os to deal with their perennial quarrels over land and pigs. Indeed, the readiness of contestants to litigate threatened to overwhelm the courts, for the DDS field staff was still seriously shorthanded.

Also during this period the elaborate ceremonies to propitiate ancestral spirits had lapsed, partly in response to the missionaries' exhortations but largely, according to Enga men, because they were no longer necessary. Clan-wide disasters, such as military defeats or the epidemic illnesses of children and pigs, now seemed unlikely. Similarly, the bachelors' associations ceased to carry out the ceremonies with which they had periodically freed themselves of feminine contamination. Domestic rituals intended to mollify specific ghosts and to cure sickness were less often performed; victims now preferred to visit native medical orderlies in the neighborhood, as well as the Administration and mission hospitals, for treatment. The Te exchange cycle was in disrepair, and its associated magical practices were dismissed as pointless. Other prestations of valuables (now mainly pigs and cash) persisted for the payment of brideprice and of death and homicide compensations; but not only were these being implemented in a more matter-of-fact, if not perfunctory, manner; they were also losing participants among the nominally Christian Enga.

In short, as Mae public life had become less sanguinary, it had also lost much of its color and excitement–in the eyes of many Enga themselves, as well as of outsiders. True, the activities of women had changed little; they were still caught up in the daily round of weeding gardens, harvesting sweet potatoes, and feeding pigs. But men now seemed much more preoccupied with matters that bore on their relationship with Europeans, with the growing of cash crops (especially of coffee), with the sale of food and timber to the missions and the Administration, with securing local jobs, especially as laborers, and with getting their young sons into Government and mission schools to ensure their subsequent employment.

In effect the situation of the Central Enga by 1960 appeared to express a colonial success story—a portrait of a people whose ready acceptance of Western values, attitudes, and technology was somehow solving the social problems that had formerly exercised them, while at the same time they were being prepared for a modest future as pacific peasants secure under the aegis of British justice.

The Return of Violence

9

Clouds on the horizon

A casual visitor to Wabag in 1960 might well have departed the area persuaded that he had encountered a network of sober rural communities whose members were coping satisfactorily with the new order as they industriously cultivated their gardens in an atmosphere of relative tranquility. But, as perceptive Administration officers and missionaries were unhappily aware, this appearance was in many respects illusory; more and more often the façade of placidity was being riven by intergroup disputes over land, which neither formal courts nor informal moots could readily resolve. Ironically enough, the increasing frequency of such confrontations was strongly rooted in conditions engendered by the earlier period of imposed peace and the extension of public services.

From the start, Administration officers had taken the position that the "proper" boundaries of the clans should be those which existed when "Government" first intervened and prohibited warfare in the area. This arbitrary freezing of what had been traditionally, indeed inherently, fluctuating borders affected different clans in different ways. Groups with small or declining populations, whose military weakness would hitherto have exposed them to total or partial eviction by stronger neighbors, were given a new lease on life. Some in fact found themselves in the pleasing situation of having arable land to spare, at least until their numbers began to rise. Small wonder that such clans tended to be strongly pro-"Government" and advocates of the new law. Others, however, took a

156

more jaundiced view. On the one hand there were those groups which had recently lost land by force or chicanery and had been poised to recapture it. On the other hand large or rapidly growing clans that had been extending their limits in order to meet their subsistence needs were now confined to territories that would soon be too small to support all their members. Accordingly, such groups, whether to recover land that they considered rightfully theirs or simply to secure any land at all, were now compelled to go to court to achieve their ends.

This litigation the Central Enga quickly defined as "fighting in the courts," and they regarded the outcomes as equivalent to military victories or losses affecting whole phratries. Thus the men of a growing clan who believed their group required more land would carefully concoct a case, often spurious, against a weaker, non-fraternal neighbor. After patiently rehearsing his followers in the statements they were to make,[1] the Big Man or the luluai took the matter to the kiap with the realistic expectation that the sheer weight of testimony would persuade the overworked officer, who had neither the time nor the facilities to sift all the evidence. The indignant defendants of course argued strenuously in rebuttal, but, given the absence of written land records and the intrinsic difficulty of determining "historical facts" on the basis of assertions about the identities of ancestors said to have planted particular trees in particular spots, it is understandable that resolute lying often carried the day. However the case was decided, the disgruntled losers would soon fabricate a counterclaim (or polish up a valid complaint) against an apparently vulnerable fraternal clan of the victors. If this was not feasible, a brother clan of the defeated group initiated a court action either against the winning clan or against one of the latter's fraternal clans. The basic assumption here was that defeat of any unit of the opponents' phratry could in the long run benefit one's own phratry and, by implication, one's own clan.

Thus, it was not merely that the initial Administration decision to freeze clan boundaries automatically and almost immediately generated a large number of court cases. In addition, such litigation inevitably stimulated retaliatory suits by the losers. It is true that while clansmen were going to court they were less likely to fight physically, and to this extent appeared to support the Administration's ideal of public tranquility; but the spate of litigation over boundaries soon had the kiaps overwhelmed. To hear all such cases in full accordance with the fairly elaborate procedural rules of CNA demanded more time than the handful of hard-pressed officers could take from their other, equally exigent duties of apprehending murderers, patrolling, taking censuses, initiating public works, supervising policemen and compiling horrendously time-consuming reports for district headquarters.

Kiaps tried to deal with the problem in several ways. One was to encourage luluais, paramount luluais, and noncommissioned police officers to hold preliminary hearings on land disputes and to attempt out-of-court conciliation and compromise. To some degree this approach was effective in intraclan quarrels. Where two lineages or subclans were at odds over boundaries, a vigorous and respected luluai could on occasion bring the disputants together and, through the lesser Big Men of their groups, persuade them to reach a settlement. Very rarely a prestigious waitpus could also induce, through the luluais, clans in his own phratry to accept a relatively peaceful, albeit precarious, compromise. But in general, when land was at stake, it was not possible for autonomous clans, even fraternal groups, to come to an agreement. For one thing, the men of a clan could not grant a luluai of the "enemy" group the right to determine their fortunes. For another, they assumed that any decision giving them less than all they claimed was proof that the waitpus or police sergeant had been suborned. Last and most important, the very nature of the issue made it impossible for the parties to agree on the basic "facts" of the case, and, in the context of informal moots, there were no techniques for making independent adjudications of what was or was not evidence.

Such considerations, then, rendered it unlikely that the contestants would wholeheartedly accept any decisions or compromises offered by such arbiters, and indeed the usual outcome of these unofficial hearings was that both parties returned to the kiap, demanding that he deal with the matter. The officer was well aware that if he failed to act, the quarrel could easily escalate into brawling and from that to armed violence, in which case he would have to spend even more time quelling the disturbance and arresting and trying the offenders. In consequence, kiaps devised their own modes of rough-and-ready arbitration, in which they briefly visited the disputed tract, summarily heard out both groups, and then with a compass and chain marked a boundary that seemed reasonable to him and give something to each side.[2] This form of inquiry and decision-making was technically an out-of-court settlement reached by the litigants themselves, a procedure that did not conform to the explicit judicial rules of the CNA and hence was not entered in the court records. Instead the kiap usually made an entry in an unofficial, *ad hoc* register, cursorily identifying the locality in question (not always accurately) and the groups concerned, and noting his decision.

Often enough busy officers who heard many such disputes, especially when on patrol, failed to record the details on their return to the station. Given that in the Wabag Subdistrict (as in most of the highlands) there was a relatively rapid turnover of kiaps, mainly of junior officers, omissions in the registers had significant consequences, which the Enga quickly learned to exploit. Although in general clansmen readily recognized the kiaps' authority and incorruptibility, this knowledge did not make unsuccessful litigants content with their misfortune. They still firmly believed that they were in the right and that they were entitled to recoup their

158

losses, honestly or otherwise. Accordingly, whenever there was a change of officers at Wabag or at any of the patrol posts, clans that had lost earlier decisions, or had secured less land than they thought they deserved, promptly descended on the newcomer to present what purported to be untried cases. With the chaotic state of the registers and, sometimes, the inexperience of the new officer, the plaintiffs stood a fair chance of success. In this way, to my own knowledge, clan titles to some pieces of land were successively reversed as many as four or five times.

During the 1950's the relative inefficiency of this mode of dealing with land, although not without its comical aspects, also served a useful function in defusing, if only temporarily, the potential for intergroup violence. As long as each clan that lost a land decision saw the defeat as one that might soon be retrieved in fresh litigation before a new kiap, it did not feel impelled to take up arms to gain its ends. The men could live with the present adversity while they planned their next moves in court. But, as we shall see, in the 1960's judicial procedures for land cases became increasingly rigid and cumbersome and thus less and less attuned to the people's needs. At that point popular recourse to violent confrontations was less easily averted.

Meanwhile, other factors were exacerbating the difficulties facing the Mae and neighboring Central Enga with respect to land requirements. As I noted earlier, the postwar Administration had perceived that the sheer size and density of this population in relation to its land resources posed problems for the future. Great care was taken, therefore, to limit the alienation of Enga land by outsiders. In contrast to its policy in the eastern highlands, the Administration did not facilitate the establishment of coffee plantations in the Wabag Subdistrict, but through the extension services of the Department of Agriculture, Stock and Fisheries, encouraged Enga to grow coffee in small plots on their clan territories. Indeed, the one European who maintained a plantation (of about forty acres near Wapenamanda) in the 1950's later turned it over to the Lutheran mission, which used it as an agricultural training center for Enga. The only other land that Enga clans sold or ceded on long lease comprised dispersed blocks, on which the Administration placed public utilities (such as patrol posts, schools, agricultural centers) or which the missions acquired (through the Administration) for their bases, schools, and hospitals. By 1960 the total area thus transferred was about 1,200 acres and by 1970 perhaps 1,500 acres—a small although not negligible fraction of the Enga arable land.

At the same time agricultural officers, both Administration and mission, were concerned to introduce additional crops suited to the mountains, which Enga could use to supplement their diet (for instance, Irish potatoes, turnips, cabbages, legumes) or to sell abroad for cash (coffee, table vegetables, pyrethrum). They also brought in European strains of pigs to improve the local herds and initiated small-scale, Enga-owned cattle projects, enabling men to produce more meat for consumption or for sale. In these ways the Administration hoped to increase the region's productivity, both to raise the current standard of living and to provide a safety margin against substantial population growth.[3]

It soon became clear that, whatever such measures might achieve in directly diversifying the Enga diet, in the immediate future they could not generate enough cash to enable families whose numbers were outrunning their land to feed and otherwise supply themselves from the trade stores that had been established in the Subdistrict. Coffee trees did not yield prolifically in the high Enga country, and in any case, coffee prices were steadily declining on the world market. Moreover, as the expatriate residents in the Subdistrict were primarily Administration officers and missionaries whose adult population grew only from about twenty in 1949 to about 100 in 1959, there was little prospect of significant local employment for these Enga. Obviously, most clansmen who wanted jobs would have to seek them elsewhere.

In 1956 the Wabag Subdistrict entered into the recently devised Highlands Labour Scheme. This institution had several explicit goals. It was primarily intended to encourage men from the highlands, especially those without dependents who came from densely populated regions, to sign on for work on coastal and island plantations that were having difficulty securing labor locally. Officers of the Department of Labour recruited the men on two-year contracts with guaranteed wages and supervised their working conditions, payment, and repatriation. In this way the Administration tried, with fair success, to prevent the abuses that had pervaded the prewar system of commercial recruiting and indentures and so make the scheme attractive to highlanders. By facilitating migration the Administration hoped not only to assist the copra and cocoa plantations whose products were significant export commodities, but also to stimulate a flow of cash and skills into the highlands. In addition, although less explicitly, the scheme was intended to drain off from these areas landless and "idle" young men who might otherwise become "troublemakers" at home.

Whereas the scheme worked well enough elsewhere in the highlands, it was never particularly effective in the Wabag Subdistrict. Relatively few Enga were willing to enlist for jobs so far afield. At no time, even in the 1960's, were there more than 500 or so Enga absent on these terms in any year, a tiny fraction of the potential labor force, and fewer still were prepared to sign a second contract. The reasons for this reluctance were clear. As I was told many times, a man residing so far away would worry constantly about his clan's or family's land. How could he learn promptly of enemies' attempts to encroach on the estates of his father or brothers? How could he, given his contractual obligations, leave his work and find

160

the money for airfare in time to help his kinsmen defend their property? In short, young men argued, they should stay home and not risk leaving their families unprotected. Thus, the very circumstance that implementation of the Highlands Labour Scheme among Central Enga was intended to change, namely, the presence of unemployed men ready to resort to violence in land disputes, was for these men a powerful reason for rejecting that scheme.

Later the scheme was further impeded in the Wabag Subdistrict by the reputation Central Enga workers on coastal plantations acquired, whether deservedly or not I do not know, as truculent and intractable troublemakers. Before long plantation managers were informing labor officers at Mount Hagen that they would not accept "those big-headed Engas" on the job, even though in their innocence they were happy to receive contingents of reputedly industrious Fringe Enga men who were recruited, not as "Engas," but under their regional names.

It was not until well into the 1960's that young Enga men began to travel abroad independently in significant numbers to seek employment, and their destinations were confined mainly to the coffee (and later tea) plantations farther east in the highlands and to malaria-control stations there.[4] Even so, there were probably no more than about 1,000 absent from the Wabag Subdistrict in any year. Once again, the emigrants were clear about their motives. As many told me, the money was welcome and the skills they acquired on the plantations could prove useful in the maintenance of their own family coffee plots. Above all, it was easy to take leaves from these jobs, and, with the many motor vehicles now plying the highlands roads, one could return home quickly and cheaply to help clansmen in fights. Indeed, men frequently demonstrated the truth of this assertion. For instance, during my sojourns with my own clan, whenever tension was rising and quarrels were proliferating with neighboring groups over land boundaries, I could be sure that within a few days some young travelers would return and start checking their weapons. The speed with which messages reached these men and the celerity with which they obeyed them were impressive.

Late in the 1960's and into the 1970's there was also a small-scale emigration of Central Enga men and their families, 60 people at most, to the island of Bougainville, where well-paid jobs were available following the development by Bougainville Copper Proprietary Ltd. of an open-cut mine at Panguna. By 1973 it appeared that some of these people were well-established in their occupations and were in no hurry to return to their homeland.

In sum, the number of Central Enga who went abroad to seek work was small relative to the total population, and their movements did little to relieve the overall pressures on land resources. The Administration was aware of this, and, from the late 1950's onward, officers of several departments proposed schemes of varying magnitude for the resettlement of Central Enga families, especially in the outlying lower valleys where the small communities of Fringe Enga lived. None of these recommendations, however, was pushed with great vigor, not only because the annual budgets of the Western Highlands District could not provide the money or the trained personnel to carry out even the most modest of them, but also because, when such suggestions were informally mooted among the Enga, their responses were not encouraging. Most clansmen stated that although they would welcome extra land within reasonable traveling distance of their own territories, they would in no circumstances give up their claims to the latter and move away permanently—an attitude that undercut the whole purpose of resettlement.[5]

Eventually, in the early 1960's, the Administration acquired several tracts of land at Kindeng, Kondapini, and Nondugl in the Wahgi valley east of Mount Hagen, which were subdivided and made available to western highlands families, primarily for the cultivation of cash crops. By 1970 fifty or sixty heads of Central Enga families (especially men of substance) had managed to secure blocks there and were providing intermittent employment for a couple of hundred kinsmen as they grew vegetables for sale at the Mount Hagen market. But none of these people ceded their rights to their natal land. Instead, they commuted regularly between the two areas. Also at this time (about 1969–70), Administration officers at Wabag purchased from Fringe Enga groups in the sparsely settled lower Lai valley two large pieces of land (about 1,800 acres in all), which were to be cut into sections suitable for intensive cattle-raising and offered to Central Enga family groups. In 1973, when I was last in Wabag, shortages of staff and financing were still delaying the implementation of this plan.

While the Administration was making these varied but often tentative and ineffective attempts to grapple with the problems posed by the large Central Enga population, the difficulties themselves were rapidly intensifying. From the late 1950's on there had been a substantial increase in the population, one that was now on the order of 2 to 2.5 percent per annum. This stemmed in part from the imposed peace, which brought a decline in war-related deaths, and in part from the people's more diversified diet. Mainly, however, it reflected the effective extension of health services (hospitals, medicines, local medical orderlies and aid posts) throughout the region, with a concomitant reduction in maternal, infant, and, also significant, porcine mortality. On the other hand, the introduction of cash cropping and of cattle projects not only removed arable land from subsistence cultivation but also redefined and increased the value of land.

In short, the ratio of people to horticultural land was now markedly higher than before pacification—and, most important, the Central Enga were becoming very aware of this. They could see clearly their growing

162

need to utilize insufficiently rested fallow areas and to extend gardens into forest reserves and swamps formerly used for grazing pigs; they also noted the alarming numbers of children underfoot.

With this recognition of greater pressures on critical resources went a perceptible heightening of intergroup tension. Many observers during the 1960's, Administration officers, missionaries, and anthropologists alike, were struck (as were Enga themselves) by the palpable atmosphere of hostility and anxiety that pervaded social relations. Quarrels over land and pigs quickened and brawls became more frequent, as did homicides, housebreaking, and arson, all tendencies aggravated by the availability of liquor following the Administration's legalizing of its sale throughout Papua New Guinea in 1961.

The widespread upsurge of violent behavior brought an obvious reversal of the changes in residence patterns evoked by the recent period of general peace, as well as a contraction of personal mobility. Once more the central clans had to look to their defenses, and the location and style of dwellings again became crucial. Isolated houses and houses near highways and clan borders were easy targets for raiders, and before long there was a perceptible movement of houses back to the safer upper terraces of clan territories. Moreover, buildings in the coastal style were not only ill-suited to the local climate; their flimsy walls offered poor protection against arrows and spears, and their ample doorways invited the entrance of axe-wielding enemies. The sturdier traditional men's and women's houses therefore returned to favor. All that was lacking from the past was the large-scale construction of palisades.

At the same time people once more were wary of journeying alone, and nobody risked passage through the domains of hostile or even neutral clans. Casual visiting noticeably diminished, and men with pressing reasons for travel preferred to move in groups, often armed with axes despite the kiaps' prohibition on carrying weapons abroad. Wayfarers no longer trusted to the Administration's authority to protect them from assault on the highways. If they needed to go to a government station or a mission, they tried to walk with as many companions as possible, or they sought seats in the Enga-owned motor trucks that now took fare-paying passengers. In short, the return of Central Enga to what was in effect their old system of violent self-help was accompanied by a revival of former modes of residence and mobility.

Meanwhile, perhaps in response to the ever-increasing number of disputes over land that field officers had to deal with throughout the highlands districts, the Administration, advised by the Department of Law, instituted changes in adjudication methods. These innovations were not merely procedural; they also shifted jurisdiction over land matters from the kiaps in their role as magistrates in the CNA's to specially created judicial bodies. The history of these modifications is too convoluted to

163

recount here, but the most far-reaching of them was the passage of the Land Titles Commission Ordinance of 1962, which gave the Commission the sole power to hear suits concerning native ownership or use of land.[6]

For the Central Enga the main result of this transfer of authority was the replacement of prompt and easily accessible *ad hoc* arbitration by elaborate, cumbersome, and time-consuming machinery. Whereas arbitration had in its disorganized fashion averted many armed confrontations, the Commission could in fact cope with very few complaints and its determinations were generally unsatisfactory to the litigants. Not the least of the new system's defects was the allocation of only one regional commissioner to handle all the land cases arising in the highlands—a manifest absurdity. In consequence, all local kiaps could do as Enga besieged them with such cases was to promise to bring these to the commissioner's attention when he next came to Wabag, which might not be for months. Moreover, so much in demand was the commissioner that often he had to cut short his sittings after hearing only two or three suits, in order to take up urgent cases in other districts.

Such limitations and postponements soon brought the new style of litigation into disrepute among the Enga, who could not believe that their pressing problems were being taken seriously even by the kiaps whose judgment they formerly had respected. This disenchantment in turn played into the hands of intransigent clansmen, men who believed in using force to achieve immediate solutions. If, as was common, the "stirrers" could persuade their fellow clansmen not to wait for the commissioner's court but to occupy the disputed land, violence followed, and the kiaps and police (still understaffed) had to spend long hours quelling the disturbances.[7] True, the field officers could arrest and imprison the rioters; but by law they could do nothing constructive to settle the issue that led to the confrontation. Their hands were tied, and the hostility between the two groups would smolder on, only to erupt afresh when the convicted men returned home from jail.

Perhaps even more important was the fact that even when the commissioner explicitly decided a particular case, neither party was likely to be satisfied with the verdict. It will be remembered that a crucial feature of the previous informal arbitration was that, like traditional Enga political dealings, it was open-ended. Given the absence of detailed records of land cases and their outcomes, together with the frequent turnover of field officers, the opponents in a dispute could usually renew the struggle and litigate again in the reasonable expectation either of reversing a previous decision or of extending its terms. This perceived flexibility of the old system was compatible with Enga thinking about land boundaries, in which no outcome was accepted as precluding further action by either contestant.

It was precisely in this respect that Central Enga found recourse

164

to the Land Titles Commission unsatisfactory. A commissioner's judicial decision on the definition and location of any land boundary was ideally unequivocal, final, binding, and permanently recorded for future reference, a state of affairs that suited neither the plaintiff nor the defendant. The losers in a land case naturally wanted an opportunity (indeed, the right) to revive the issue at an appropriate time when they might recover the disputed tract; the winners, confirmed in their opinions by their victory, did not want to be prevented from securing more land from adversaries whose weakness had been exposed by their defeat (military metaphors are wholly apt here). Without reactivating the matter through a legal appeal to a higher authority (an expensive and uncertain procedure), neither party could continue with that particular battle in court, and in effect had little choice but to turn to the old patterns of chicanery and forcible dispossession. For all these reasons, then, the Central Enga were increasingly disinclined during the late 1960's to litigate over such important matters as the possession of land, trees, and pigs, and violent self-help became commonplace.

Finally, mention must be made of another administrative innovation that was intended not only to help establish a regular system of "native" land tenure throughout Papua New Guinea but also to aid in settling disputes over the ownership and use of specific domains. In 1965 the Land Titles Commission was empowered to create across the whole country "areas of adjudication," within each of which several "demarcation committees" were to be set up. It fell to the district commissioners and their field officers to define the adjudication areas in their districts and to devise feasible methods for selecting (or electing) the committees. Each committee was to comprise no fewer than three members, the majority of whom were to be native residents.[8]

In the Wabag Subdistrict the adjudication areas were made to coincide more or less with the boundaries of the existing Local Government Councils (a reasonable decision on the part of overworked officers), and the Councils played an important role in proposing members for the demarcation committees. Indeed, almost without exception, the committee members (confirmed in their office by the Commission in 1966) were local government councillers, that is, mainly mature men of status in their own clans, many of them former Big Men and luluais. Moreover, the Councils agreed to pay the chairman of each committee a small weekly stipend in compensation for the time lost from personal affairs.

The Land Titles Commission intended each committee to work systematically through its section of the adjudication area, defining and indicating with permanent markers the recognized boundaries, first of the larger local groups such as clans, and later of their constituent units, which in the Enga case could be subclans, lineages, or families. The bounded domains were then to be surveyed accurately (by whom was never really made clear—trained surveyors were in short supply), and the information on location and ownership recorded in district land registers that would eventually make up a national register. In the event that particular groups or men could not agree upon the common boundaries or the rightful ownership of certain tracts of land, the committee was to call on knowledgeable men of the neighborhood for independent evidence and advice, while at the same time it attempted to persuade the adversaries to accept the committee's demarcation. Differences that could not be reconciled were to be adjudicated by the Land Titles Commissioner. In this way it was hoped that relatively prompt out-of-court settlements would be reached through informal arbitration and that fewer land cases would fall to the hard-pressed commissioner.

Obviously, given the circumstances that were then exercising the Central Enga, there was little likelihood that demarcation committees could achieve the goals set them. It does seem that at first the Mae committees undertook their duties conscientiously and with the best intentions. Thoughtful members were perturbed by the increasing incidence of violent confrontations over land and by the climate of hostility that was blighting social relationships, and they were willing to try the new scheme as something that might help. Accordingly, with the aim of attracting public support by chalking up some early successes, the Mae committees began by dealing with clan boundaries, especially those between fraternal groups, over which agreement was likely to be reached without delay. There were, however, all too few of these relatively easy tasks, and before long they had to pass on to the difficult ones.

Almost at once the committees were in serious trouble. Inevitably people viewed each public discussion as a legal proceeding, in which the contending groups firmly rejected all suggestions of arbitration or conciliation and were concerned only to reiterate vehemently what they asserted were their rightful claims to their opponents' land. Whenever the committee members proposed what seemed to them a fair boundary, the group that saw itself as the loser announced that the other party must have bribed the committee (with pigs or cash) to make such an outrageous determination. Sometimes both clans, equally disgruntled, launched such accusations. Either way there was no hope of reaching a peaceful decision, and the dispute had to be referred to the commissioner for a future hearing. In many cases, when the disputing groups were adversaries of long standing, either or both simply refused to heed the committee's summons to attend a demarcation meeting, stating that the committee had no authority over their land. The committee could return to a location several times to no avail. None of the landholders would appear. Moreover, although the committees were empowered to have police enforce attendance, they were reluctant to do so, believing rightly that such an action would only provoke a bloody confrontation between the two clans.

166

The Administration officers were also unwilling to push these issues; the CNA's and the jail could not have coped with the consequences. It is not surprising that the committee members' enthusiasm for their task quickly waned. By 1970 they were attempting very few demarcations, and these only perfunctorily, for they well know that the groups concerned would not abide by any decision that did not suit them.

Obviously, the deployment of demarcation committees among the Central Enga achieved little or nothing. Not only were the committees unable to contribute anything of significance to the land register, they also failed lamentably in their role as informal arbiters. Their presence did not reduce the number of violent interclan disputes over land. Indeed, in the opinion of many Mae and of some Administration officers, far from alleviating the peoples' preoccupation with these problems, the very actions of the committees stimulated overt quarrels over land boundaries that otherwise might not have come to a head. I am inclined to agree with this view.

However that may be, from the early 1960's onward the Central Enga displayed an increasing tendency to take matters into their own hands and to turn to physical force to settle their land disputes. In the circumstance they could hardly do otherwise. The escalation of violence can readily be verified by perusal of the CNA records for this period, as well as the annual reports to the district headquarters from the Wabag, Lagaipu and, later, Wapenamanda Subdistricts. In the latter one can perceive the growing urgency with which the Administration officers reported their observations of a steadily deteriorating situation.

In the earlier reports (around 1960) there were references to sporadic brawls and the riotous behavior of men contesting the occupation of garden lands, disturbances that the limited numbers of kiaps and police could resolve relatively easily while coping with their other multifarious duties. Ten years later the reports spoke almost with desperation of the failure of crop innovations, of labor migration, of settlement schemes, and of new legal procedures to ameliorate local conditions. None of the officers doubted that the swelling tide of violence was correlated with the rapid growth of the large Central Enga population, which was outrunning its horticultural resources. They noted that most of the confrontations involved groups among the dense population that exploited the valleys of the Lai and upper Lagaipu rivers between Wapenamanda and Laiagama, whereas the sparsely settled Fringe Enga in the outlying areas were less preoccupied with land issues and in general fought less often.

Thus the reports of the late 1960's referred to the frequent outbreaks of large-scale, organized warfare between central clans, which the few available officers and police had more and more difficulty in controlling as combatants either ignored their presence or fired arrows at them to discourage their intervention. In the face of this "complete disregard for law and order," the kiaps were now forced to devote more time and energy to trying to contain these battles than to their other tasks, and they often had to summon the special riot squads stationed at Mount Hagen to help them disperse the warring groups.

I turn now to a description and analysis of warfare in which Central Enga, including the Mae, have been engaged in recent years.

The resurgence of warfare

The data I present here refer to sixty armed conflicts in which various Enga clans were engaged between late 1961 and late 1973. They mainly concern Central Enga, but some Fringe Enga disputes are included. These are by no means all the violent confrontations that occurred among local groups in these years, and the period 1961–69 is underrepresented. Nevertheless, I believe that overall my material represents a significant proportion of the collisions that took place during the twelve years. The evidence for the cases in the sample is drawn both from my own inquiries and, importantly, from Administration records held at Wabag, Laiagama, and Wapenamanda. The accounts of particular clashes vary in depth of detail, for instance with respect to the phratry affiliations of contending groups, duration of combat, and the number of casualties, so that I have had to abstract several subsamples from the larger corpus in order to answer different questions. I am confident, however, that the conclusions I reach hold for the state of affairs existing among the Central Enga, including the Mae, at that time.

Before I tabulate these data, I shall indicate the form that this fighting has taken; and in this I can be brief, because in many basic respects the pattern of recent warfare among Central Enga resembles the traditional pattern described earlier. True, some technological innovations are apparent, such as the reliance on steel rather than on stone axes (although as yet not on firearms), experimentation with arrows and shields, the participation of some men who, as trained medical orderlies, fight by day and, with purloined drugs, treat their wounded clansmen by night. At the same time, the account given above of, for instance, the ways clan assemblies decide on war or peace, the planning and execution of strategy, the implementation of tactics in the field, the scale and intensity of combat—all this holds good for contemporary warfare. Given that a relatively large number of men who were warriors before are again actively fighting and devising strategy and tactics twenty years later (1973), this should not be surprising. Their aims have changed little, if at all.

The main difference between past and present warfare concerns the duration and outcome of engagements, and this is directly attributable to the intervention of Administration forces. Traditionally, war between

168

clans had its own "natural" course of development, leading either to a stalemate, or, more commonly, to a partial or complete victory for the aggressors. The sequence of events might take weeks or months to reach its conclusion. Nowadays, depending on the numbers of combatants and of officers and police, outbreaks of fighting are usually contained within one to four days, as the authorities break up the contingents of warriors into smaller groups and arrest as many as they can.

Moreover, the continuing presence of police in the area, sometimes for weeks after the battles, effectively prevents the invading clan, at least for the time being, from holding the land it has overrun. Initially successful groups therefore view the actions of the police as an unwarranted interference, which not only denies them the fruits of a well-earned victory but also unfairly furthers their enemies's interests. More particularly, if either side has incurred deaths in the fighting, it wishes to continue until these are avenged. In consequence, a disgruntled clan is likely to wait until the police have gone and its men have returned from jail, when it strikes again to settle what it sees as unfinished business. Indeed, as long as the pressures on home resources remain, a growing clan has little choice but to reopen hostilities with weaker neighbors. As a result, there are several notorious Central Enga "trouble spots," centers of high population density where, despite frequent Administration intervention and scores of jail sentences, warfare has erupted almost annually between the same groups.

It may also be that, in the absence of alternative solutions to these peoples' problems, constant reliance on the police to choke off confrontations merely increases the ferocity with which the next round is fought. Men remark on the readiness of combatants nowadays to mutilate fallen enemies, and they say that formerly this practice was less common. The casualty rates and the incidence of arson and other destruction of property in these curtailed conflicts support popular opinion.

Since the late 1960's the manner in which police have been employed to control intergroup fighting among Central Enga has altered, partly in response to the growing intensity of warfare, partly because of changes in the deployment and command of police throughout the country. Especially important has been the creation of specially trained mobile riot squads, several of which have been allocated to centers such as Mount Hagen to deal with the now endemic public disorder in the highlands.[9]

Until that time the task of quelling disturbances in the Wabag Subdistrict had devolved on the few officers and the local police. The duties of the police were varied. Not only did they arrest offenders at the kiaps' direction, they also accompanied the latter on patrols, supervised labor engaged in public works, manned the jails, and heard informal courts. There was a policy (unofficial I believe) of assigning police outside their home districts to remove them from pressures that might have induced corruption or injustice. However, some served long terms among the Enga and a few married Enga women, circumstances that could lead to their active participation in local affairs.

By and large the relations of the police with the Enga were tolerably friendly. The Enga viewed their behavior with amiable cynicism, frequently included them in prestations of wealth, and, whenever they could, tried to exploit to their own advantage the foreigners' connections with the kiaps. Some police, such as efficient noncommissioned officers or men married to clanswomen, were indeed treated with respect. The general absence of pronounced hostility toward the police greatly facilitated the maintenance of order during the period of peace, and, even for some time after conditions worsened and violence increased, few Enga saw these locally based police as the enemy. Rather, they regarded them as a minor nuisance. The police in turn, except for a few martinets, were not inclined to provoke Enga unnecessarily. They depended on local people for luxuries and services that made life in the field more comfortable, they drank with Enga men in the council clubs, and they knew that Administration authority could not in the long run protect them from the retaliation of clansmen whom they pushed too hard. In short, the police and the Enga developed over the years an intentionally ambiguous but satisfactory *modus vivendi*.

From the earliest days, however, Administration officers had complained, with good reason, that they were never allocated enough police to carry out all the tasks assigned them. And as the Enga and European populations grew, public services expanded and duties diversified and multiplied, the police establishment became relatively less adequate, in terms both of numbers and of the proportion of experienced constables. Thus, in 1946, when civil administration was resumed, there were 21 policemen in the original Wabag Subdistrict. By 1956 these had been increased to 68, and in 1965 there were 66 policemen (including 24 prison warders) in the new, smaller Wabag Subdistrict and forty in the recently created Lagaipu Subdistrict. Up to this point the kiaps and police, by working long hours, were able more or less to meet every-day administrative demands. But in succeeding years the number of police among the Enga actually declined as constables were diverted from the highlands to cope with emerging problems elsewhere, such as the rising crime rates in the rapidly growing coastal towns. By 1970, although there were now 46 police in the Lagaipu Subdistrict, the Wabag Subdistrict, whose 87,000 inhabitants included most of the Central Enga, had only 26 field police and 31 prison warders.

The situation deteriorated. As the frequency and scale of interclan confrontations increased among Central Enga, the limited resources of the kiaps and police were stretched too thin for them to control all the clashes promptly. In addition, the paucity of field staff raised serious legal

170

difficulties with respect to the rules of evidence in the CNA. In the swirling confusion that marked the engagements of hundreds of disguised warriors it was well-nigh impossible for outsiders to secure positive identifications of more than a few participants, identifications that would meet the requirements of a court in which the arresting kiap could not serve as magistrates. In effect the court had to depend largely on the defendants' willingness to admit their guilt, an anomaly Enga soon learned to turn to their own advantage. It became common for a clan that was ready to cease fighting to select some of its younger men to surrender as scapegoats in order to speed the departure of the police. Thus, valued fight leaders and experienced warriors stood a better chance of evading arrest and of being available to renew the struggle. In any case, no matter who was arrested as a combatant, in the absence of solid evidence there was almost no way prosecuting officers could obtain indictments for such grave offenses as homicide, grievous wounding, or arson. The usual outcome of the trials was the conviction of several unimportant clansmen on charges of riotous behavior. Since their sentences could only be for six to twelve months in jail, the fear of arrest hardly served as a deterrent to groups that were determined to attack their neighbors.

The perceived inability of the Administration to deal severely with existing public disturbances not only stimulated other clans to take matters into their own hands but also encouraged them to disregard the kiaps and police when these did attempt to intervene. More and more often the warriors of invading forces who scented victory discharged arrows at the intruders, both officers and police, and warned them to stand aside until they had finished fighting. Only when they had occupied the land they claimed or avenged outstanding deaths, they said, would they yield men for arrest. Sometimes, when contending groups were evenly matched and the issue remained in doubt, both sides would shoot at the police.

These reactions placed the kiaps in an impossible position. They were, as agents of the law, bound to continue their endeavors to prevent bloodshed, but their numbers were too few and their former moral authority was rapidly eroding. Shots fired in the air no longer intimidated anyone, and the recently issued tear-gas projectiles were ineffective against swarms of mobile warriors sweeping up and down the mountainsides. At the same time stringent official sanctions forbade their using firearms directly against the combatants except in the direst emergency. A kiap who killed an Enga in these or indeed in any circumstances knew he would face a formal trial, and, even if he were exonerated, would probably find his career permanently blighted. Similarly, he would be culpable if he placed his policemen in jeopardy and any were killed while obeying his orders to hold their fire.[10]

With all these constraints, there was little the exasperated kiaps and police could do except hover on the outskirts of the battles, seizing such stray warriors as came their way, while they waited for the initial flush of fighting to subside. Then they tried to get between the contending groups, to hold them apart as they attempted to identify and arrest participants, especially the leaders and "stirrers." Sometimes two or three days elapsed before the officers could intervene physically, and even then, if 400 or 500 men were opposed over a wide area, combat might continue between detached units in several sectors of the front as arrests were being made elsewhere. When finally the skirmishing slowed to a halt and the warriors who had not been taken (usually the majority) slipped away into the forests or into territories of friendly clans to plan their next moves, small detachments of police occupied the disputed areas, often for weeks. Their presence was intended to discourage fresh outbreaks, while their patrols also scoured the neighborhood in search of escaped culprits. Angry police were understandably ungentle in their interrogations of local people, and, when they took prisoners, handled them roughly. Such behavior further hardened attitudes among the Enga, reinforcing their intransigence. No wonder then that the official reports frequently referred to the apparent decline of the people's respect for law and order.

In the early 1970's the Administration implemented changes in the functioning of rural courts and police, that were aimed at relieving the intolerable burden on the officers and at increasing the efficiency of the legal institutions. Thus, a full-time European magistrate and two Enga assistant magistrates were posted to Wabag to hasten the hearing of court cases.[11] An experienced district officer was also charged with the task of identifying impending interclan disputes and of attempting to head them off with informal conciliation or arbitration. When armed confrontations did occur, his job was to pick up the pieces afterward, especially to persuade adversaries to offer prompt payment of homicide compensation and restitution for the destruction of property such as coffee plots and trade stores, in order to remove at least some of the reasons for fighting again.[12]

Command of the field constabulary was transferred to a European police officer, who had a small Criminal Investigation Branch unit to aid him in his inquiries. The strength of the police detachment was somewhat augmented, but more significantly, efficient communication procedures were devised to ensure that any or all of four squads of mobile riot police (about 120 men in all, directed by Europeans officers) could quickly be flown from Mount Hagen to quell major outbreaks of fighting. Provision was made for their remaining in the Subdistrict for as long as it took to cope with recurring or extended conflicts.

These innovations had not long been in operation when I last conducted research in the area in 1973, and my information concerning the situation in my absence has been limited. Moreoever, one would not expect the changes to have immediate effects. Nevertheless, some interim assessment of their consequences can be offered. The presence of a full-time magistrate and a police officer (with his CIB aides) apparently did help check the surge of violence and crimes against property in the environs of the "townships" (the former Administration stations), much of which was directly related to a growing consumption of alcohol and to gambling. The important factor here was the professional speed with which offenders were apprehended, tried, and sentenced to terms in the new jail at Baisu, near Mount Hagen.[13]

The release of the kiaps from such duties enabled them to devote more time to investigating and trying to compose disputes over land that were coming to a head, and this frequent showing of the flag may well have averted some potential clashes. At any rate the officers were now in a better position to intervene quickly in armed conflicts and to summon riot police promptly when matters got out of hand. Finally, the ready availability of the mobile squads apparently was beginning to act as a deterrent, however partial, to interclan warfare. For instance, whereas in 1972 there were at least 17 serious outbreaks of fighting among Central Enga clans, in 1973 (until October) there were only about nine.

This decline, however, is not to be attributed simply to the superior efficiency or expertise of the riot police. Essentially, they were trained in techniques for containing urban disorders and, even with their specialized equipment, they were not at their best when called on to control hundreds of fleet-footed, experienced warriors who were maneuvering on their native heath. Riot police, like the kiaps and regular police, were forbidden to fire on combatants. They could use tear gas, an unreliable aid in open countryside, but for the rest batons and shields were their arms. Enga men told me emphatically that, in head-on collisions, they were certain they could hold their own against the riot squads. Nevertheless, whenever the latter were brought in, with the assistance of local police, they eventually broke up the clansmen's forces, choked off the fighting, and made arrests. The main reason for their success seems to lie in their numbers and their persistence. Once established on the battlefield they could hold the adversaries apart and systematically harry them, dispatching parties to pursue fleeing warriors. At the same time, Enga told me, they treated noncombatants in the area, the dependents of the participants, with considerable brutality. Before long men were prepared to surrender rather than endure such harassment and, equally important, see their families suffer.[14]

However effective these various innovations may have been in reducing the incidence of warfare, they were at best treating the symptoms of the problem facing the Enga, not the problem itself—namely, the persisting popular view that land resources were in critically short supply. I return to this issue later.

Cases in point

To illuminate the tables that follow and also to support my contention that recent warfare among the Central Enga significantly resembles that of the past, I briefly describe a confrontation between Mae groups that occurred in 1971. The case is typical of many that appear in Tables 12–16.

The two owners of the quarrel were neighbors, and at the time clan A of phratry I had about 320 members and clan T of phratry II about 230. For several years in the late 1930's and early 1940's these clans had combined to attack and finally to oust a weak contiguous clan (now extinct) of phratry III, whose land and trees they partitioned. There was, however, a small but productive arable tract (perhaps twenty acres) on the new, common border about which they could not agree. Although from the beginning clan A occupied this portion, clan T refused to recognize the *fait accompli* and from time to time attempted to cultivate fallow land or to build houses there. These incursions led to constant arguments, culminating in hectic brawls in which clan A would drive out the squatters. The confrontations continued into the 1950's, and men of both clans were several times jailed for riotous behavior. In 1956 an Administration officer arbitrated the issue on the spot and, after hearing spokesmen of both groups, awarded most of the land to clan A largely on the basis of prior occupation. More disputes and arrests followed, and 1960 another kiap went there to adjudicate the matter. Once again the verdict favored clan A.

Believing that "Government" had verified the essential rightness of its position, clan A was willing to live in peace with its neighbors, but clan T persisted in its demands. Brawling and retaliatory pig thefts continued, more often initiated by disgruntled clansmen of T with the result that each time more of them were imprisoned than men of clan A. These outcomes further infuriated the leading men of clan T, who saw them as an unbroken series of humiliating defeats and worked on the passions of their followers.

By 1970 the situation had deteriorated sorely, and normal intercourse between the groups was at an end. Both had evacuated their women's houses around the disputed area, and younger men patrolled regularly. Clansmen of A were sure that stirrers in clan T would soon force an armed confrontation, something they wished to avoid. Not only did they believe they could retain the land if the issue remained in the courts, but also, with many young men away at work, they feared that a military action would cost them dearly. Early in 1971 men of clan T began tilling gardens on the disputed land, while their leaders tried unsuccessfully to persuade the local demarcation committee to define a new boundary to their advantage. Spokesmen of clan A at once went to the senior kiap in Wabag and charged the intruders with trespass. He called in the two groups several times in attempts to achieve some kind of conciliation and eventually visited the site to hear the matter. The men of clan T flatly rejected all the officer's suggested compromises. He finally gave a decision for clan A and warned the men of T to leave peacefully or face arrest. He then returned to Wabag.

That same day clan T armed and swept in force over the border, felling trees and burning houses of clan A. The men of A mobilized and sent many of their families and pigs to shelter with relatives; but, having "won" the arbitration, they were still reluctant to retaliate with violence. When, however, the police and kiaps arrived, alerted by the smoke, clan T refused to withdraw and continued its destructive rampage. By then dozens of trees were down, gardens torn up, and 14 houses in flames. Clan A could stand no more. Attacking vigorously, they pushed back clan T, and, outflanking the enemy, crossed the border and put 15 of its houses to the torch.[15] The police fired tear gas and shots in the air to no avail. The fighting went on furiously until dusk, when both sides withdrew to safe positions. Many men had been wounded with arrows, including allies from clans nearby. Clan A already had at least a dozen casualties among its own sixty or seventy warriors.

Each group patrolled through the night and its medical orderlies patched up the injured. During the night, an ally of clan T died of an arrow wound in the groin. Incensed, his comrades returned to the battle at dawn and struck deep into clan A's territory. Soon the men of T sent up the victory shout as they cut down and dismembered a wounded ally of clan A, a sister's son from the fraternal clan D I. Clan A retrieved the corpse and rallied strongly. Heavy fighting went on all day as allies streamed in to aid each side. At least 18 men of Clan A and its allies were wounded that day, some several times. One, an ally, died of his wounds about four months later. By now riot police and officers from Mount Hagen had joined the local kiaps and police but were unable to contain the combat, which raged until darkness fell. Both forces were determined to avenge their dead and to secure the disputed land. The authorities had to stand aside and watch the action as they tried to identify combatants for later arrest.

Fighting resumed at dawn on the third day and before long clan A was getting the better of it, pressing its enemies back to the border and threatening the territory of clan T. At this a group of men from the neighboring clan F of phratry III who had been assisting clan A suddenly changed sides. Clan F was no friend of clan A, for the two had long disputed their common boundary and had several times gone to war over it. These men of F had unenthusiastically supported A because the father's mother of the Big Man of their lineage had been a clanswoman of A and they maintained exchange relations with some men of that clan. However, the mother of one of the men of F was from clan T, and they feared for the safety of her agnates, whom they now went to help.

Men of clan A were angered by this duplicity and singled out the defaulters for particular attention. They soon managed to shoot the Big Man in the belly, a wound from which he was lucky to recover. Hearing the news, other men of clan F, who so far had remained neutral, charged across the undefended border of clan A and burned four houses before defenders could muster to push them out. Meanwhile the remainder of the combined forces of A and its allies, despite taking many casualties, were able to hold those of T at the other border until nightfall.

The 500 or so warriors entered the fray again on the fourth day. Although the tempo of the fighting was slowing as tired men felt the effects of their wounds, the police were still unable to halt them. In the morning a party from clan A buried in a safe place the ally from clan D I who had been killed on the second day. Inflamed by the funeral oratory, the forces of A counterattacked savagely and before long cut off a detachment of the enemy, several of whom they wounded and one, an ally of clan T, they slew. The killers dismembered and mutilated the victim, cutting off his penis and fixing it in his mouth (a traditional embellishment) before throwing the remains to the police for disposal. The victory songs spurred on the dead man's comrades, but for all their outrage they could not dislodge the men of A and their allies from their positions on the border before daylight failed.

On the fifth morning, as the weary combatants once more moved into action, the officers judged that the time was right for a strenuous effort to break up the groups of warriors. When the police charged the lines in force, the men of clan A, exhausted and suffering many casualties, were ready to call a halt. They had reoccupied the land that they believed rightfully theirs and, also important, they and their supporters had killed two of the enemy against the loss of only one "brother." The leaders of clan A thereupon told their allies to withdraw promptly to escape arrest, while they informed the kiaps that they were satisfied with the outcome and would fight no more. They then surrendered as prisoners ("rioters") 13 young men whom they had already asked to volunteer as scapegoats. These were chosen on the grounds that each had few or no immediate dependents and that no two came from the same family. Indeed, one man offered himself because his current disability (twisted knees) had prevented his fighting and he felt he owed his clansmen a service for defending his land.

Meanwhile, the men of clan T and their supporters, incensed by the imbalance of deaths and by their failure to hold the territory they had invaded, announced their intention of continuing the combat. This intransigence called down on them the full strength of the exasperated riot police and by the end of the day they were dispersed, with 29 of them (including allies) being arrested.

The sequel to this sanguinary engagement was that the special police were billeted in the area, which they patrolled for about six weeks, until officers thought it safe to remove them. The men who had been arrested were sentenced to six to twelve months imprisonment with hard labor in Baisu jail. Popular opinion in clan A was that these men actually got the best of the bargain. While they were eating well and sleeping peacefully in jail, their clansmen at home had to spend anxious nights guarding the border lest the irate men of clan T struck again without warning.

Throughout all this, Administration officers, assisted by an Enga representative in the national House of Assembly, worked to negotiate payments of homicide compensation by the owners of the quarrel. Later in 1971 the men of clan A gave an interim installment of about sixty pigs to the clansmen of D I for the ally who had died in their cause, and clansmen of T gave compensation (I do not know how much) to each of the two clans that had lost a man helping them. Then, under the supervision of a kiap, clan A handed over 122 cooked pigs to both the allied groups of clan T, while at the same assembly clan T (with no good grace) gave 110 cooked pigs to clan D I. Later that year, when another ally of clan A died of his wounds, clan A distributed fifty or sixty pigs to his agnates. In the absence of pressure from the kiaps, clan T refused to make any payment for this death, asserting (correctly) that in the past a clan was not bound to offer compensation when it killed allies of its enemies. Finally, on 1973 clan A gave as the definitive ally compensation to its fraternal clan D I the enormous amount of 219 pigs, one cassowary, and Australian $692 (then worth about $900 U.S.).

All of which in effect settled nothing. Clan T in no way relinquished its claim to the disputed land, and men of clan A were still constantly on the alert for another attack.

I now present in tabular form data bearing on interclan fighting among Enga between 1961 and 1973. Although the tables are largely self-explanatory with respect to what was happening in those years, they should be compared with tables 1 and 5 (pp. 13 and 109) which summarize analogous features of traditional Enga warfare. In this way we may see more clearly the important continuities and differences between the two periods.

The figures in Table 12 refer to confrontations among both Central and Fringe Enga groups. Moreover, these are certainly not all the outbreaks of fighting that occurred in these areas during this period.[16] Nevertheless, the temporal distribution of the sample cases clearly shows the erosion of the general peace in the late 1960s, as the available modes of litigation proved less and less adequate to settle disputes over land. Moreover, comparison of the categories and frequencies in Table 12 with those in Table 1 (the "traditional" situation) indicates a substantial increase in the later period in the significance of land disputes as a primary stimulus to intergroup violence (see Table 13). In the light of what we know of the recent growth of the Enga population and of other social changes, this difference is to be expected.

177

Table 12 Ostensible reasons for warfare among Enga clans, 1961—1973

Ostensible reasons

Year	Land	Pig theft	Homicide	Brideprice	Others and uncertain[a]	Total
1973	7	—	1	—	1	9
1972	17	2	3	1	1	24
1971	7	—	—	2	—	9
1970	6	—	—	1	—	7
1969	3	—	—	—	—	3
1968	1	—	—	—	—	1
1967	—	—	—	—	1	1
1966	—	—	—	—	2	2
1965	1	—	—	—	1	2
1964	—	—	—	—	—	—
1963	1	—	—	—	—	1
1962	—	—	—	—	—	—
1961	1	—	—	—	—	1
Total	44	2	4	4	6	60
%	73.3	3.3	6.6	6.6	10	100

[a]The following reasons were each cited once: assault, pandanus theft, Te payment, and death payment. In two cases the reason was uncertain.

Table 13 Reasons for Enga warfare, c.1900—1950 and 1961—1973

Period	Ostensible Reasons				
	Land	Other property	Homicide	Other	Total
c.1900–1950	41	17	11	2	71
%	57.7	23.9	15.5	2.8	100
1961–1973	44	9	4	3	60
%	73.3	15.0	6.6	5.5	100

With respect to the distribution of cases among the various Enga areas (see Table 14), the frequency of fighting in general is, as might be predicted, higher in the densely populated territories of the Central Enga than in the sparsely occupied territories of the Fringe Enga. However, and this is somewhat surprising, the sample shows little difference between the two categories of Enga with regard to the proportion of warfare arising out of land disputes. It is difficult to say whether this similarity is a mere artifact of selective reporting in the Administration records or

178

Table 14 Frequency of warfare among Enga clans, 1961—1973, by region and by ostensible reasons

Region	Ostensible reasons					
	Land	Pigs	Homicide	Other	Uncertain	Total
Central Enga	37	2	4	5	2	50
%	74	4	8	10	4	100
Fringe Enga	7	—	—	3	—	10
%	70	—	—	30	—	100

whether it actualltects an increased preoccupation of growing Fringe populations with land matters. I believe it to be the latter.

For 38 of the sample of fifty Central Enga conflicts, the affiliations of the owners of the quarrel can be reliably identified (see Table 15). Here again interesting differences emerge when these figures are compared with those from Table 1, differences that are readily understandable in the light of the changes discussed above. Whereas in the past (c.1900–1950), less than 40 percent of the armed confrontations took place within the phratry, more recently (1961–73) 50 percent of them have been between fraternal clans. On the other hand, whereas 10 percent of the fights previously opposed subclans of the same clan, nowadays no such warfare is reported. I believe that here we are observing the differential effects on Central Enga social organization of the groups' growing concern over resources. Clans that formerly were guided to some extent by fraternal comity in choosing the directions in which they pushed back their boundaries can no longer afford the luxury. Now a group is more likely to go after any land that appears open to encroachment. By the same token, clans nowadays are experiencing such serious pressures that they see

Table 15 Affiliations of contending groups among the Central Enga

Contending groups	Period		
	c.1900–1950	1961–1973	Total
Clans of different phratries	44	19	63
%	62.0	50.0	57.8
Clans of same phratry	20	19	39
%	28.2	50.0	35.8
Subclans of same clan	7	—	7
%	9.8	—	6.4
Total	71	38	109
%	100	100	100

179

themselves as being surrounded by rapacious enemies, against whom they cannot relax their guard and to whom they dare not expose any internal weakness. As I have often heard men say, this is no time for the clan's constituent groups to fight among themselves for any reason. In short, the heightening of the struggle for land has acted to enhance the solidarity of the Central Enga clan while undermining the cohesiveness of the super-ordinate phratry.

Finally, I abstract from the larger sample of Enga confrontations between 1961 and 1973 several sets of data that give us (in Table 16) an

Table 16   Features of Enga warfare, 1961–1973

	Central Enga	Fringe Enga	All
Number of warriors engaged			
Number of cases	29	4	33
Total number of warriors	10,540	650	11,190
Mean number of warriors	360	160	340
Range	50-1,000	50-250	50-1,000
Duration of conflict (days)			
Number of cases	40	5	45
Total number of days	58	7	65
Mean number of days	1.4	1.4	1.4
Range	1-4	1-2	1-4
Number of deaths in combat			
Number of cases	46	10	56
Total number of deaths	72	4	76
Mean number of deaths	1.6	0.4	1.3
Range	0-7	0-1	0-7
Number wounded in combat			
Number of cases	25	8	33
Total number wounded	490	100	590
Mean number wounded	19	12	18
Range	5-75	4-35	4-75
Number of houses burned			
Number of cases	33	—	33
Total number burned	425	—	425
Mean number burned	13	—	13
Range	0-77	—	0-77

Note: All numbers except numbers of cases are estimates.

overall view of significant features of recent warfare, some of which may be compared with the evidence from earlier times. Several points may be made here. First, some of the figures given in Table 16 obviously and seriously underestimate the true state of affairs. For instance, men do not parade their wounds before the authorities to be counted, for these would be *prima facie* evidence of their status as combatants and so render them liable to arrest. Similarly, it is difficult to assess with any accuracy the subsequent mortality rate among the wounded. By and large, in this kind of sampling one can only include those who succumb shortly after the conflict.

Nevertheless, the figures given here for casualties and for arson can be regarded as a conservative index of the extent of the death and destruction accompanying present-day warfare among the Enga (and that without even attempting to estimate the substantial losses of pigs, trees, and garden crops). The evidence indicates that, despite the intervention of Administration officers and police, the Central Enga are still conducting warfare in much the same way and on much the same scale as they did in the past. And, as the other tables demonstrate, their reasons for doing so have not materially altered; they have simply become more pressing.

Epilogue

10

The evidence I have set forth demonstrates that among the Central Enga, in the present as in the past, the desire of local descent groups to gain and to hold arable land has been the most powerful motive impelling them to make war on each other. On occasion the immediate provocation may be the obligation to avenge a killing or a dispute over movable property; but, as Enga men plainly state, most of these confrontations are symptomatic of a deeper enmity generated by the adversaries' continuing endeavors to encroach on each other's land. The prevalence of this pattern naturally raises the question, Why in these communities is land so highly valued? Why are clansmen willing to go to such painful lengths to defend or appropriate it?

Enga men have no doubt about their reasons. We must have the land, they say, to feed our people and our pigs. The land is the basis (root, cause) of everything important in our lives. A clan whose territory is too small cannot expect to survive. It is not simply that its members may go hungry in bad seasons; they will also be vulnerable to the pressures of neighboring groups. A clan that lacks sufficient land cannot produce enough of the crops and the pigs needed to obtain the wives who are to bear future warriors to guard its domains and daughters whose brideprice will secure mates for their "brothers." Other groups do not dispose of their women simply to establish affinal connections of dubious worth; they seek a more rewarding investment. And without wives, how can this clan tend its gardens and pigs? How can we contribute sufficiently to exchanges of

182

pigs to attract military and economic support in times of trouble? Therefore, men say, a clan has no choice but to use all means at its command to acquire more land as quickly as possible, or it will have a short life.

Assertions in this vein unambiguously proclaim the Enga view of the universe and of their own motives for acting as they do, and the evidence I have adduced is in general consistent with these statements. Nevertheless, the Enga here are advancing an essentially "sociological" analysis of the circumstances that give rise to interclan fighting, that is, they generally invoke social (including political and economic) circumstances to account for each outbreak. Perhaps their explanations simply reflect a culture-bound definition of relative scarcity, i.e., a definition in terms of their society's traditional system of values, in which local groups maximize their prestige and political influence by expanding prestations of wealth and extending territorial boundaries. Given such expectations, then land, like pigs and other valuables, must always be in short supply relative to the culturally approved aspirations of clansmen. But recognition of this truism does not answer the kind of question a hard-nosed exponent of cultural materialism might wish to ask, namely, whether in any "objective" sense of the phrase the Central Enga really have been short of land. For instance, have clans, even in the most densely populated areas, been so lacking in arable land that they have been driven to seize land by force to ensure that their members do not starve?

Obviously, we cannot specify the nutritional status and horticultural productivity of Central Enga clans in earlier times. Indeed, in the absence of intensive, reasonably representative, and sophisticated studies of demography, health, diet, cultivation regimes, and monetary incomes throughout the region, little more than informed guesses can be offered about the adequacy of food consumption and productivity among the Enga today.[1] It seems probable that formerly, in part because of the effects of endemic and epidemic sickness and of warfare on population size and movements, Central Enga in general were not so lacking in land, and hence in subsistence, that in normal seasons they would have been in real danger of starvation. But without quantified evidence, this can only be speculation, which moreover introduces as a conditioning variable the warfare whose incidence is to be explained.

In effect, the one reliable datum is that in the past Central Enga judged arable land to be a scarce and valued good, and each local group asserted its right to control as much land as it deemed necessary for its survival in a fashion befitting true Enga. Such perceptions of scarcity were thus part of the total social, technological, and environmental context within which the people operated (or to which they adapted) and, through processes of feedback or interaction, determined their relationship to the land no less significantly than did topography, the pattern of rainfall, or the range of indigenous plants. That is to say, ideas

183

are also causally efficient components of human ecosystems, and in this instance they appear to have contributed importantly to reinforcing an adaptation of the whole Central Enga population that helped maintain the system for perhaps two or three centuries in a slowly shifting equilibrium (see Meggitt 1967, 1974).[2]

With the arrival of the Administration, some variables in this complex changed, especially the size of the Enga population, which increased at first slowly and then rapidly. At the same time, for most Enga the culturally acceptable delineation of the good, or at least the satisfactory, life did not alter greatly. In particular, concepts of prestige and power continued to be expressed in terms of transactions in wealth (notably pigs) and, ultimately, of access to land. But the amount of land available to the growing numbers of people of course did not grow commensurately; rather, the initial cession of tracts to the Administration and the missions and the planting of coffee trees somewhat reduced the area suitable for gardens and pigs.

At the same time almost all landholders continued with the traditional horticultural techniques and food crops, mainly because they had few viable alternatives. The physical characteristics and climate of the region, together with the size and distribution of gardens and the paucity of cash incomes, all combined to render pointless most innovations that were proposed to increase subsistence returns.[3] The only way most owners of limited amounts of land could achieve short-term increases in the output of staples was to cut into areas currently reserved for pig foraging and to shorten fallow periods. Both practices would lead to a decline in soil fertility and hence in productivity, a consequence understood by many Enga gardeners ("land used too often loses its vital essence and yields less").

In short, by the 1960's the Central Enga, who had long believed that their land was a scarce and essential commodity, could point to such "objective" facts, especially to the continuing rise in their numbers, as proof that land was now in even shorter supply relative to the demands being made on it. It is not surprising that they were also of the opinion that local groups must therefore compete more vigorously to secure their share of this necessity.

The circumstances that were perturbing the Enga did not go unnoticed either by local field staff of the Australian Administration or by their superior officers in Port Moresby, and both were concerned lest the situation grow worse. Various measures were suggested and some of them implemented, to no great effect. Even discounting for the benefit of hindsight, some of the Administration's responses to "the Enga problem" were *ad hoc* and ill-conceived. Perhaps their most significant weakness was that officials so often viewed both the problem and its possible solutions primarily in terms of law and order, rather than as a state of affairs that

184

demanded the making of difficult economic and, to a lesser extent, political decisions in collaboration with the people. Given the authorities' general orientation, this may not be remarkable. Papua New Guinea was then a colony with no immediate prospects of independence, and it seemed better to strive for a repressive public tranquility than to launch risky social experiments. Moreover, the few venturesome proposals that envisioned significant socioeconomic changes were constrained by limited budgets. These in turn were severely constrained by imbalances in the wider economy of Papua New Guinea, which meant that public services throughout the country depended largely on annual subventions from the Government of Australia.

Whatever the reasons, the reactions of the Administration, both in Port Moresby and at the local level, to what it regarded as the disturbing behavior of the Central Enga were usually imperfectly coordinated attempts to deal directly and unilaterally with the most visible symptoms of these people's difficulties. Thus, over a period of about twenty years, there were frequent changes in the legal procedures, including the use of police, that were intended to facilitate the settlement of disputes over land, none of them notably successful: among other goals, the Highlands Labour Scheme aimed at attracting young men away from potential trouble spots, but few were willing to work far from home and leave their land undefended; cash crops were introduced to stimulate a flow of money into the region, but market prices declined steadily; new forms of animal husbandry either cost too much to be efficiently sustained or withdrew even more land from subsistence cultivation; the extension of educational opportunities to the secondary level was meant to fit at least some young people for non-rural employment, but there were few or no jobs for them. Meanwhile, the Central Enga population increased apace, as did the incidence of overt conflicts.

Some of the Administration's actions, as well as being particularistic and reflexive, were informed by the kind of thinking so typical of experts in colonial or postcolonial "development," namely, that when presented with what outsiders have defined as rational alternatives, people will at once perceive these to be superior, discard cherished traditional values, and radically reorganize their way of life to incorporate the innovations. Obviously most Enga did not respond this way. Instead, they not only examined the new options in the light of their strongly held views about what constituted the basic social verities (group solidarity, prestige, influence, circulation of wealth, landownership) but also tested them against the realities of the wider economic world (labor costs, commodity costs, incomes, employment opportunities). On both counts people judged the innovations to be deficient: they did not solve problems within the social system to which Enga were committed, and they certainly could not provide the means for living outside it. This reasonable assessment of their

185

condition persuaded most Central Enga that they had little choice but to cleave to the old ways, even if these also entailed a continuation of the old patterns of aggressive self-help.

Thus, one compelling conclusion the people have reached over the past decade or so is that, whatever changes may take place in the world at large, whether they are subjects of a colonial administration or citizens of an independent nation, the majority of them are, and will long remain, bound to a rural economy that functions on a relatively small scale under severe technological disabilities. This recognition, together with their continuing inclination to resort to traditional definitions of, and solutions to, the difficulties posed by their growing population, has further reinforced the attachment of local groups to their patrimonial land. As men have often said to me, what else have they but their land, and what else can they do but fight when covetous neighbors encroach on their domain?

The predicament of the Central Enga is not peculiar to them, and theirs is not the only society in Papua New Guinea that has been racked by violent disputes among local groups. During the past decade there has been a marked resurgence of armed confrontations in other parts of the country, to the extent that by 1970 fears of a major breakdown of public order became widespread (see Oram 1973, Standish 1973). Such anxieties were most loudly voiced by European residents and the journals serving them, and as the date set for national independence (eventually 1975) drew near, they became increasing concerned about the likelihood of attacks on the lives and property of expatriates. In the event, no such calamities occurred.

Nevertheless, it would be a mistake to dismiss these apprehensions as the exaggerated reactions of an insecure minority that saw its interests threatened by a transfer of political power. There was indeed a proliferation of public disturbances, especially throughout the highlands, not merely of drunken brawls but also of large-scale pitched battles in which numbers of men were killed and many wounded. Field officers and police could scarcely keep up with the outbreaks, and cases overwhelmed the district courts. In consequence, in 1972 the interim "home rule" government then in charge of the country's domestic affairs appointed two working parties (most of whose members were indigenes, some of them public servants) to make exhaustive inquiries, the one into land matters in general, the other into "tribal fighting" in the highlands.

Although the committees' terms of reference differed, their findings and recommendations for action (see Papua New Guinea 1973a, 1973b) overlapped in significant respects and were mutually supporting. This is not the place to examine in detail these valuable and informative studies, but several of their complementary conclusions bear directly on issues I have already raised. Indeed, the whole of the report on tribal fighting

186

illuminates my account of what was happening to the Central Enga.

The reports conclude that disputes over the ownership and use of land are the prime cause of intergroup violence in the highlands, notably in heavily populated regions such as that of the Enga, where people believe they are under heavy demographic and economic pressure.[4] In some areas quarrels over sorcery, homicides, women, and pigs are also important. With respect to conflicts over land, their escalation is partly attributable to the manifest inability of the Land Titles Commission to dispose of suits promptly and simply. There is an urgent need for village courts, backed by village law officers and rural police, to deal with these matters quickly and with emphasis on informal arbitration and conciliation. In cases of trespass and armed aggression, ways must be instituted to assess the liability of whole social groups and to penalize them (for instance, with large fines of pigs), as well as to jail individual offenders.

However, the reports note, improved judicial procedures and more efficient use and control of police will achieve little as long as the people concerned remain short of land.[5] Repossession and redistribution of European plantations in the highlands would be inadequate, even as a short-term measure. Inasmuch as, for the foreseeable future, the economy of Papua New Guinea will not be able to provide many of these people with alternatives to a rural life, it is essential that the Government take steps to facilitate their movement from overpopulated areas to those where arable land is available. Unless economically viable resettlement projects of varying magnitude are undertaken, serious disturbances will continue to plague these communities.

The national House of Assembly received the reports, and the Chief Minister of the Government promised to study the recommendations carefully. He also warned that what the Government could do to implement them, and how rapidly, would in part depend on their legal implications and on budgetary considerations; and to date (1976) much of the necessary legislation is still being drafted. It is highly likely, however, that before long the Government will produce plans for the permanent resettlement of at least some of the highlands people.

Such a prospect, of course, raises the question of the willingness of the Central Enga to participate. I agree with the import of the committees' findings, that given the present and probable future circumstances of the Enga, the migration of a considerable number of them out of the region to take up, with government assistance, rural activities elsewhere appears to offer the only economically feasible means by which the population as a whole can avoid a declining standard of living and a continuation of intergroup hostilities. Nevertheless, the manifest attachment of Central Enga men to their clan estates may well place great obstacles in the way. Indeed, similar attitudes among the Enga in the past deterred the Australian Administration from actively pushing even modest proposals for their resettlement (budgetary constraints were also a factor). Had the postwar Administration then firmly grasped the nettle before the increase in the Enga population became so pronounced, it might perhaps have been able to induce groups to move to sparsely occupied regions, in particular to the north and west of the Lai valley.

Now, one must wonder whether such schemes, which to make any significant difference will have to be carried out on a large scale and will entail intimidating financial outlays, can be pursued in the western highlands without causing considerable social upheaval and perhaps in the short run more conflict among local groups. Nevertheless, it appears that at this point the Government and the Enga have little choice but to take the risk.

Notes

Chapter 1

1. For a general account of traditional Mae society see Meggitt 1965a; for details on the history of Enga-European contacts see Meggitt 1971, 1973.

2. Formerly the Enga occupied several subdistricts in the western part of the Western Highlands District of the (Australian) Territory of Papua and New Guinea. These, with the exception of that containing the Kyaka Enga, were combined in 1974 to form the Enga District of Papua New Guinea.

Chapter 2

1. Definitions of this kind have long had wide currency; for discussion and references see Wright 1965, and compare Fried, Harris, and Murphy 1967, Schneider 1964, and Turney-High 1971.

2. See Pospisil 1968 for a discussion and references. Elsewhere when dealing with conflicts among the Enga, I have sometimes loosely and metaphorically used the term feud; I now believe I was wrong to do so.

3. In Western society arbitration generally connotes the possession by the intervening party of some statutory authority to settle a dispute and to that extent is perhaps too strong a term to apply to the traditional processes of mediation within Enga groups. On the other hand, Enga Big Men have more *de facto* power to force the resolution of quarrels than is usually implied in the Western notion of conciliation.

4. One cannot treat lightly such restrictions on the free gathering of data. In the eyes of that neighborhood I am identified closely with my own clan of residence and to a lesser degree with other clans of that phratry; consequently, it would be foolish,

189

indeed suicidal, of me to attempt nowadays to seek information (particularly about land matters) in the territories of our more intransigent enemies.

5. Stealing from gardens is in a different category; the one instance I know where this led to warfare concerned, significantly, subclans of a clan that was rapidly growing in size. Normally, a man who filches food from another's garden is derided as a "rubbish man," whose action betrays his own poverty, sloth, or incapacity. In consequence, although men cheerfully destroy the crops of an enemy group during a fight, they do not remove them, for theft would leave their own clan open to insults. Moreover, if a man is detected stealing food from the gardens of another clan and those men severely injure him in return, his own clansmen are too humiliated to make an issue of his maltreatment.

For instance, a young bachelor of clan X often visited his father's sister's son in clan Y of another phratry. Men of clan Y suspected him of stealing from their gardens. When they surprised him in the act of cutting their sugarcane, they held the young man while the owner of the cane chopped off both his hands at the wrists. They turned the thief loose, and somehow he managed to reach his home three miles distant, where a curer saved his life. The assailants refused to offer compensation to the bachelor's agnates. The latter did not protest the refusal but quietly gave the conventionally required injury compensation to his mother's agnates. The mutilated man led a long and active (albeit celibate) life until his death in 1955; aided by a complicated arrangement of armlets, he could effectively wield an axe or digging stick.

6. Members of defeated and dispersed groups who have gone to live elsewhere have good political and economic reasons not to draw attention to their immigrant status but instead to try for relatively rapid absorption into the host clan. Similarly, the new occupants of the disputed territory are not disposed to draw attention to their usurpation. In consequence, the identities of extinguished clans or subclans are soon lost to public knowledge and in time such groups drop out of the genealogies of their former phratries. Thus the investigator's sample probably underrepresents the number of groups that have actually disappeared in this way.

Chapter 3

1. There are some exceptions to this rule, which the people account for in terms of (putative) past migrations of particular groups in search of land or following military defeats.

2. Comparison of the general form of a Mae "great fight" and of the constraints attending it with those of mediaeval tournaments, as described for instance by Painter 1964:47*et seq.*, reveals significant similarities between the two. The skirmishing that characterizes such battles among the Mae seems in many ways to resemble, despite differences arising from peculiarities of terrain, etc., that of the Dani as depicted in the film *Dead Birds*.

3. Obviously these figures are at best informed estimates. I arrived at them as follows. In 1949, the first year for which I have reasonable albeit partial census data for Central Enga, six phratries in and around the neighborhood in question included 12,000 or so people, of whom roughly one-third were men over the appar-

190

ent age of 16. I also know that when a clan goes to war (nowadays as well as in the past), almost all its men capable of bearing arms do so. Accordingly, I calculate that each of the six phratries had *on the average* some 600 potential warriors in 1949. Moreover, the growth of the Central Enga population following the temporary cessation of warfare and the spread of European medical services apparently was not marked until the 1950's, when it climbed. By 1959 the same six phratries numbered about 15,000—a population increase of perhaps 3 percent per annum. The rate of increase among the Central Enga in the decades before 1949 appears to have been much lower, so that the total population in the 1930's was probably little less than that of the late 1940's.

The picture of local communities joining to place 1,000 men in combat may cause surprise. Yet for at least three of the inter-clan (not inter-phratry) battles fought by Central Enga during the 1960's and early 1970's, Administration observers have judged the number of men engaged to be 1,000 or more; indeed, their estimates indicate that the *mean* number of warriors engaged in 21 such conflicts was about 400.

4. If by accident one champion kills the other, the slayer's clan is not obliged to pay compensation to the victim's agnates. Considerations of personal and group prestige, however, may impel the killer and his clan to make a "voluntary" offer of compensation, which of course is happily accepted.

5. After an engagement of any kind the lightly wounded men walk or run home, helped by their clansmen. Those more seriously injured but still conscious may be carried on the back of the strongest "brothers." For an unconscious or otherwise immobilized casualty, if conditions permit a rough litter is quickly made by tying tough vines and cordyline leaves between two poles. But if there is no time for this refinement, the injured man is simply trussed like a corpse to a pole and borne off at a jolting trot.

6. Unfortunately I can provide only an inferential estimate of casualty rates in great fights. Men who had participated in them said that in some, certainly in the one involving four phratries, more men were killed in the day's combat than died in the usual interclan conflict. This may imply a toll of five to ten deaths, hardly excessive in view of the large number of combatants.

7. After the inception of the government's system of courts, no clan ever conceded that defeat (however defined) in a great fight gave the winning side any claim in litigation whatever to any of the losers' land.

8. I quote a pertinent paragraph from Scott's *Ivanhoe* (ch. 12): "Thus ended the memorable field of Ashby-de-la-Zouche, one of the most gallantly contested tournaments of that age, for although only four knights, including one who was smothered by the heat of his armour, had died upon the field, yet upwards of thirty were desperately wounded, four or five of whom never recovered. Several more were disabled for life; and those who escaped best carried the marks of the conflict to the grave with them. Hence it is always mentioned in the old records, as the Gentle and Joyous Passage of Arms at Ashby."

9. More accurately, men refer to their clansmen (and subclansmen) by a conjunctive term that means "fathers and brothers," whereas the men of other clans in their phratry are simply "brothers." That is, they recognize differences in authority between generations in the first category of agnates who are clansmen but not

in the second. Within the lineage, however, they make specific kinship distinctions and refer to that group as a whole as "those who share one blood" (see Meggitt 1964b).

10. Mae men disburse and receive pigs in so many transactions, including distributions of brideprice, death and homicide compensations, and Te exchanges, that the size and composition of their herds constantly change. In consequence, particular pigs are not usually identified with specific owners and indeed are rarely given individual names. Nevertheless, popular metaphor equates pigs with men and, when men of one group illicitly kill a pig belonging to another, they clearly see the animal as a surrogate; in dispatching it they are, notionally at least, killing a man of that group.

11. Given that, as Mae men themselves assert, groups at odds over land readily seize on almost any pretext to force a fight, the rarity of sexual grounds for intergroup conflicts is interesting, although in view of the sexual attitudes of Mae Enga men and the status of their women (see Meggitt 1964a), perhaps understandable. Moreover, in such sex-based conflicts as do occur, the situation tends to be defined in political or economic terms. Thus the rape of a wife or daughter of a current or potential enemy is seen, as I noted earlier, as an act of provocation rather than of lust. Similarly, a husband's killing of an adulterous wife (an uncommon occurrence) usually has military consequences only if he and his clansmen refuse to pay homicide compensation to her agnates and the two groups are already disputing other issues.

12. Cross-checks with data on fatalities drawn from genealogies indicate that, even with reference to my own or other friendly clans, the figures derived from accounts of warfare that occurred before I began my fieldwork are almost certainly *underestimates*.

13. Usually the mutiliation of an enemy occurs in the heat of battle or ambush as part of the act of killing. The Mae do not take prisoners in order to torture them at their leisure or indeed for any other reason. They abhor cannibalism.

14. Although a rape precipitated the intraclan conflict occurring about 1940 in which 16 died, the subclans (of a clan with some 450 members) were in fact fighting over land. Two of them, with about 60 percent of the population, combined to attack two others, with about 20 percent of the population, while men of the remaining subclan, unable to compose the dispute, fought on both sides, as did external allies. After the initial attack, sporadic raids and pitched battles continued for some (perhaps four) months, until in a final thrust the two larger groups ousted the two smaller, who sought refuge with fraternal clans. In all, the victors lost seven dead (including an ally and a woman), the losers nine (including two allies and a woman). Why was the smaller force routed even though the deaths on both sides were roughly equal? It may be that a group's losses relative to its size are more significant than the absolute number of casualties. This, however, seems to be an exceptional case.

15. Indeed, this obligation to signal one's intentions to a fraternal clan can lead to the postponement or even total abandonment of plans for an attack. For instance, if the intended opponents reply that they are about to engage in major rituals to propitiate their clan ancestors, the other group should stand aside at least until these lengthy activities are completed.

192

16. The boasts and responses may be couched in highly metaphorical terms, but often are quite straightforward: "We shall sweep you from your land so quickly that afterward we shall have time to smoke at leisure and still return home for our evening meal!" Rejoinder: "You only have five fingers on your hand; we also have five fingers [that is, we are your equals]. If you had six fingers we might have reason to fear you."

17. In intergroup fighting a man is not obliged to spare an opponent who bears the same personal name if the latter is neither a relative nor a friend. If he does kill this man, he may change his own name lest its continued use attract the attention of the victim's ghost.

18. Some Fringe Enga men told me that at the conclusion of combat military allies usually were given pigs as payment for their services; I could not determine whether these transactions involved individuals or groups. Mae informants, on the other hand, stated explicitly and unanimously that among them allies did not receive payments *per se* for military aid, because (1) allies share in whatever spoils of battle there are; (2) men should freely help relatives and exchange partners on these occasions; and (3) Mae men in any case welcome opportunities to fight. Nevertheless, when the "owners of the quarrel" distribute pork and pigs as compensation for the deaths of enemies and allies, they generally make small "good-will gifts" of pork to those outsiders who fought beside them. However, such small pieces of meat can hardly be regarded as adequate rewards for men who have risked their lives in prosecuting another's dispute.

19. The conflict that took 24 men's lives, which occurred about 1936, displays several interesting features. Clan A of phratry I and clan B of phratry II had for some time been at odds over the land on their common border. Men of A surprised and wounded a man of B who was stealing their pandanus nuts. He escaped to his home ground, and a raiding party from clan B, supported by kinsmen of the adjacent clan C, *also of phratry I*, that day killed a man of clan A. Clan C was willing to aid clan B in this attack on its "brothers" because it, too, was disputing with clan A over land. Clan A, however, had expected such a raid and accordingly laid an ambush, helped by kinsmen of the neighboring clan D of phratry III. Clan D had earlier also been fighting over land with clan B and had deaths to repay. In the ambush the raiders lost a man from clan B and one from clan C, and they retired in confusion. Next day men of clans A and D attacked clan B in force, and clan C came to the aid of clan B. When at the urging of other allies, peace was negotiated some months later, clans A and C were each in possession of part of clan B's territory. By then A had lost seven men (including an ally from a maternally related clan) and C four, while B had lost three men and D ten. Not only are the high casualty rates among C and D noteworthy, so also is the fact that six of the men of clan D died at the hands of their "brothers" from clan A and five of clan A were killed by clan D. This fraternal slaughter suggests that clans A and D were using the dispute between clans A and B as a pretext to weaken each other, a view also held by my informants from clan C who had participated in the fighting. Indeed, years afterward they still commented on this breakdown in phratry comity. Finally, I should note that clans A and C, since their occupation of the land of clan B, have constantly quarreled and occasionally fought (most recently in 1971) over the division of spoils.

20. One could perhaps argue here that such a belief in the danger of ghostly re-

prisals serves the useful function of deterring the men of the clan from acting in a manner (that is, by passively accepting the insult) that might publicly reveal the military weakness of their group to interested and rapacious neighbors.

21. Some Mae say that the ghost of a man who has been murdered in an ambush may appear in a dream to his brother or other close agnate and warn him that the killer will soon be near their clan territory. The chosen relative should then, on pain of ghostly displeasure and attack, keep a sharp lookout for the intruder and ambush him in turn.

22. There are, of course, conflicts in which a clan totally defeats and dispossesses its opponent; the latter, its surviving members dispersed and unable to regroup, disappears as an autonomous unit.

23. Different Mae men express different opinions about the effects of this pattern of selective enmity on marriage choices. Whereas most assert without qualification the formula "we marry the people we fight," some believe that while two clans see themselves as "real" enemies they do not intermarry, and that they resume intermarriage only as the level of violence between them abates and each clan acquires new "real" enemies. Other men, on the contrary, state that marriages are and should be made during the intermittent periods of peace with "real" enemies in order to facilitate travel (which seems somewhat optimistic to me); to sustain the connections that in peacetime mediate important exchanges of wealth; and to provide multiple channels for negotiating future truces, for instance, to enable the opponents to perform undisturbed their ancestral rituals.

Granted the difficulties in dating wars and marriages accurately in pre-European times, Mae genealogies give some support for both arguments. Marriages with "real" enemies do not occur when fighting is in progress, but they do take place (albeit rarely) in the periods between bursts of actual warfare. That is to say, the popular assumption that "we marry the people we fight" is in general confirmed.

24. The apparently obvious alternative of not inviting both the contending clans to be present at the same time does not really exist for the hosts. Each group has the right to be there and to receive its due. For the host to deny this would establish the basis of a lasting quarrel with the offended clan, one in which the host is in the wrong. I know of several occasions, some recent, when men of Mae and Laiapu clans who had not been asked to distributions of wealth to which they had claims suddenly arrived in force and fired on the startled hosts and guests, killing some of them.

Chapter 4

1. Although Mae houses are solidly built, to be maximally effective in this climate and in relation to the horticultural regime they should be replaced about every three or four years (see Meggitt 1957a). It follows that a man has to make many decisions about house sites during his life.

2. Cane grass, even when it is growing, burns fiercely in dry weather. Hence a screen, if it is dense and too near the house, can be a serious hazard. Mae raiders on occasion set fire to such defenses in the hope that the flames will leap to the house thatch, but normally householders take care not to expose their dwellings to this danger. Indeed, Mae raiders are not given to the wholesale burning of inhabited areas that, for instance, the Waka, Aruni, and Kandepe Enga undertake. During in-

194

tergroup fighting among these peoples, areas of fifty acres or more, each including several houses, are reduced to ashes.

3. The tunnel generally runs from the rear part of the house, because raiders usually first set fire to the thatch over the front doorway in the hope of preventing the occupants from breaking out through this exit.

4. Nowadays such disguises are also intended to prevent the Administration officers and the police from identifying in court trials those who have been fighting; without a positive identification of the defendant, the magistrate must throw out the case. Men who are supposed to be upholders of law and order, namely, councillors and Administration and mission employees, are especially careful to remain anonymous when they fight lest they jeopardize their jobs.

5. I am aware of only one authentic instance of the "military" use of a bamboo knife: some years ago a man of our clan stalked an enemy scout and cut his throat.

6. Roughly fashioned clubs are, however, employed to kill pigs on festive occasions and are put aside for future use. Moreover, men also hew from hardwood specially designed heavy mauls with which to hammer into place the planks that form the walls of houses.

7. The Enga propensity for experimenting with novel kinds of arrow heads was given point in a recent conversation among Administration officers concerning suitable weapons for the police, who are now called on to control interclan battles. One officer suggested that the police be equipped to fire tranquilizing darts at the fight leaders. The reply was: "Not a hope! Those bloody Enga would simply mount the darts on their arrows and knock out all our police."

8. During the early days of contact with Europeans, Enga men willingly accepted large steel "bush knives" (machetes) as payment for goods and services. They still use these primarily as domestic and horticultural implements and occasionally as weapons in brawls. For serious warfare, however, they prefer axes, which they regard as more durable, better balanced, and hence more reliably lethal.

9. Following the establishment of general peace in the 1950's, men tended to shorten this period of avoidance, at first to about a month, later to only the five days of the mother's post-parturition seclusion. With the subsequent resumption of intergroup fighting, the period of avoidance apparently has not regained its former length.

10. I should remind the reader that the ethnographic present here halts at the mid 1950's. As I have indicated elsewhere (Meggitt 1964a), the form and content of relationships between men and women later changed perceptibly in response to pressures exerted by the Administration and the Christian missions, as well as by such impersonal factors as the increasing monetization of the economy. Nevertheless, the "traditional" elements did not disappear entirely, and indeed there has of late been an obvious revival of interest in the bachelors' associations.

11. A mild father warns the offending boy once, then punishes him for a repetition of the misdemeanor, whereas a stern father (and there are many) strikes on the first occasion. The father's punishment can be harsh by Western standards—flogging, tying with pig ropes, smoking the lad for a day over a slow fire, slicing his hand with a knife, or cutting off and cooking his ear lobes and making him eat them so that in future he will heed his father's commands.

12. One index of a strong man's self-confidence is his willingness to alert and intimi-

date a man he plans to kill. For instance, a strong man who wishes to avenge the death of a brother slain by someone in a distant clan, does not deign to enlist an agent. Instead, he makes a series of night-time forays into the killer's territory, and each time places fern or other "significant" leaves outside the house door of the intended victim, or he disturbs the grave of one of his close kinsmen. In this way he clearly notifies the killer that he can dispatch him whenever he chooses, which gives the latter much to think about.

13. Among the Yandapu Enga to the west, men place the plumes of the white cockatoo *(Kakatöe galerita)* on their wigs to mark military exploits. I have been told, but am uncertain of this, that among several western Fringe Enga peoples a headdress of black tail feathers of the *Astrapia femina* bird of paradise indicates a man who has killed a woman. Finally, some Waka and Maramuni Enga men wear a hornbill skull and beak as a pendant; this is not to my knowledge a military decoration or a homicide's badge.

14. Thus, one elder of my acquaintance, who had at various times killed three men in battle, said he would not dare to affect the knotted string, for none of these deaths was in any way remarkable. My late "brother" and closest friend, who was both a true Big Man and a former luluai, had earned the name "man-killer" before he was about thirty. By the time of the Australian peace, when he was about forty, he had slain single-handed at least seven men in combat and had wounded or helped dispatch many more. Although other men told me he was fully entitled to wear the knotted string, he himself did not believe he was and would not do so. In short, I estimate that in the average clan only one or two men were so distinguished.

15. Whereas among the southern Fringe Enga such tally trees may be fenced around the base and hung with ornamental ferns and leaves, the Mae do not decorate their trees.

16. Webster's Third New International Dictionary (1966), defines strategy as "the science and art of military command exercised to meet the enemy in combat under advantageous conditions," and tactics as "the science and art of disposing and maneuvering troops, ships, or aircraft in relation to each other and the enemy and of employing them in combat"; . . . "Strategy wins wars; tactics wins battles." See also von Clausewitz 1968:173–4. Whereas I believe one can fairly distinguish between strategy and tactics in the Enga prosecution of war, even though I would be reluctant to regard the utilization of either as a science, as far as I can tell the Mae have only the one phrase to cover both situations, "skillful warfare."

17. Moreover, although the Mae do not explicitly make the point, some of the "true" or major Big Men are of an age that might make them liabilities in combat, as contrasted with those Big Men who were also current fight leaders, who seemed to me in general somewhat younger and fitter.

18. The Mae view of war is in general largely compatible with that of von Clausewitz, and they would subscribe wholeheartedly to such statements as: "From the outset there is a play of possibilities, probabilities, good and bad luck, which . . . makes War of all branches of human activity the most like a gambling game" (1968:117). "Everything is very simple in War, but the simplest thing is difficult. These difficulties accumulate and produce a friction which no man can imagine exactly who has not seen War" (p. 164). ". . . This enormous friction . . . is therefore everywhere brought into contact with chance, and thus incidents take place upon which it was

196

impossible to calculate" (p. 165). "In War more than anywhere else in the world things happen differently to what we had expected" (p. 263).

19. The high density of Central Enga population means that men engaged in nefarious activities, even by night, frequently are observed by members of adjacent clans, who, if they have relatives or friends among the victims, promptly pass on the information. The flow of intelligence does much to fuel existing hostilities between groups.

20. "For Warre, consisteth not in Battell onely, or the act of fighting; but in a tract, wherein the Wille to contend by Battell is sufficiently known: and therefore the notion of Time, is to be considered in the nature of Warre." (Hobbes 1651/1968: 185/61).

21. One reason Mae give for their dislike of the introduced "coastal"-style dwelling is that a raider can easily thrust his spear through the thin cane wall into a sleeping resident. This was brought home to me during one field sojourn when our clan was seriously at odds with a neighboring group. Our clansmen insisted that my wife and I move our pallets at least a spear's length from the outer wall of our coastal-style house, and for some weeks sentries watched the building to ensure that no nocturnal prowler could exploit its obvious vulnerability.

22. A Lutheran missionary, Marvin Sackschewsky, has published (1970) a careful description of clan meetings among Mae Enga of the Ambumu valley. His observations closely parallel my own of Mae meetings in the Lai valley, and I refer readers to his account for more details.

The house may be chosen simply because it is the largest or most secluded; it may, however, be the house of the most important convener or of the clan's major Big Man. If, as is likely, it cannot accommodate all the participants, much of the business is transacted in the porch yard.

23. Mae warriors do not, at this or any time before a battle, engage in ceremonies aimed at cleansing or strengthening them, nor do they celebrate purificatory rituals after the fighting.

24. No doubt men who make a meal of pork and vegetables on the eve of battle go into action in better shape than men who do not, and perhaps they are in consequence able to fight more vigorously than the latter. However, given the small amounts of meat consumed, and that lightly salted, if at all, I do not think the situation here is comparable with that which Rappaport (1968:135*et. seq.*), analyzes for the Maring, where the physiological effects of precombat feasts of heavily salted pork fat appear to be considerable.

Chapter 5

1. It should be remembered, however, that many Mae clans range from 600 members to over 1,000, and that these larger groups are particularly prone to trying conclusions with weaker but nevertheless relatively sizable neighbors, so that considerable forces are involved in some interclan combats.

2. It might appear that Mae houses, being stoutly constructed (see Meggitt 1957a), could serve as temporary fortresses from which the occupants could stand off besiegers until reinforcements arrived. In fact, they are so well built they are unsuit-

able for defense. It is nearly impossible to remove planks quickly from the firmly lashed, doubled, and insulated walls in order to make openings through which archers could fire; nor could the men easily clear away the complicated roof structure to use their bows freely. In short, given that the houses with their single small doorways are almost hermetically sealed, they are more likely to be traps for their occupants than defensive strongholds.

3. One can perceive in the Mae tacticians' reliance on this mode of attack a recognition, however limited, of the need to achieve at once a favorable "critical imbalance" and to maintain it throughout the action. See Bretnor 1969: ch. 4 for an explication of this concept.

4. It is worth emphasizing here an important difference between "modern" warfare and that of the Mae. When a Mae army is routed in the field, the clan is largely destroyed, for that army effectively comprises *all* the clansmen; there is no one left to constitute a relief force (cf. Bretnor 1969:124–5).

5. "Refusing the center" has occupied an important place in military tactics at least since 216 B.C., when Hannibal employed it to destroy a Roman army at Cannae (cf. Polybius 1966:184 *et. seq.*; Wintringham & Blashford-Snell 1973:55).

6. If the invaders are numerous and their leaders awake to the ruse, they may from the start of the action detach small scouting parties to discover and break up any attempts to infiltrate the rear of their main force.

7. A further incentive to the invaders' continuing hostilities, a motive their opponents usually share, is their wish to avenge any deaths already suffered. This is not simply a matter of prestige. Men have a very real fear that the clan ancestors, angered by impairment of the group's strength, will harm or kill them if they are dilatory in balancing or, better, exceeding the account. One should not underestimate the strength of the Mae concern to escape ghostly malice as a complementary stimulus to military action.

8. Scouts and raiders do not, of course, talk while reconnoitering. They may use a predetermined code to pass information to one another. Thus, the lead man on entering an uncertain area whistles softly once to indicate "all clear—close up quickly," or twice to warn "there are enemies about—fall back." Silence signifies "the situation is unclear—stand fast."

9. This calling of the roll occurs often in times of tension, as well as at the end of a day's fighting. If a man is missing, a scouting party at once searches the area where he was patrolling or was last seen in action (if this is feasible), in case he has been wounded and is hiding from the enemy. Had the latter killed him outright, their exuberant shouts would have informed his clansmen.

10. Present-day Mae warriors have made this point to me in up-to-date terms: "Just as a truck cannot move without benzine, so a man cannot fight on the run for several days if he does not take in enough food and water each night."

Chapter 6

1. The imputation of malicious action to an agnatic ghost does not absolve the clan of the (physical) killer from later paying homicide compensation to the deceased's clansmen.

198

2. Receiving an arrow in the buttock, however, is thought to indicate a certain lack of valor on the part of the victim, who may afterward be the butt of his companions' heavy-handed jokes.

3. Indeed, death in these circumstances does not absolve the "killer's" clan from the responsibility of paying homicide compensation.

4. A young friend of mine who recently participated as a branch holder in such a divining told me that at the outset he was skeptical of the whole procedure. Nevertheless, he said, at the appropriate question the branch became extraordinarily heavy and without his intending it began to swing vigorously. Thinking that his partner was doing this, he looked around to see that the latter was equally helpless and puzzled. My friend was forced to conclude somewhat reluctantly that the ghost of the dead man was indeed present.

5. Koch 1974 describes in considerable detail the kinds of fighting pursued by the Jalé of Irian Jaya, a highlands people in some respects similar to the Mae. Although he does not tabulate the numbers of deaths occurring in these confrontations, I estimate, after a tentative examination of 27 of his cases, that on the average some two or three Jalé men are killed in each encounter.

6. Since the 1960's accusations of sorcery appear to have become more common among the Mae.

7. The practice of conducting an autopsy to determine the "cause" of a death whose circumstances puzzle the deceased's relatives is widely known through the western and southern highlands of Papua New Guinea; see, for instance, for the Huli, Glasse 1968: plate I, for the Ipili, Meggitt 1957b:46, for the Waka and the Kandepe Enga Meggitt 1956:108, 131, for the Laiapu Enga Westermann 1968:198–9.

Among the Mae Enga such investigations, which are not frequent, are occasioned solely by deaths of men (I have not heard of any being performed for a woman or child). Mae autopsies are confined to two main categories of situations: those in which a man dies suddenly for no apparent reason and sorcery is suspected, and those in which death may be attributed to the effects of an earlier wound.

The dead man's close agnates summon a specialist ("one who sees") to act as coroner, and they pay at least a pig for his services. Such experts are few, but it is an advantage if the man chosen is a respected member of a neutral clan; then both the agnates and the members of any group he may nominate as responsible for the death are more likely to accept his findings with less argument. Should the deceased's clansmen believe beforehand that the death may be due to a particular wound incurred in warfare with another clan, they invite men of that group to be present at the autopsy. The latter, however, are unlikely to attend because if the coroner's decision goes against them, the angry agnates may attack them then and there. Accordingly, they prefer to send as representatives relatives from an uninvolved group. Similarly, if the bereaved suspect that their "brother" died as a result of sorcery, they ask his maternal kinsmen to observe the operation, and these people usually do appear. In any case only mature men participate in an autopsy. Younger men and women are thought to be too vulnerable to attacks by the victim's incensed ghost.

With a bamboo knife (and if necessary an axe) the expert cuts across the corpse's thorax below the ribs and loosens the sternum. Assistants use hooked sticks to wrench up the sternum and to hold the rib cage open to expose the heart

199

and lungs. In a sorcery inquiry the coroner examines the organs for small black excrescences "like fragments of charcoal" (blood clots?). If they appear on the victim's right lung, one of his living agnates or an agnatic ghost is responsible for the death, and men of his subclan are bound to pay his mother's subclansmen additional compensation. Marks on the left lung indicate that the sorcery emanated from the mother's agnatic group, and these men should give compensation to the deceased's agnates. Whether or not the latter in turn make the usual death payment to the maternal kin is largely up to them and the value they place on the connection. In neither case is any attempt made to specify a particular individual or ghost as the "killer," a restraint that obviously reduces strain on future relations between the two groups.

If the expert perceives no unambiguous signs on the outside of the lungs, he opens them and examines the interior. Should this prove unrewarding, he slices the heart and searches for indications in the right and left ventricles. Failure here leads to other modes of divination. Thus, the coroner may place a rolled-up Cordyline leaf in each hand of the victim or in each armpit. Next morning he inspects the inside of the leaves for the presence of foreign material (moisture, dirt, insects), which he interprets in order to allocate the blame matrilaterally or patrilaterally. Or the dead man's agnates may resort to the services of another expert skilled in grave or other divining, who questions the ghost. Whatever the outcome, the coroner is paid for his work.

When the matter is one of determining whether the victim died from the effects of a wound received earlier, and whose weapon caused it, the investigation bears more resemblance to a Western coroner's inquiry. The specialist interrogates all clansmen with first-hand knowledge of the deceased's military career and from their replies constructs a case history of battles fought, wounds incurred, their bodily locations, and their previous treatment and consequences. Thus informed he opens the torso of the cadaver and seeks "evidence" in the form of arrow points, cassowary claw spear tips, lesions, and pockets of suppuration that will identify a specific injury to which the death can plausibly be attributed. If the coroner encounters such conditions, he considers them in the light of his other knowledge and nominates the clan, indeed sometimes even the actual "killer," responsible. The victim's agnates then chant or send messages to that group, demanding prompt payment of homicide compensation. Occasionally a coroner may hold that the combined effects of two separate wounds killed the man, whose "brothers" make their claims simultaneously on two different clans. Whether in any of these cases the designated group admits liability and pays, either a full or an interim and partial compensation, depends on other circumstances such as the phratry affiliations and the current political and exchange relations between the clans.

8. Note, however, that when an old man dies, especially one of little social consequence, even if he has previously been seriously wounded and his agnates assert that his injury has contributed to his demise, they are unlikely to press for an autopsy. In practice a statute of limitations operates here; nobody really expects the clan responsible for the original wounding to concede homicide payment for a death decades later. If the elderly deceased had been an important man, his "brothers" may formally make such a claim but with no great hope of success, unless their own clan has recently paid homicide compensation to the other group for another death or has aided them substantially and at cost in warfare.

9. Glasse's figures (1968:98) for the Huli, neighbors of the Enga, indicate that 19.5 percent of males there die in or as a consequence of combat. Heider (1970:128) estimates that among the Dugum Dani of Irian Jaya (another highlands society that importantly resembles that of the Mae) 28.5 percent of all males die violently. Similarly Chagnon (1974:160–1) states that among the Shamatari Yanomamö of Venezuela, over 30 percent of the men die in warfare and that among the Namowei-teri the figure is about 24 percent. The convergence of these statistics with those I have adduced for the Mae is interesting.

10. There is also a marked difference between the rates of male and of female war-induced casualties in figures cited for other societies: for Huli, 19.5 percent of male deaths and 5.2 percent of female deaths (Glasse 1968:98); Dugum Dani, 28.5 percent and 2.4 percent (Heider 1970:128); Shamatari, 37.4 percent and 4.4 percent, Namowei-teri, 23.7 percent and 6.9 percent (Chagnon 1974:160).

11. Mae men of my acquaintance state unanimously that raiders do not attempt to rape women they surprise during a foray into enemy territory, and I have no evidence to the contrary. The common view is that a man who wastes time in such behavior not only jeopardizes the expedition but also exposes himself to the imputation of cowardice, both from his comrades and later in his opponents' songs—"He plays with women because he is afraid to fight men!" Apparently, he should either kill the woman or leave her alone entirely.

12. There still remains the puzzling question why among western Fringe Enga more women appear to be direct victims of warfare than among the Mae. I can only suggest that among the former, whose smaller populations are much less dense on the ground, the paucity of immediate neighbors and the possibility of physical mobility may combine to persuade men that they and their dependents can more readily evade the retaliatory consequences of their own unrestrained violence.

Chapter 7

1. In urging the peace Big Men of both sides may also invoke the calendar of distributions in the Te exchange cycle. For instance, it may soon be the turn of clans in the neighborhood of the warring groups to receive and to give large numbers of pigs in ceremonial prestations (see Meggitt 1974). A clan caught up in fighting can be bypassed, with a consequent serious loss both of pigs and of prestige. Moreover, clans can readily incorporate payments of homicide compensation in these disbursements. Similarly, if a clan in the neighborhood plans a major ritual to propitiate its ancestral spirits, fraternal clans have the right and the obligation to participate (to their own advantage), and other clans nearby share profitably in the large-scale exchange of game and pork that accompanies the celebration (see Meggitt 1965b). Obviously a neighboring clan that is busy fighting stands to lose on either score.

2. Although such promises may be "more often honored in the breach than the observance," a recognized Mae term denotes this compensation for the killing of an enemy's ally; it may be translated as "additional homicide compensation [to maintain] a connection or friendship."

3. Unlike some groups in the Mount Hagen area, the Mae do not commemorate either interim truces nor final ratification by piling up weapons at the meeting site.

Indeed, apart from the public distributions of valuables, no formal or ceremonial gesture marks such occasions.

4. In general, to put a complex matter simply, every prestation demands a return, though there are often disputes over what constitutes an acceptable counteroffering.

5. There is an important difference between homicide compensation paid by the killer's clan to the victim's agnates and the death compensation that the agnates of any deceased person give to the latter's maternal kin (and sometimes certain affines). Not only do homicide payments as a clan obligation ideally take precedence over death payments made by subclans, they also are usually larger. Moreover, in the case of a man killed in battle, his agnates try to delay giving death compensation for him until they have received the homicide payment due them, part of which they can then divert to his matrilateral relatives.

6. The singers refer to the dead man by his father's name or other circumlocutions, for they fear that his given name may attract the unwelcome attentions of his angry ghost.

7. On public and relatively formal occasions of this kind bachelors are very much at the beck and call of their seniors, and they do a great deal of laborious fetching and carrying.

8. Enga, like some other New Guinea highlanders, have a fairly elaborate counting system. Numerals run from one to ten, then proceed through ten named sets of four up to fifty. Each set of fifty is also numbered, so that in theory a man could continue up to 2,500 (50 × 50). In fact, I have not seen more than about 200 objects counted on any occasion.

9. Donors try, of course, to distribute pigs whose loss will not impair the balance and breeding potential of their own herds, just as recipients hope to secure useful beasts to substitute for expendable pigs of theirs. The most prized animals are mature sows of proven reproductive worth, and men part with these most reluctantly. Gilts (young females) are more freely given. Boars are thought to be basically intractable, dangerous to children and to other livestock, as well as destructive of gardens. Accordingly, each clan normally keeps only a few unaltered males on hand for breeding purposes. The rest are gelded young and, as fattened barrows, are disbursed in, or killed for, prestations. Thus, in a sample of 400 Mae pigs distributed on various public occasions, 12 were boars, 243 barrows, 45 sows, and 100 gilts. See Meggitt 1958a:286–298 for an account of pig husbandry among the Mae.

10. Another important stimulus to this activity was the frequent and unpredictable interruption, during the 1950's, of the normal cycle of Te exchanges by government prohibitions of such assemblies (see Meggitt 1974). Mae Big Men, who had a vested interest in promoting Te transactions, soon perceived that they could continue to do so under the guise of making homicide compensations to appropriate clans, prestations not banned by government officers. Indeed, the Administration and the missionaries may well have encouraged such distributions, believing them to contribute to peaceful relations between clans.

11. Thus, the mean number of pigs disbursed in homicide compensations in my sample in 1955–57 was 36; between 1959 and 1962 it rose to 47. Similarly with money, which to the best of my knowledge was not part of homicide payments made before 1955. However, in those prestations of 1955–57 in my sample the average cash component was 20/- (about $2.00); by 1959–62 it was 41/- (about $4.00).

Chapter 8

1. "European" is shorthand for all those who were exponents of the values, attitudes, and technologies of Western industrial society. In fact, whereas most of the Administration officers were middle-class Australians, the missionaries (Roman Catholic, Lutheran, and Seventh Day Adventists) came from Australia, the United States, and several European countries. The early prospectors were also mainly Australians.

2. See Meggitt 1973:14*et seq*. Souter 1963 gives a general account of the entry of Administration officers, missionaries, and prospectors into the highlands of Papua and New Guinea. See also Jinks, Biskup, and Nelson 1973, Sinclair 1969, U.P.N.G. 1969, and White 1972.

3. I am most grateful to Robin Hide for making copies of Downs's reports available to me.

4. My reconstruction of Administration actions in the Enga region during this period depends in part on ANGAU patrol reports still extant in the Wabag Subdistrict Office in 1955–57. I am grateful to the (then) Department of District Services for allowing me access to them. Unfortunately, because of the war, the files at Wabag were often moved and many of them apparently were lost (those remaining are now in the Papua New Guinea national archives). There are therefore gaps in my record for 1943–46. However, the surviving patrol reports tally well with what I was told by Mae men active at that time.

5. The Mae did not consider a spell in the stockade (with assured food and light work) an undue hardship, an attitude that has persisted and still undercuts the efficacy of legal sanctions.

6. Although I believe these statements generally to hold true (certainly for the Mae Enga whom I know best), I hardly want to give the callous impression that this was a time of light-hearted gamesmanship. Some clans *were* "shot up" with an outrageous indifference to the rights and wrongs of the case, especially by the one ANGAU officer; some human beings *were* killed for reasons they could not be expected to understand—after all, they were not at war with the Japanese, of whom they had never heard. And the deeply grieving kinsfolk of the dead were left, uncomprehending, to mourn their passing and to bear the knowledge that they had no way of exacting retribution.

7. After some years the term native was seen in Government circles to have pejorative overtones, and various alternatives were tried. For a brief period in official usage all foreigners became "expatriates," and indigenes, incredibly, "non-expatriates." Eventually, the obvious terms Papuan and New Guinean were adopted.

8. The Administration in Port Moresby successively broke up extensive administrative regions into smaller units with more local autonomy as the resources, the social and economic "development," and the problems of each became more differentiated. Thus, in 1960 the western half of the Wabag Subdistrict became the Lagaipu Subdistrict of the Western Highlands District, and in 1963 the western portion of the latter became the Lake Kopiago Subdistrict. In 1972 the eastern (Laiapu) part of the Wabag Subdistrict became the Wapenamanda Subdistrict. Meanwhile, in 1971 most of the original Wabag Subdistrict was given the status of the Enga Division under a Deputy District Commissioner, in recognition of the common interests

203

of the people who were the majority of its residents. In 1975 the Division became the Enga Province, with its own Commissioner.

9. From 1948 to about 1951 officers established small police posts for short periods in various Enga localities in order to spread their limited resources and to give some continuity to Administration influence in the patrolled areas. They abandoned the practice, partly because warfare was declining but mainly, I believe, because the presence of such intermittently supervised constables raised more problems than it solved.

10. Compare Marilyn Strathern's excellent monograph (1972) on the operation of official and non-official courts among the neighboring Melpa of the Mount Hagen area, where the development of these institutions closely paralleled that observed in the Wabag Subdistrict. Much of what she says about the Melpa situation is relevant to that of the Enga. See also Reed 1943, Rowley 1966, Brown 1969, A.J. Strathern 1970, 1974, Oram 1973, and M. Strathern 1974.

11. Smaller clans, especially fraternal groups, were often paired, with a luluai chosen from one and his tultul from the other. If the two clans were old opponents, the members of one resisted taking orders from an official of the other, and indeed quietly worked to place obstacles in his way.

12. The appointment of luluais among the Enga continued until the 1960's, when the Administration in Port Moresby instituted in its place a system of elected Local Government Councils, the first at Wabag in 1963, then at Wapenamanda and at Laiagama in 1964, at Kompiama in 1966, and in 1967 at Kandepe, a patrol post established in the new Lagaipu Subdistrict in 1960. Initially, many luluais and Big Men were elected as councillors and as *komitis* (ward lieutenants), but in subsequent elections younger men with more experience of the Western world began to replace them. Although women can vote, no women councillors were elected, a state of affairs wholly consonant with traditional Enga views of women's place.

13. In the mid-1950's I accompanied several Administration patrols among Fringe Enga in what was then "uncontrolled" country, where we were occasionally the targets of such hostile demonstrations. To the novice these armed displays could be somewhat unsettling, and I was impressed by the cool manner in which the kiaps refused to let the warriors provoke them or the policemen into physical retaliation.

14. It is perhaps worth emphasizing in this respect the relativity of the term peace. For instance, in the year July 1949 to July 1950, the small Government hospital at Wabag treated 769 in-patients (most Central Enga were then still suspicious of Western medical practices); of these cases, 331 (43 percent) were fight injuries. Moreover, from mid-1949 to mid-1951, 41 homicide cases were brought to trial; in many others the guilty parties were not apprehended.

15. Pacification among some of the Fringe Enga and, in particular, among the more distant Ipili of the Porgera valley farther west progressed less rapidly. Given the sheer extent and the difficult terrain of the Wabag Subdistrict and the small number of field officers available (rarely more than five or six then), it was simply not possible for them to patrol the outlying areas more than once or twice a year. In consequence, in some places intergroup warfare persisted, although with decreasing intensity, until the late 1950's.

204

Chapter 9

1. As an anthropologist living on the land of a clan with which I was identified, I soon learned that I had a strong obligation, not only to men of that clan but also to all its "brothers," to act as a kind of "preview" audience for such rehearsals. The men would argue their case passionately and at length, and if, with my local knowledge, I did not look skeptical, their leader would decide they were ready to go to court. At no time was I expected to coach or otherwise advise the actors about court procedures, nor was I ever asked to try to influence an Administration officer's decision. Indeed, these men were quite rightly convinced that kiaps could not be suborned.

2. In some situations about which I had reasonable background knowledge, decisions reached in this apparently offhand manner rendered fairly adequate justice. Thus, when the assertions of the two groups about the "correct" location of the common boundary were greatly at variance, a shrewd kiap might take both marks as reference points, select a creek or other natural feature midway between the two to divide the enclosed land into two roughly equal parts, and make this the official border. Men of other, uncommitted clans on such occasions have told me that in their opinion that was indeed the former boundary, and that the claims of both groups had been outrageous.

3. It may be argued that the expertise of the agricultural officers would have been better employed if from the start they had concentrated on enhancing the productivity of traditional Enga high-altitude crops instead of devoting so much effort to the introduction of potential cash crops whose monetary returns were at the mercy of external market conditions. Similarly, improving the health and husbandry of the small but hardy indigenous pigs might well have produced more meat in the long run than did experimentation with larger exotic or crossbred pigs that do not thrive in the Enga area.

4. It appears that the demand for Enga workers on these highlands plantations arose as fewer local men signed on. Some of the latter, especially Chimbu, were now occupied with their own small holdings and businesses, while others (again notably Chimbu) had gone to the coast in large numbers in search of higher wages. Why, when Enga generally were reluctant to take employment far afield, were Chimbu, who also resided in a densely populated highlands area, willing to move out? I suspect the answer involves differences in the corporate nature of landholding among descent groups in the two societies and the pressures these groups can bring to bear on their members.

5. One cannot overestimate the intensity of an Enga man's attachment to his patrimonial land, as the following incident shows. I was present at a formal sitting of the CNA in which several men were convicted of riotous behavior for attempting to occupy land in a neighboring clan territory. When the kiap informed them that not only were they going to jail for six months but also they had no claim to this tract, their spokesman, a lesser Big Man, shouted: "You can put me in jail many times, you can kill me, cut off my head if you will, but my body will walk back to that land—it is ours!" There was no doubt he meant every word.

6. Hide 1972 in his analysis of the Land Titles Commission in Chimbu (central highlands) describes in general terms the antecedents of the Commission. His ac-

count of the Commission's operations among the Chimbu clearly reveals its deficiencies and could, with little alteration, be applied to the situation among the Central Enga. See also Papua New Guinea 1973b.

7. Opinions of my Mae acquaintances (and of some Administration officers) were divided on the identity of these "stirrers." Some Mae asserted that the pressure for violent action came from younger men who feared that their shares of existing patrimonial estates would be too small to support them and their families in the future. Consequently, these men wished to see their clan territories extended by any means possible, and they urged their senior clansmen to reject litigation and to support the immediate occupation of land nearby. Other Mae, however, noted that behind the scenes certain men of substance (even councillers and Administration and mission employees) played on the anxieties of their juniors and fueled their passions. One argument commonly attributed to these secret stirrers was that young men without dependents could jointly resort to violence, even to killing, with relative impunity because at most they would spend a year or two "living well" in jail and, on their release, would be guaranteed part of the land secured by their clan. I believe that whereas some Big Men were covertly pushing junior clansmen into such acts, many younger men did not need encouragement; they were sufficiently motivated by their own perceptions of the situation.

8. See Hide 1972 for further details of this innovation and for a description of its operation among the Chimbu. Once again, his account of events in that region parallels closely what I observed among the Central Enga.

9. For a general survey of the highlands situation see Papua New Guinea 1973a and also Standish 1973, who refers particularly to the Chimbu District.

10. I know of occasions on which sorely beset kiaps were forced to fire shotguns at the legs of men who were shooting arrows at them at close range. Formal investigations followed. Officers and police went to great lengths to avoid shooting at combatants, who in turn showed considerable restraint in their attacks on the kiaps and police.

11. Government legislation precluded their hearing cases involving landownership, as distinct from trespass. They still had to go through the cumbersome procedures of the Land Titles Commission. All the local magistrate could do was to hear the many criminal cases of violence that stemmed from the delays in the Commission's adjudication.

12. In the late 1960's some kiaps were already pursuing this approach—that is, calling the leaders of opposed groups together when fighting halted to negotiate reciprocal compensations for combat deaths. When amounts were agreed upon, the kiap and police supervised, indeed enforced, their public payment. Large numbers of pigs were distributed. I do not believe, however, that such transactions did much to alleviate tensions. The donors saw them rather as involuntary fines whose payment did not absolve them from the obligation to avenge their brothers' deaths and to continue the struggle for the disputed land.

13. The appointment of the two Enga assistant magistrates was not a success. Their court decisions frequently evoked accusations of corruption (quite unwarranted) and even threats of violence from dissatisfied litigants. Faced with these pressures, the assistant magistrates became understandably reluctant to determine cases and soon relinquished their office.

206

14. Apparently there was no love lost between the riot squads and the local police, who did not care for the former's elitist attitudes. They also deplored their maltreatment of Enga, in part because it offended their sense of fair play, in part because they knew that, after the outsiders departed, they would have to face the victims' resentment. Regular policemen sometimes intervened to protect friends among the warriors from what they saw as unnecessary injury.

15. I remind the reader of the considerable investment of time, labor, and materials that goes into the substantial Enga houses. The loss of 14 or 15 dwellings at once is a severe blow.

16. The distribution of these outbreaks suggests a slightly marked seasonal patterning: there appears to have been rather more fighting in the dry season (June through August/September). Not only are conditions better then for combat, but also more new gardens are cultivated then and more new houses built—both occasions for making claims to land. Thus:

Month	J	F	M	A	M	J	J	A	S	O	N	D	Total
Frequency	1	4	7	4	4	8	6	5	6	6	4	5	60

Epilogue

1. Nutritional studies in tropical horticultural societies have not always agreed on minimal requirements for an "adequate" diet. On the other hand, presumably a group of people does not require nutritional tables to know when its members are constantly hungry.

2. I emphasize the term "whole population" for the history of clan dispersal or extinction indicate that the overall dynamic equilibrium could be supported only by the intermittent destruction of some component units. The pattern of clan collisions may thus be seen as expressing something analogous to Gausse's principle of competitive exclusion, although here the competitors' definition of "environmental resources" obviously includes more than mere subsistence.

3. Thus, few men could afford regularly to buy chemical fertilizers, or the dietary supplements needed by European breeds of pigs. Although some kinds of farm machinery might be suited to the local terrain, fewer men could meet the initial cost or even that of fuel and maintenance. Such exotic crops as would grow successfully in this central region (for instance, Irish potatoes, turnips, maize) offered no appreciable advantages in productivity (nor, perhaps, in nutrition) over the existing combinations of sweet poatoes, taro, and other indigenous plants.

4. In some parts of the highlands, especially Chimbu (cf. Standish 1973) a widespread belief that national independence would presage a wholesale return by local groups to violent self-help clearly motivated many of them to secure as much land as possible before independence. Whereas Central Enga were ill-informed and uneasy about the implications of independence, this apprehension did not, to my knowledge, lead them to encroach on neighbor's land.

5. The Commission on Land Matters looked at the possibility of introducing birth control measures as a long-term solution to demographic problems in certain areas. It concluded that popular opinion in general was then firmly opposed to such ideas.

Glossary

affines   persons related by marriage.

agistment   the care and pasturing of another person's livestock in return for payment.

agnates   kinspeople who trace their relationship through male links only.

Big Man   the recognized leader or organizer of a local group, who achieves his status through his skill in managing the public activities of the members of the group.

bos boi   member of a local group chosen informally by government officers to act as an intermediary between his group and representatives of the central government. Cf. *luluai*

brideprice   the valuables or wealth given by the bridegroom and his kinsfolk to the bride and her kinsfolk in order to ratify or legitimize the marriage.

cognates   kinsfolk; persons who are related by actual or assumed consanguineal ("blood") links.

descent group   a set of kinspeople who may or may not live together and who believe they are descended from the same ancestor. A cognatic descent group comprises people who trace their descent through males or females; an agnatic or patrilineal descent group traces descent through males only, a matrilineal descent group through females only.

eponymy   giving a person's name to the group formed by his or her off-spring or descendants.

exogamy   the rule or custom prohibiting marriage within a specified group, whether a clan or a local community.

kiap   Melanesian pidgin term for an administrative or government officer, thought to be derived from the English word "captain."

leviratic marriage   the custom whereby a man is expected to marry the widow of his actual or classificatory brother or of his fellow clansman.

luluai   member of a local group formally chosen by government officers to represent his group in its dealings with the government; among Enga, luluais were frequently former Big Men.

matrilateral   on the mother's side, especially with reference to relatives, whether kinsfolk or affines.

phratry   a "brotherhood"; the largest named patrilineal descent group that the Enga recognize; a set of fraternal clans.

prestation   the public and formal handing over of wealth or valuables by one individual or group to another.

Te exchange cycle   an elaborate, public and formal series of prestations in which over a period of about four years clans exchange pigs, pork and other valuable objects.

tultul   member of a local group formally chosen by government officers to act as the assistant or lieutenant of the local luluai in managing the group's public activities.

usufruct   the right to enjoy the use or benefit of property without an absolute right to the property itself, as when a person may plant and harvest crops on land belonging to another.

waitpus   paramount luluai; a luluai formally chosen by government officers to coordinate the activities of a number of luluais in one neighborhood.

References

Bretnor, R. 1969. *Decisive Warfare*. Harrisburg, Pa.: Stackpole Books.

Brown, B. J., ed. 1969. *Fashion of Law in New Guinea*. Sydney: Butterworths.

Chagnon, N. A. 1974. *Studying the Yanomamo*. New York: Holt, Rinehart & Winston.

Chappell, J., and M. Strathern. 1966. Stone Axe Factories in the Highlands of East New Guinea. *Proceedings, Prehistoric Society*, 32, 96–121.

Clausewitz, C. von. 1968. *On War*. Harmondsworth: Penguin.

Fried, M., M. Harris, and R. Murphy, eds. 1967. *War*. New York: Natural History Press.

Glasse, R. M. 1968. *Huli of Papua*. Paris: Mouton.

Hallpike, C. R. 1973. Functionalist Interpretations of Primitive Warfare. *Man*, 8, 451–70.

————. 1974. Reply to Netting. *Man*, 9, 488–89.

Harris, M. 1974. *Cows, Pigs, Wars and Witches*. New York: Random House.

Harrison, R. 1973. *Warfare*. Minneapolis: Burgess.

Heider, K. G. 1970. *The Dugum Dani*. Chicago: Aldine.

Hide, R. 1971. Land Demarcation and Disputes in the Chimbu District. . . . In *Land Tenure and Economic Development*, ed. M. Ward. New Guinea Research Unit Bulletin No. 40, pp. 37–61. Port Moresby.

————. 1973. *The Land Titles Commission in Chimbu*. New Guinea Research Unit Bulletin No. 50. Port Moresby.

Jinks, B., P. Biskup, and H. Nelson, eds. 1973. *Readings in New Guinea History*. Sydney: Angus & Robertson.

211

Koch, K.-F. 1974a. *The Anthropology of Warfare*. Module in Anthropology No. 52. Reading, Mass.: Addison-Wesley.

————. 1974b. *War and Peace in Jalémó*. Cambridge, Mass.: Harvard University Press.

Leahy, M.J., and M. Crain. 1937. *The Land That Time Forgot*. New York: Funk & Wagnalls.

Meggitt, M.J. 1956. The Valleys of the Upper Wage and Lai Rivers. . . . *Oceania*, 27, 90–135.

————. 1957a. House Building among the Mae Enga. . . . *Oceania*, 27, 161–76.

————. 1957b. The Ipili of the Porgera Valley. . . . *Oceania*, 28, 31–55.

————. 1958a. The Enga of the New Guinea Highlands. . . . *Oceania*, 28, 253–330.

————. 1958b. Salt Manufacture and Trading in the Western Highlands. *Australian Museum Magazine*, 12, 309–13.

————. 1958c. Mae Enga Time Reckoning and Calendar. . . . *Man*, 58, 74–77.

————. 1962. Dream Interpretation among the Mae Enga. . . . *Southwestern Journal of Anthropology*, 18, 216–29.

————. 1964a. Male-Female Relations in the Highlands of New Guinea. . . . *American Anthropologist*, 66, 4(2), 202–24.

————. 1964b. The Kinship Terminology of the Mae Enga. . . . *Oceania*, 34, 191–200.

————. 1965a. *The Lineage System of the Mae Enga of New Guinea*. Edinburgh: Oliver & Boyd; New York: Barnes & Noble.

————. 1965b. The Mae Enga of the Western Highlands. In *Gods, Ghosts and Men in Melanesia*, eds. P. Lawrence and M.J. Meggitt. 105–31. Melbourne: Oxford University Press.

————. 1967. The Pattern of Leadership among the Mae Enga. . . . *Anthropological Forum*, 2, 20–35.

————. 1971. From Tribesmen to Peasants. In *Anthropology in Oceania*, eds. L.R. Hiatt and C. Jayawardena. 191–209. Sydney: Angus & Robertson.

————. 1973. The Sun and the Shakers. . . . *Oceania*, 44, 1–37, 109–26.

————. 1974. Pigs Are Our Hearts! . . . *Oceania*, 44, 165–203.

Netting, R. McC. 1973. Fighting, Forest and the Fly. *Journal of Anthropological Research*, 29, 164–79.

————. 1974. Functions of War. *Man*, 9, 485–87.

Oram, N.D. 1973. Law and Order. *New Guinea*, 7, 4–22.

Painter, S. 1964. *French Chivalry*. Ithaca: Cornell University Press.

Papua New Guinea. 1973a. *Report of the Committee Investigating Tribal Fighting in the Highlands*. Port Moresby: Government Printer.

————. 1973b. *Report of the Commission of Inquiry into Land Matters*. Port Moresby: Government Printer.

Polybius. 1966. *The Histories*, ed. E. Badian. New York: Washington Square Press.

Pospisil, L. 1968. Feud. In *International Encyclopedia of the Social Sciences*, ed. D.L. Sills. Vol. 5, pp. 389–92. New York: Macmillan.

212

Rappaport, R. A. 1968. *Pigs for the Ancestors*. New Haven: Yale University Press.

―――. 1969. Population Dispersal and Land Redistribution among the Maring of New Guinea. In *Ecological Essays*, ed. D. Damas. 113–26. National Museum of Canada Bulletin No. 230. Ottawa.

Reed, S. W. 1943. *The Making of Modern New Guinea*. Philadelphia: American Philosophical Society.

Rowley, C. D. 1966. *The New Guinea Villager*. New York: Praeger.

Sackschewsky, M. 1970. The Clan Meeting in Enga Society. In *Exploring Enga Culture*, ed. P. Brennan. 51–101. Wapenamanda: Kristen Press.

Sinclair, J. 1969. *The Outside Man*. Melbourne: Lansdowne Press.

Souter, G. 1963. *New Guinea: The Last Unknown*. Sydney: Angus & Robertson.

Standish, W. 1973. The Highlands. *New Guinea*, 8(3), 4–30.

Strathern, A. J. 1970. Kiap, Councillor and Big Man. In *The Politics of Melanesia*, ed. M. Ward. 549–67. Canberra: National University Press.

―――. 1974. When Dispute Procedures Fail. In *Contention and Dispute*, ed. A. L. Epstein. 240–70. Canberra: Australian National University Press.

Strathern, M. 1972. *Official and Unofficial Courts*. New Guinea Research Unit Bulletin No. 47. Port Moresby.

―――. 1974. Managing Information. In *Contention and Dispute*, ed. A. L. Epstein. 240–316. Canberra: Australian National University Press.

Taylor, J. L. 1940. Hagen-Sepik Patrol 1938–1939. *Annual Report of the Mandated Territory of New Guinea*. 130–49. Canberra: Department of Territories.

Turney-High, H. H. 1949. *Primitive War*. Columbia: University of South Carolina Press.

Vayda, A. P. 1971. Phases of the Process of War and Peace among the Marings of New Guinea. *Oceania*, 42, 1–24.

―――. 1974. Warfare in Ecological Perspective. *Annual Review of Ecology and Systematics*, 5, 183–93.

Vial, L. G. 1940. Stone Axes of Mount Hagen. . . . *Oceania*, 11, 158–63.

Westermann, T. 1968. *The Mountain People*. Wapenamanda: Kristen Press.

White, O. 1972. *Parliament of a Thousand Tribes*. Melbourne: Wren.

Wintringham, T., and J. Blashford-Snell. 1973. *Weapons and Tactics*. Harmondsworth: Penguin.

Wright, Q. 1965. *A Study of War*. Chicago: University of Chicago Press.

Zorn, J. G. 1974. The Land Titles Commission and Customary Land Law. *Melanesian Law Journal*, 2, 151–77.

Index

Adjudication. *See* Litigation

Administrative districts, 148, 203–4 n. 8

Adultery, 148, 192 n. 11

Affines, 25, 28, 32, 36, 182

Agistment, 32, 36, 142

Agnates, 44, 59, 60, 68, 77, 105, 107, 118, 199 n. 7; close, residence pattern of, 49–50; conflicts among, 22, 79–80, 175; defined, 5, 49; distant, 28, 32; and exchange relationships, 44, 45, 106, 117, 122; ghosts of, 107, 194 n. 21, 198 n. 1, 200 n. 7; homicide compensations by, 79, 80, 126, 133, 137, 141, 200 n. 7, 232 n. 5; homicide compensations to, 38, 41, 79, 80, 114, 119, 123–24, 126, 130, 133, 134, 138, 177, 191 n. 4, 192 n. 11, 200 n. 7, 202 n. 5; injury compensations to, 190 n. 5; refuge among, 25; and retaliatory homicide, 46, 79

Agricultural services, 147, 159

Agriculture. *See* Crops

Alcohol. *See* Liquor

Ambumu valley, 16, 197 n. 22

Ancestors, clan: ghosts of, 38, 106, 116, 126, 155, 198 n. 7, 201 n. 1; propitiation of, 28, 81, 155

Arrows, 54–56, 57, 59, 62, 168; wounds made by, 63, 101, 102–4

Aruni Enga, 194 n. 2

Australian Administration, 11, 27, 44, 140–41, 144–88 passim, 195 n. 10; attitude toward, 144, 147, 149; basic weakness of, 144, 184–85; confrontations with officials of, 145, 146–47, 152, 171, 173, 186; labor scheme of, 160–61; officials and agents of, 27, 148–76 passim, 185, 186, 204 n. 12; redistricting under, 148, 203–4 n. 8; resettlement scheme of, 162, 167, 187–88. *See also* Pacification program

Australian New Guinea Administrative Unit (ANGAU), 146–47

Autopsies, 105, 110, 199–200 nn. 7–8

215

Axes: as commodities, 8, 58, 117, 134; as weapons, 19, 22, 24, 57–58, 59, 101, 103, 119, 130, 168

Bachelors, 28, 101–2, 130, 131, 141; associations of, 63, 77, 122, 155, 195 n. 10; high loss of, in warfare, 110–11; homicide compensations for, 138; social status of, 138; as young warriors, 18, 95, 110–11, 116
Baisu, 173, 177
Big Men, 8, 9, 45, 59, 73, 77, 106, 139, 142, 147, 157, 158, 165, 175–76, 197 n. 22, 204 n. 12, 206 n. 7; as bosbois, 150, 152; role in peace-making, 20, 25, 27, 29, 92, 116–36 passim, 141, 142, 189 n. 3; role in warfare, 18, 19, 20, 34, 39, 41, 68, 69, 70, 78, 79, 80, 82, 83, 86, 95, 97, 98, 108, 128, 196 n. 14; as top leaders, 68, 69–70, 151
Birip Enga. *See* Laiapu Enga
Birth control, opposition to, 207 n. 5
Biskup, P., 203 n. 2
Black (patrol officer), 145
Blashford-Snell, J., 198 n. 5
Bosbois (government agents), 150, 152
Bougainville, migration to, 161
Bougainville Copper Proprietary Ltd., 161
Bows, 54–55, 57, 59, 101, 119, 130, 132
Bretnor, R., 198 nn. 3–4
Brideprice, 58, 122, 123, 140, 155, 182
Bridges, 48, 153
Brown, B. J., 204 n. 10
Burial, 105–6, 107; 125; payment for, 106, 125

Cane grass, 48, 50, 154
Cannibalism, 192 n. 13
Cash economy, 141, 155, 159, 160, 161, 162, 184, 185, 195 n. 10
Casualties. *See* Death; Warfare: casualties in; Wounds, combat
Casuarina plantations, 7
Cattle-raising, 160, 162
Central Enga, 1, 2, 10, 11, 12, 14, 17, 114, 197 n. 19; under Australian

Administration, 141–86, 187–88; under Papua New Guinea Administration, 186–87, 188
Chagnon, N. A., 201 nn. 9 and 10
Chappell, J., 57
Children, 45, 61, 77, 155, 199 n. 7; boys as combatants, 93; and early paternal contact, 60; evacuation of, 30, 35, 80, 99, 175; increasing population of, 163; military education of boys, 61–64; mortality rate of, 112, 162; as noncombatants, 18, 30, 35, 80, 93, 102; as war casualties, 24, 30, 111–12
Chimbu people, 205 n. 4, 206 nn. 6 and 8
Chimbu region, 205 n. 6, 206 n. 9, 207 n. 4
Christians. *See* Missions and missionaries
Clan, 42, 182; assemblies of, and decision to fight, 76–79, 98, 168; composition of, 4; exogamy in, 4, 28, 39, 42; founders of, 5, 28; freezing of boundaries of, and consequences; interclan enmity, patterns of, 42, 43, 45; interclan fighting, 10–14, 16, 17–21, 27–43, 70, 74, 113, 152, 167–73 passim, 174–81, 183; interclan mutual obligations, 28; intraclan fighting, 10–14, 16, 17, 21–28, 113, 179, 192 n. 14; parish of, 4, 88, 108; patrilineal, 2, 5, 49; political autonomy of, 11, 31, 33, 38; rituals of, 28; size of, 30, 32, 197 n. 1; territory of, 2, 11, 47–48, 92
Clausewitz, C. von, 196 n. 16; quoted, 196–97 n. 18
Coca plantations, 160
Coffee and coffee-growing, 149, 155, 159, 160, 161, 184
Cognates, 25, 28, 32
Commission on Land Matters, 207 n. 5
Commodities, export, 155, 159, 160
Commodities, traditional: ceremonial exchange of, 8; clashes over control of, 12; hierarchy of, 121–23; trade

216

Fringe Enga, 1, 25, 57, 143, 145, 147, 161, 162, 167, 168, 178–79, 193 n. 18, 196 nn. 13 and 15, 204 nn. 13 and 15; women as war casualties among, 201 n. 12

Funerals, 105–6; feasts at, 106, 123; prestations at, 23, 25, 37, 106, 142

Gambling, 173

Gardens, 7; stealing from, 190 n. 5. *See also* Crops; Land

Genealogies, of clans and phratries, 5–7, 31, 190 n. 6

Ghosts: agnatic, 107, 194 n. 21, 198 n. 1, 200 n. 7; ancestral, 38, 106, 116, 126, 155, 198 n. 7, 201 n. 1; of enemy, 81, 107–8; exorcism of, 60; of newly deceased, 38, 60, 81, 106, 107, 193 n. 17, 194 n. 21, 199 n. 7, 202 n. 6; pro-pitiation of, 5, 38, 81, 104, 107, 116, 155, 198 n. 7, 201 n. 1; retribution by, 60, 107, 109–10, 126

Glasse, R. M., 199 n. 7, 201 nn. 9 and 10

Gold, 145, 149

Gold-prospectors, 144, 145, 149, 203 n. 1

Hannibal, 198 n. 5

Harris, M., 189 ch. 2 n. 1

Heider, K. G., 201 nn. 9 and 10

Heroes, 66–67, 74–75

Hewa people, 149

Hide, R., 203 n. 3, 205–6 n. 6, 206 n. 8

Highlands Labour Scheme, 160–61, 185

"Highways," 153–54

Hobbes, Thomas, 73; quoted, 197 n. 20

Homicide, 14, 22, 44, 70, 163, 171; com-pensation for (*see* Homicide com-pensations); as political issue, 123; responsibility for, 20, 30, 38–39, 41, 46, 110, 123, 140, 200 n. 7; retalia-tory, 37–41 passim, 46, 106, 107, 116, 123, 128, 152, 169, 175, 182, 196 n. 12, 198 n. 7

Homicide compensations, 14, 20, 23, 25, 27, 30, 38–46 passim, 65, 69, 70,

Homicide compensations (Continued) 92, 98, 108, 110, 114–21 passim, 141, 155, 172, 177, 191 n. 4, 192 n. 11, 198 n. 1, 199 n. 2, 200 nn. 7–8, 201 n. 1; case studies of, 126–28; importance of, 142–43; nature of, 21, 22, 24, 26, 78–79, 121–28; size of, 139; statis-tics of, 137–43; as transaction, 129–37, 144

Hospitals, 148, 155, 159, 162

Houses, 2; burning of, 24, 30, 31, 51, 52, 62–63, 75, 76, 81, 87, 90, 94, 112, 152, 175, 176, 180, 181, 195 n. 2; cult-, 31, 48; men's (*see* Men's houses); protection of, 50–51, 154, 163; women's, 2, 24, 47, 48, 49, 50, 51, 112, 134, 163

Huli people, 54, 199 n. 7, 201 nn. 9 and 10

Hunting, 8, 58

Illness: endemic and epidemic, 112, 155, 183; treatment of, 104, 155

Inflation, 141

Insults, 105, 190 n. 5; as preliminary to warfare, 18, 29; as reason for war, 17–18, 38, 120

Intermarriage. *See* Exogamy

Ipili people, 54, 149, 199 n. 7, 204 n. 15

Ivanhoe, quoted, 191 n. 8

Jailings, 150, 152, 153, 167, 169, 171, 173, 174, 177, 187, 206 n. 7

Jalé people, 199 n. 5

Japanese troops, 146, 147

Jinks, B., 203 n. 2

Kandepe area, 111, 204 n. 12

Kandepe Enga, 194 n. 2, 199 n. 7

Kiaps (government officials), 149, 150, 151–52, 153, 157, 158, 159, 163, 167–75 passim; constraints on, 171–72, 173

Kindeng, 162

Knives, 54

Koch, K.-F., 199 n. 53

Komitis (government officials), 204 n. 12

218

Murder. *See* Homicide

Murphy, R., 189 ch. 2 n. 1

Mutilation: of fallen enemies, 20, 24, 31, 36, 58, 76, 105, 169, 175, 176; as punishment, 190 n. 5, 195 n. 11; self-, 106, 115

Namowei-teri people, 201 nn. 9 and 10

National independence, and fears of violence, 186, 207 n. 4

Native Administration Ordinance of 1921, 150

Nelson, H., 203 n. 2

Nondugl, 162

Old people, 141; death of, 109, 110, 112, 200 n. 8; men as combatants, 93; men in public exchanges, 141; as noncombatants, 18, 80, 104, 112

Oram, N. D., 186, 204 n. 10

Oven-divination, 81–82

Pacification program, 44, 140–41; acceptance of, 11, 144, 147–55; rejection of, 156–81

Pai-era people, 149

Painter, S., 190 n. 2

Pandanus nuts, 7; theft of, 14, 33, 70, 71, 73, 128, 152

Panguna, Bougainville, 161

Papua New Guinea, 11, 188; armed conflicts in, 186; economy of, 185, 187; government of, 188; government reports of, 186–87, 206 nn. 6 and 9

Patriclan, 2, 3, 10, 22. *See also* Clan

Patrilineage, of clans, 2, 5, 49

Peace-making, 98; ceremony after, 20; complexity of negotiations and compensations in, 113–43; in interclan warfare, 12, 29, 30, 31, 70; in interphratry warfare, 20, 36; in intraclan warfare, 12, 22, 23, 24, 25, 27, 31. *See also* Homicide compensations; Pacification program

Phratry: composition of, 4, 28; founders of, 5, 28; size of, 4, 28, 151, 190–

Phratry (Continued)
91 n. 3; warfare between clans of different phratries, 10, 12–14, 33, 36–43, 74, 113, 179; warfare between clans of one phratry, 10, 12–14, 28–36, 70, 113, 179; warfare between phratries, 10, 16, 17–21, 70, 113

Pigs, 11, 48, 61, 121, 163, 166, 182, 184, 187; breeding and numbers of, 7–8, 36, 80, 141–42, 160, 162, 183, 192 n. 10, 202 n. 9; compensation in, 21, 22, 23, 24, 25, 30, 41, 65, 72, 108, 114, 115, 116, 123–42 passim, 155, 177, 192 n. 10, 193 n. 18, 199 n. 7; evacuation of, 30, 35, 80, 92, 99, 153, 175; in exchanges, 7, 8, 9, 117, 140, 155, 182–83, 184, 192 n. 10, 201 n. 1; in funerary distributions, 23, 25, 142; for ritual purposes and feasts, 81, 123; theft of, 14, 17, 23, 33, 41, 44, 66, 70, 72, 73, 76, 78–79, 127, 149, 152, 174; trespassing by, 23, 31, 71–72, 142; as war casualties, 24, 30, 31, 90, 181. *See also* Pork

Plumes, 8, 112

Police, 148, 149, 151, 152, 155, 157–58, 167–76 passim, 185, 186, 187; attitude toward, 170; duties of, 169–70, 173; numbers of, 170, 172

Polybius, 198 n. 5

Polygyny, 4, 49, 111

Population figures: Central Enga, 1; clan parish, 4, 88, 108; clans, 30, 32, 197 n. 1; Enga-speaking peoples, 1; Mae Enga, 2; men's and women's houses, 50; phratries, 4, 28, 151, 190–91 n. 3; police, 170, 172

Population pressure, 1, 142, 156–63 passim, 167, 184, 185, 186, 188; and mortality, 11–12, 162; and warfare, 11, 14, 23, 25, 26, 27, 31, 32, 36, 42, 43, 169, 183, 187

Porgera valley, 149

Pork, 66, 105, 106, 123; compensation in, 24, 25, 198, 123, 125, 127, 193 n. 18; exchange of, 8, 20, 117, 201 n. 1;